"bands, those funny little plans, that never work quite right…"

'Holes', Mercury Rev

Written by Adam T. Walton

http://onmakingmusic.co.uk

http://twitter.com/adamwalton

Cover designed by Caroline Duffy

http://www.carolineduffy.co.uk

£13.00

80.
WAL.

Version 2

October 2014

©Adam Walton 2014

2014,

083553

Contents

<u>Disclaimer</u>

The views expressed in this book are my own and are
not the BBC's.

This book contains occasional swearing.

Foreword

You can read the liner notes on the first Kinks album and it says, Ray Davies: "I listen to everybody's advice, take all the ideas from other people on board, then I make my own decisions." I think that's the key thing with writers. Don't be afraid to be dangerous; don't be afraid of failure because you're going to fail a few times. And never give up.

Ray Davies, The Kinks

How easy is it? If you're magical, it's easy. If you do all the right things, it's easy.

Kim Fowley, record producer

My name is Adam Walton. I have been making new music programmes for the BBC since 1993.

I fell into radio after a spectacularly unsuccessful career as a musician and a songwriter. I dedicated most of my teenage years and early twenties to making music, trawling the UK and Europe in an average band and a far-worse-than-average Transit van. We made every elementary mistake possible: signed bad contracts; jumped rusty bandwagons; recorded our newest – rather than our best – songs, and then didn't bother sending them to anyone.

That's right, *anyone*.

So I'm not a successful musician / songwriter / DJ here to share the secrets of my success or to reveal to you a magical path to fortune and critical adulation. I failed in all three departments, but failure is a fine teacher.

Artists who become world-straddling colossi might

1

have difficulty passing on the secrets of their success; those of us who've had doors slammed in our face with the regularity of Andy Dufresne in The Shawshank Redemption, have pondered long and hard why our musical dreams turned to dust.

On Making Music is about encouraging, nurturing and realising your musical dreams so that they don't turn to dust too.

The focus in this book is on you and your music. Taking that music to an audience, and expanding their number, will be treated as a secondary concern.

I am evangelical in the belief that being yourself and making music primarily for your own satisfaction – ignoring trends, bandwagons and the tastes of an audience – is the only way to ensure success, but my definition of success is an artistic one: measured in terms of how much pleasure, and a sense of satisfaction, you derive from the process, and how true your music is to your own vision.

I also believe that this is the route most likely to bring you actual, material success, if selling tens of thousands of albums is your desire.

But there are no guarantees. Of course there aren't.

All too frequently, artists are their own worst enemies. If I can help you avoid some of the most common pitfalls then this book will be worth the time you spend reading it.

The majority of the advice I have to share comes from my firsthand experience of twenty years of listening to new artists and their demo recordings. I've appraised tens of thousands of demos. I've been fortunate enough to support some incredible artists from very early in their evolution: Super Furry Animals, Cate Le Bon, mclusky & Future of the Left, The Joy Formidable, Georgia Ruth, Skindred, Gorky's Zygotic Mynci.

At a rough estimate, I have played about 10% of the

recordings that have been submitted to me. The 90% that fall by the wayside do so because they're flawed by elementary mistakes. For the most part those flaws are due to a lack of inspiration, a lack of quality control or a failure of execution. I'll share with you everything I know about how to recognise and avoid these flaws.

Fortunately I've also been privileged to speak to many truly influential and internationally-renowned artists during my tenure at the BBC. I've trawled back through many of those interviews and gathered every nugget of advice that's pertinent to other music-making people that I can find. Every section of this book has been shaped and bolstered by their words of wisdom.

I wouldn't blame you for being cynical about any words I offer on the subject of songwriting, for example, but I imagine that the words of Ray Davies, Black Francis, Martin Carr, Andrew Falkous, The Joy Formidable, Georgia Ruth, Elliott Smith, Kristin Hersh – and many others – will hold more authority for you.

You may not recognise all of the names of the people that contribute their hard-earned wisdom to this book. They're not all 'famous'. However – to a person – they are artists who have had the courage to trust their own instincts and to follow an original vision.

Courage and instinct are two of the cornerstones of On Making Music.

In short: On Making Music is a free, downloadable guide for original music-makers.

On Making Music resolutely is *not* a rulebook. I'm so tired of people with good intentions interfering with music, chopping the corners off, planing all of the interesting knots and grains out. I believe that we musical apparatchiks (the media) would better serve this wonderful force by... well, serving it rather than trying to mould it. Music is bigger, more varied, frightening, and replete with possibilities than any of us can imagine.

Frequently the things that don't fit become the things that are worth celebrating most of all.

This book has bad intentions. It wants you to ignore the rules, treat the media with diffidence, stick two fingers to the world, and make whatever sounds you please.

These are not prescriptive demands chiselled onto tablets of stone. You're invited to discuss each and every point: to nod your head, to bang your fist on the table, to swear at your screen, to cheer and to boo! This book is all about sparking an inner debate that will help refine your vision as we progress.

I want this book to encourage your individuality. I want it to inspire you to have the courage to make music that thrills you, *then* an audience.

I'm firmly of the belief that this – right now – is the most challenging, yet potentially exciting, time to be a musical artist in my lifetime. As a music-maker in the 21st century you have ready access to technology that will help you refine, compose, record, distribute and promote your music. The era of large advances, logistical support from a label and unimaginable wealth may well have passed but you can have more control over what you do than any artists that have preceded you. I find that an inspirational thought. I hope it's inspirational to you too.

On Making Music will talk about many of the challenges you will face as an original music-maker. We'll start right at the very beginning, as your interest in music coalesces from the sounds and instruments spiralling around you. We'll talk about finding your own sound; about songwriting; about arrangement and recording.

Then, and only then, we'll consider how to take your music to labels, venues, the media and an audience.

The book will also deal with how you can exploit your

own music and its commercial potential by registering with the requisite agencies (PRS, MCPS, PPL etc.)

Some very wise, music industry voices recommended that that particular chapter (**Chapter 40:** *Paper Work(s) - Making Money From Your Music*) should have more prominence, and come earlier in the book; that it might, indeed, be the most useful chapter in the whole of On Making Music.

I think it is key. But I also think that the philosophy of On Making Music is that we focus on making the music first. That has to have ultimate precedence.

However I recommend that you pay particular attention to **Chapter 40** when you are ready for it. Many music-makers don't. They assume that the paperwork is too opaque and confusing for them and that contemplating financial reward for their music is, somehow, selling out. It isn't. If the singular and original 'sound of you' encouraged by this book manages to find support on the radio, why shouldn't you be paid for it? You, of all people, standing out from the anodyne karaoke throng, deserve those royalties.

On Making Music is intended for original music-makers, regardless of their genre or whether they're a solo artist or in a Sly & the Family Stone-like musical collective. I make no assumptions about how old you are, your gender, your race, your hair colour... none of this matters when it comes to music-making. In these pages, at least.

I have given some thought to the ordering of the chapters, imagining ('hoping' would be more accurate) that you'll read through from start to finish.

However you should be able to just dip into chapters as and when you need their advice.

Be aware, though, that the chapters are rather broadly-titled. Advice on music-making isn't an exact science. Go straight to the chapter on Songwriting, for example, and you'll read fine advice on that particular subject, but you'd also miss an overlap of songwriting-related advice in the chapter on Arrangement.

The sequence of chapters reflects one logical path through music-making but is not intended to dictate the order in which you approach your music. Some of the chapters, although split to make the book more digestible, work better when considered in parallel with each other (the chapters on 'Songwriting' and 'Lyrics', in particular.)

I very much hope that you'll find the time to read all of On Making Music. I appreciate it's long and unwieldy, and a little verbose in places. That was inevitable: it's a reflection of me, my love for music, and my rather peripatetic and wordy way of enthusing and writing about the subject.

A key part of On Making Music's philosophy was for it to be 'free'.

Doesn't 'free' undermine any potential value the book has? You can't get something of any value for nothing, can you? Other than a load of rhetorical questions, seemingly?

Well, I think it has real value.

I think it contains enough hard-earned advice from enough respected music-makers for it to help you.

It won't write a killer song for you but it will remind you that that is what you should be doing, first and foremost.

It's free because music-makers are too skint to buy music, let alone books about music. Its 'freeness' might mean that people actually read it. Hopefully, lots of people.

It's free because I want to help as many music-makers as possible, to create, record and distribute their noise effectively. This altruism came into sharper focus last year when I celebrated my 20th year in radio. That's two decades of living off other people's creativity. This is my rather high-minded gift back to music and music-makers.

Having said that, if On Making Music helps you, and you can afford to, there is a donation link at: http:// onmakingmusic.co.uk

I hope sincerely that this book inspires you. It has taken a year to research and write. That's a lot of time sat at the table in my kitchen when I could have been trying to master MarioKart 8.

Please feel free to share the download link with whoever you see fit.

If you quote from the book, please credit the source and link back to: http://onmakingmusic.co.uk

I'd love to hear what you think. Feel free to tweet me @adamwalton

Good luck. Have fun and happy music-making!

PLAYLIST:
Mercury Rev - Holes
Super Furry Animals - The Man Don't Give A Fuck
Cate Le Bon - Wild
The Joy Formidable - The Greatest Light Is The Greatest Shade
mclusky - To Hell With Good Intentions
Future of the Left - Notes On Achieving Orbit
Georgia Ruth - In Luna
Skindred - Warning
Gorky's Zygotic Mynci - Patio Song
The Kinks - Waterloo Sunset
Frank Black - I Gotta Move
Pixies - Gigantic
The Boo Radleys - Wish I Was Skinny
Elliott Smith - Condor Ave
Kristin Hersh - Your Ghost

1: <u>No Rules</u>

So, you want to be a rock 'n' roll star, do you? Well, if I were you I wouldn't bother. It's not all it's cracked up to be. Yes, there are perks... you'll be as rich as Croesus, you'll date film-stars and supermodels, and you'll buy a holiday island in the Caribbean, but you'll soon find the constant adulation tiresome. And feeling intimidated by the burden of expectation placed on you by public acclaim, you'll retreat into yourself. You'll become a recluse. Only glimpsed occasionally through the long lens of the paparazzi.

You'll enjoy a sad and lonely death surrounded by empty vodka bottles and the paraphernalia of drug abuse.

So, ask yourself... is it worth it?

Deke Leonard, Man

If you're in a rock 'n' roll band, enjoy it. It's the best job on earth. It will take you around the world, if you're lucky, or it will keep you occupied for the rest of your life in a local rehearsal room.

It's always a source of wonder and I try and pass on to any young band who ask for me any advice this: I tell them that most importantly they should just enjoy what they do, and let the music that they create take them wherever it is meant to.

Mike Peters, The Alarm

The idealist within me want to proclaim that the first and most important 'rule' of contemporary music-making is that there are no rules. This is (broadly) rock 'n' roll[1], for

God's sake, not accountancy.

Our daily lives are governed by enough bureaucracy. Rock 'n' roll still has a validity, an allure and a romance in the 21st century because it exists beyond the mundanities of everyday life. Occasionally music elevates us above such mundanities by celebrating them... bringing an irresistible noise to the daily struggle: The Kinks, The Specials, The Smiths, Pulp, Dizzee Razcal, are just some of the UK artists who have elevated us from the grind by singing about the grind. Robert Johnson, Springsteen, Motown and hip hop did similarly for working class Americans.

So some music speaks to us because it's escapist and frequently it's most effective when it rolls around in the very details we want to escape from.

Popular music is riddled with and thrives on these contradictions.

There are no rules.

Well, there are some rules.

Apply the 'no rules'-approach during a formal music theory exam and you'd be very unlikely to pass. Random pitching in a vocal, or vocal harmonies that are out of tune, are unlikely to please anyone other than the most contradictory listener.

So there are some rules worth familiarising yourself with (how to tune an instrument, harmony / disharmony, timing and tempo). But these aren't dictates from the gods.

I started playing music when I was an art student in Leeds in 1977. The Clash, The Sex Pistols and the Damned all came round on a tour and the message we got was that anyone could do this and – maybe – you didn't have to be able to play the guitar or the drums really good to make something interesting.

That was always the premise behind The Mekons. Anyone could do it.

Jon Langford, The Mekons

So punk grew out of the ethos that anyone could make rock 'n' roll music. You didn't need to be able to play an instrument. It was a liberating and inclusive philosophy after years of virtuoso snobbery from rock's prog monoliths. But punk's lack of musicianship has been exaggerated. Other than Sid Vicious, the Sex Pistols could all play more than competently. The Clash were no beginners on their instruments either. The Slits – who were at the vanguard of the 2nd wave of bands inspired by the punk – had an instinctive musicality, just one that wasn't predicated on technical ability.

The Ramones stripped everything down to the absolute basics of chugging power chords and choruses but there isn't an out of tune, or out of time, note on any of their records.

Rock 'n' roll is misleading, economical with the truth and downright contradictory. It would have you subscribe to the belief that there are no rules to foster its air of accessibility and rebelliousness – when, in fact, there are many rules. And – to add a final layer of mystery and confusion – rock 'n' roll is rarely as thrilling as when it is bending or breaking those rules.

If you let the rules – or the technicalities – dictate the spirit of the music you make then that spirit will desert you. It's spirit that we're all listening for. Even when electronic artists like Kraftwerk tried to remove every ounce of human spirit from their recordings, they did so with such grace and conviction that it imbued the clinical sounds with a life all their own.

No rules, see – but we're getting close to something important here. It'd be more accurate to say that there isn't one rule for all. These are Schrodinger's Rules: it all depends on how you look at the rule and whether the rule is in a box that you need to open.

I don't mean to be oblique. It's important that we're not clear about these things because they aren't clear. But we're getting closer to an understanding.

Daniel Johnston can bash away on a guitar that probably hasn't ever been subjected to a digital tuner because he writes phenomenal, fractured songs that suit a certain amount of laxness in the technical details because the spirit of the songs has nothing to do with technical details. But if Yngwie Malmsteen was to finger-tap himself through an out of tune version of Flight of the Bumblebee his entire audience would notice and tut themselves to near death because his music is all about precision and technique and his audience revere that precision and technique.

So it's rarely about rules – it's almost always about context.

Context tells us whether an out of tune guitar is acceptable. Context tells us whether a burst of atonal noise partway through an otherwise rhapsodic piece is a fascinating musical development or a misstep. Context gives us the loose set of expectations that define genre for us: hitting the off beat may lead us to expect reggae or ska; a four to the floor, sampled kick drum is a signature of techno music; a bottleneck guitar will give a flavour of the blues.

A sloppy, out of tune vocal might work in the context of an underground lo-fi self release but it would have given Brian Wilson nightmares.

Understand the context of what you want to do. If you're a rock 'n' roll band, capture spirit and energy first and foremost. If you want soul, make and record your music soulfully. If you make electronic music and desire soullessness and precision, make it soulless and precise. These may appear to be statements of the bleedin' obvious but I cannot tell you how many times I've heard new artists who get their context all wrong and subsequently make their music impossible for others to invest their belief and their time in.

I have a deleted files folder filled with weedy, overly precise, lifeless rock recordings with less atmosphere than an accountancy convention on the dark side of the moon. I have an almost equal amount of messy, formulaic electronic recordings built with dead sounds that moved me two steps closer to my own end, when I listened to them.

Whatever type of music you make it has to be convincing. First and foremost, it has to convince you, the writer, and then, if you want it to reach a wider audience, it has to forge a link to other people's hearts via their ears.

Every weakness in your whole – the composition, the performance, the recording – will move that potential audience a step further away from you. One   too many badly-pitched vocal phrases, or out of time drum beats, will make it entirely impossible for them to suspend their disbelief long enough to believe in you and your music.

So there are some rules but it's up to you to recognise which apply to you and the context of what you're doing.

And, of course, context and rules are there to be messed with and treated with irreverence – as long as you have a sense – whether through instinct or learning – of what you want to achieve.

By the time you've finished reading this book you will have read through a mass of advice, some of it contradictory, from a range of different artists. These snippets of advice are not rules. You don't have to follow any of the advice offered here. If you're clear about what you want to do with your music, and where you think it fits within the grand scheme of things, then finding advice that's relevant to you and planning a path through the music industry will be easier.

Not easy... just easier.

A fundamental question for me is this? Do you want to be famous or do you want to be in a great band? I think the answer – probably – is 'yes' to both of those. But they're often not compatible with each other.

David Gedge, The Wedding Present

A good start would be for you to identify your aims for your music. Define yourself... whether you're a solo artist, a band member, looking to form a collective, a prospective label owner, a guitarist, a producer, a programmer, a rapper or a flautist.

Perhaps you decide that you're a guitar playing singer-songwriter who wants to build their fanbase by doing as many gigs as possible, who would appreciate radio play to extend that audience and who is eventually planning to self-release their music, via one of the many different digital outlets, because you value your own autonomy.

Maybe you're a singer looking for a band to help you find worldwide acclaim via the few opportunities still offered by the traditional recording industry. You want to find someone to collaborate with to write that killer song. You're interested in finding a good manager, eventually, because you have no business acumen of your own, and you're not sure you want to learn it... running counter – as it does – to your understanding of what rock 'n' roll is.

Or you're an electronic artist who isn't particularly

interested in gigging or seeking a record label. You just want to hone your sound until you feel confident enough to press up your own 12" promo, and take it from there – with the eventual ambition of running your own record label.

Write down who you are, what you do and what you want from music, and do that now. Referring to it will help you to recognise the advice that will best help you.

If you seek it, you will find lots and lots… and lots… of advice. The music section of your local library or bookshop will feature a trove of experience in the form of biographies and autobiographies. There are millions of artist interviews online. That's not an exaggeration. Read what you can, when you can. Other people's experiences and working techniques can be both inspirational and educational.

Meet other music people. Hang out at venues, independent record shops, the music room at school or any local rehearsal facilities. Talk to, and listen to, whoever you can.

Maybe you're not that garrulous. Many of my favourite artists would baulk at the idea of what I've recommended above: Elliott Smith, Nick Drake and the like. In our enlightened age you can hang out in the digital equivalents of these places and learn things without having your natural sensibilities challenged.

Do all of these things and you will end up with reams of well-intentioned advice.

I'm sure you'll get loads and loads of advice from people like me. So the first thing I would say to you is listen to everyone but then take a consensus of opinion and draw on that and take what's relevant to you.

Ultimately you have to make your own mind up about things that you think are important and –

generally – if you get a few people telling you something and that matches up with your gut reaction then you'll know where the truth lies.

Paul Draper, Mansun

Paul's band went from making one of the most original and successful albums of the Britpop era – Attack of the Grey Lantern, No.1 in the album charts in 1997 – to recording one of the most influential and experimental, certainly on a major record label – Six.

When it comes to advice about your art, it's likely that you'll already have an idea of where you want to go and what you want to do with it. Trust your instincts but be wise enough to seek objective advice from people who don't have a vested interest in you or your music.

One of my favourite bands, Badfinger, became the ultimate, tragic epilogue to artist exploitation, bad contracts and mismanagement. It's hard to imagine that any of the advice they ever received was good, constructive advice. Read their story, it's a salutary tale of the worst things that can happen when remarkable talent is subsumed by a cold-hearted industry. Although the more exploitative aspects of that industry are now hopefully a thing of the past, it's worth knowing what happened to Badfinger. When you're faced with adversity, their story – and the tragic denouements – will make you realise that things aren't that bad after all.

Tjinder Singh, co-founder of one of the UK's most enduring leftfield bands Cornershop, is more dismissive of other people's advice:

I don't think there is any advice that you can give bands starting out. I think things change at each stage of the way: from starting out, to building up your audience, to getting somewhere, and I think the parameters always change.

Tjinder Singh, Cornershop

I respect Tjinder more than most of the people I have made acquaintance with in the last couple of decades. I think he's right to say that everyone's musical situation is unique but that's just life in microcosm. Look at the amount of books, magazines and websites dedicated to offering us advice on every aspect of our lives: from personal relationships through to financial advice. Advice is valid and can keep up with an ever-changing world if it has a kernel of truth to it.

And that's the very nature of the advice I have sought out for you.

But this book offers no guarantees. In fact I imagine that if you follow the advice set out in these pages, you'll probably have a difficult time trying to get yourself playlisted on any radio station; you'll end up befuddling at least half of any audience that turns up to your gigs; your releases will – if you're lucky – sell in the 1000's rather than the 100,000's and family and your more sanctimonious friends will ask you with increasing regularity when you're going to get a 'proper' job.

Ah, the 'proper job'...

This is a phrase that, for time immemorial, has haunted every music-maker. I'm writing this at a time when youth unemployment is at its highest level for decades. I don't want to be blithe about paid work.

If someone offers you an opportunity at a young age there will be a crowd of people, headed by parents, advising you that you'd be better off getting an education first, that you can do anything once you have a good solid foundation of qualifications. Parents are duty bound to say this. So are teachers. Basically any voice of authority that a teenager hears will recommend the safe route and understandably so.

However I say, go with your heart. You'll know deep down if you're any good. And by 'deep down' I don't mean the bravado that fuels your self-written biography. Be honest with yourself. If you're good and you're willing to forego hot food, friends, family and an income to chase your dream, then fucking do it.

This country is full of further education colleges. You can get qualifications any time you want but, like being a striker in an FA Cup Final, you'll be lucky to get two sightings of the net of musical opportunities, at most. Being wily enough to recognise those opportunities, and brave enough to seize them, is what sets many esteemed artists apart; they just had the guts to do it.

Quit whatever day job you have, quit whatever university you're enrolled in, whatever it is, to give it all up like a monk gives it up for God — and get in the van, or the car, or the train, or whatever it is that moves you from A to B and to get out there in the world and do your thing, however you make it happen.

That's my biggest advice. More than anything — think about your art, dig deep and think about your art and be great and don't worry about your website, or your management, or your flyers, or your band photos, or your band name, or your mailing list, or your street team, or your stickers, or your t-shirts, or anything else that doesn't really have anything to do with music.

Frank Black, The Pixies

[1]**Rock 'n' roll** - *The term 'rock 'n' roll' may strike you as quaint but it's one that I will use throughout this book as a catch all. I know that labels and genre tags may be*

important to you but in here they won't have a lot of validity.

PLAYLIST:

Man - Spunk Box
The Alarm - Sixty Eight Guns
Dizzee Rascal - Fix Up, Look Sharp
The Specials - Ghost Town
The Smiths - Still Ill
Pulp - Babies
The Supremes - Stoned Love
The Velvelettes - Needle In A Haystack
Syreeta Wright - Black Maybe
Stevie Wonder - Living For The City
NWA - Straight Outta Compton
The Mekons - Where Were You?
The Sex Pistols - Bodies
The Clash - Safe European Home
The Slits - Typical Girls
The Ramones - Blitzkreig Bop
Kraftwerk - Computer Love
Yngwie Malmsteen - Flight of the Bumblebee
Irma Vep - One Eye On Everything
Daniel Johnston - True Love Will Find You In The End
The Wedding Present - Nobody's Twisting Your Arm
Mansun - I Can Only Disappoint U
Badfinger - Baby Blue
Cornershop - Sleep On The Left Side
Pixies - Bone Machine

2: <u>First Notes</u>

Probably the most valuable lesson that I've learnt since I've started is to be passionate about what you're doing because I think that gives you the strength to not give in, and to overcome the obstacles – emotional obstacles, financial obstacles – that you might encounter in the music industry.

Clive Langer, record producer

Let's start at the very start. I assume that the majority of people reading this will be some way along the path of learning and expressing themselves through their instrument of choice (including voices and using software.) Don't ignore this chapter. It's never a bad idea to remind yourselves what drew you to that instrument, or the desire to make a musical noise, in the first place. And for anyone reading this who hasn't yet chosen an instrument but who feels a need to make music, this chapter will give some illumination as to how other people made the first steps towards making their own noise.

Other than taping the Top 40 every Sunday evening and wrecking my dad's records by listening to them over and over again, I hadn't shown any interest whatsoever in making music or learning an instrument. My Granddad Walton had been the Viceroy's bugler in India prior to the Second World War and my dad had learnt the trumpet when he was a youngster (the minute he was old enough he swapped his trumpet for a motorbike – a more rock 'n' roll gesture than any I've managed to make). Despite the family history, no one was making music in my house as I grew up, but music was a constant presence.

Then, aged 11, I went away with school to Glan Llyn, a

First Notes

Welsh language training camp on the cold and misty shores of Llyn Tegid in Bala. I don't know if it was because it was my first trip away from home without the parents but everything that week was charged with excitement.

There was a kid in our year called Graham Devine. I didn't really know him. I was mesmerised more by our footballing peers and the retinue of cooing girls that would trail in the wake of their nascent mullets and Old Spice fumes. That changed – immediately – the moment I walked into one of the reception rooms in Glan Llyn and heard Graham playing the classical guitar. It was nothing short of an epiphany. That moment was the single most important catalyst in my entire life. Something about the wonderful sound that was coming out of his guitar rang my soul like nothing had before – and little since. It completely enraptured me.

All I could think about after that was getting my own guitar. I begged and badgered my mum and dad half to death when I got back home and – eventually – they relented and my hands spent the next 20 years on, or near, a fretboard. It didn't lead me to fame or, even, notoriety but it led me here: to radio, and expounding my wisdom, and I still get more satisfaction out of being able to play the guitar than I do from almost anything else.

Maybe your instrument will call to you in a similarly Damascene way. Maybe a random lottery of instruments in a well-heeled primary school brought you your first instrumental love. Perhaps it was seeing someone like Bowie or Hendrix on the TV. Or (and I type this through gritted fingers): Matt Bellamy. Maybe it was a different kind of music-making: Grandmaster Flash on the wheels of steel or Skrillex with his headphones plugged into a laptop. Or maybe the inveterate coolness of the bands you listened to in your formative years bewitched you and you had no choice but to follow in their wake.

For many a key factor in leading them to music was the

fact that family members already had musical instruments in the house.

My dad's bass guitar was always lying around the house and I would have been watching him play. I'd have been about 5 or 6 and I just started messing about with it. But at that age there was something big and clunky about the bass guitar and it probably wasn't melodic enough to keep me interested.

Ritzy Bryan, The Joy Formidable

So Ritzy took up the opportunity to learn flute at school but that didn't work out either:

It went dreadfully. I was so frustrated at not being able to make it sound good quickly and also it used to make me want to faint. It definitely felt as if I didn't have the lung capacity for a wind instrument, so I ditched that and I moved on to harp.

The only reason I decided to do harp in school was because I think the lessons fell half-way through maths and if there was one thing in school that I absolutely hated it was maths. It was a good excuse to get out of that. But then the harp teacher was actually psychotic. She was a right bitch.

I never practised at all. I just used to sight read from week to week and she could tell. She was like, "this little shit hasn't done anything…"

Ritzy Bryan, The Joy Formidable

Gruff Rhys from Super Furry Animals started off as a drummer because of the musical topography in his family:

First Notes

My older brother already played the guitar and if there's a guitarist in the house already, you try a different instrument, you know? I decided I wanted to play drums so I started to collect buckets when I was about 6 years old and I had a collection going and then I joined the band – to play drums – when I was about 13.

Gruff Rhys

Musical topography extends beyond your family too. If you're a drummer or a bassist, you're going to be more in demand because there are hundreds of thousands of guitarists out there. Obviously follow your heart first and foremost, but it can save you frustration and heartache if you're objective about what you decide to play and the opportunities that that choice will present to you.

Once you have chosen your instrument – or it has chosen you – there is the small matter of learning how to play it. Nowadays the vast resource of the internet gives you access to a bewildering array of free tutorials, tabs and pieces of music – as well as any information you may need to break and understand either of those codes. This is a world away from teenagers huddling around Dansettes in the 60's, slowing their favourite 45's down to 33 r.p.m. so that they could work out what was being played.

There are those who would advise you to not learn your instrument at all – at least in a formal sense. Learn too much and technique and knowledge may start to get in the way of you having your own style.

I don't much subscribe to that point of view. Some of my favourite musicians received a certain amount of formal training: The Joy Formidable, Sweet Baboo and Georgia Ruth, chief amongst them. The techniques and musical understanding they picked up has helped them broaden their musical palette. I've never interviewed a musician who said that classical lessons, or a knowledge of musical theory, hampered them.

Neither, though, is it necessarily an advantage or a prerequisite. John Lennon and Paul McCartney couldn't – initially at least – read a note of music. Of course The Beatles were in the fortunate position that by the time they were given access to string sections and brass they were working with a producer and arranger par excellence in George Martin. The key thing to recognise here is that a formal knowledge didn't make the Beatles songs any more extraordinary. It was their imaginations – and informal musical knowledge – that inspired and formed their songs.

Kim Deal, the eventual bassist for the Pixies, turned up to her first rehearsal completely unable to play the bass guitar.

As we learnt in the last chapter, there are no hard-fast rules.

It's also worth noting that having some kind of formal musical training or knowledge can open doors for you in the future, doors that may help your own music progress. Carwyn Ellis, from an acclaimed band called Colorama, studied music at college to degree level. He's subsidised his own music through playing sessions, and being a guitarist / keyboardist for hire, for the likes of Edwyn Collins. Edwyn Collins released Colorama's most recent album – at the time of writing – on his own independent label, AED Records.

Session work can be a fruitful way to bolster your own income and a very useful way to get you and your music introduced to people who can help you progress. But you have to be a very accomplished musician, certainly with regards to a proficiency for sight-reading sheet music, to make a living in that very competitive field.

Someone has to do it, though. All areas of music production, certainly when it comes to finding an audience, are competitive and challenging. Taking the short cut every time is likely to lead you down blind and inescapable alleys.

If you can find a decent teacher – one who has an understanding of what you want to learn from the instrument and who can take you in that direction – then that teacher is a godsend and will help you learn much more quickly than if you were teaching yourself. However if you get the impression – or even a whiff of an impression – that your teacher is there just to take your money; that they don't seem engaged or enthused by sharing knowledge with you; or they insist on taking you down blind alleys you know are completely unrelated to what you want to learn, then ditch them.

Lessons are expensive. Teachers are plentiful. It's worth going to the effort of finding the right one for you.

Your best teacher will always be your own enthusiasm for the instrument. You could go to the best music teacher in the world but if you have no hunger to learn then you won't progress. If you're reading a book like this I think it's safe to assume that you have a deep, and probably insatiable, appetite for music and learning more about music.

Absorb as many aspects of your chosen instrument as you can. Listen to inspirational recordings by noted exponents so that you learn the possibilities of the instrument and the range of sounds that the instrument can produce. Dedicate yourself to finding a technique that matches what you want to express. You're learning how to use a tool through which you can express your soul. The better you do that, the quicker you'll find personal satisfaction in your music and – ultimately – an audience for that music.

Deke Leonard was guitarist, songwriter and founder of the legendary Man band, Wales' most successful progressive rock group. He's written a series of autobiographies that thrum with his love for music, his wit and insight, books that are brimful of anecdotes and wisdom that anyone embarking on an artistic adventure in music can learn from, even though the goalposts have moved many times in the six decades he has been making music. This is what Deke told me about what he learnt from one of his heroes, perhaps the most inspirational guitarist of all time:

I had a friend who once shared a flat with Jimi Hendrix. He told me that Hendrix never stopped playing the guitar. He played while cooking, while talking on the telephone, while rolling a joint and even when sitting on the toilet.He loved the guitar so much he couldn't put it down.

This is what you're up against. Work tirelessly on your instrument of choice. The more you do it the better you'll get.

Deke Leonard, Man

But it's not just about individual instruments. Nurture a love for music per se. We'll talk much more about this in a forthcoming chapter, suffice to say that narrow-minded listening will lead to narrow-minded music-making, and although focus can be a good thing – it's best to keep your private horizons as broad as possible. If you spend 10 years listening to nothing but minimal house music, you'll be chasing an ever decreasing muse, for ever diminishing returns.

The real innovators of any genre that tends to attract purists and music snobs are rarely purists or music snobs themselves.

John Lydon would have been derided as he dragged punk up the Mall in Silver Jubilee year if it had been more widely known that he liked Abba or Pink Floyd (both artists he's subsequently admitted to listening to). Viv Albertine[1], guitarist and songwriter in The Slits, had remarkably broad musical tastes: The Beatles, Captain Beefheart, Edgar Broughton Band, The Kinks, Hawkwind.

Another key catalyst for people learning to express themselves musically is their peers. If you have friends who are also learning to play an instrument, the natural sense of competition and camaraderie that exists between you can be a great motivating force to learning and sharing new songs, new techniques and tricks. Keep your ears open whoever you're playing with. And watch their fingers, or their feet, or whatever bodily part it is that's responsible for the music-making to hear how they make something sound good, or new, or – indeed – bad.

Steal everything you can that you like. Be a musical magpie and do not be ashamed of it. This is how music and musicianship has grown and spread for centuries. No one owns music: certainly not a technique or an effective mannerism. The more different ways you learn to express yourself you have in your kitbag, the better and more broad-ranging your music-making will be. It's no different to learning a language. Every technique is a word; every riff a phrase; every song a quotable paragraph. The bigger your musical vocabulary, the better able you will be to express yourself uniquely and with a compelling grace.

From early on, record yourself. The most rudimentary mobile phones allow you to do this easily. It's not always easy to listen to your own playing objectively when you're caught in the moment of performance. Frequently the sense of achievement in getting through a new song, or a riff, can override any critical faculties you have.

Listen back to what you've played and aim to improve the flaws. A teacher can help you identify those flaws, as can friends. But be unstinting – without being anal to the point of hobbling your enjoyment of music-making – in trying to improve yourself.

One of the mantras of this book – certainly when you come to recording finished songs and pieces that you want people to hear – will be for you to 'be your own worst critic'. Listening critically to the music you make starts now. It needn't hamper you or constrain you. Getting things wrong is all part of the process of learning and extending yourself. Accept that and understand that the quicker you can identify your weaknesses – whether they be in timing or phrasing or flow or technique – the quicker you can eradicate them from your playing, and *get better*.

Some creative writing courses recommend that aspiring writers learn a new word every day. The same general advice can be given to music-makers, with regards a riff or a song or a part of a song. Now writers aren't expected to use every new word they learn – in fact, some of the worst writing committed to print is done by people who flex their vocabulary for vocabulary's sake, but along the way a good writer will learn when is the right time to use a new word and every new word learnt will move them closer to having their own voice. And that's what we're after, here: you – as a music maker – having your own voice, your own sound.

For the vast majority of music-making people, the path to their own sound is through other people's music. So many great artists started off in very transitory, mayfly school bands butchering the hits of the day. These are bands formed with the schoolmates I mentioned earlier. Sometimes these school bands – The Stereophonics are an example – do go on to fully-fledged international recognition and acclaim. Mostly they break up in bitter acrimony after the school dance, or whatever engagement it is that they formed for, is over.

You can learn a lot about band dynamics – how to replicate, to the best of your abilities, your favourite songs – from being in a school band or a covers band. You can also learn an awful lot about band politics: the tangle of egos, the amplifier wars, identifying deadwood, that are the constituency of every young band ever. These are important lessons.

However you can't form a band unless you have a rough idea of what you want to play – that comes from having a restless spirit fuelled by a love for music. And you get a love for music by listening to it.

[1]**Viv Albertine** - *I highly recommend Viv's brilliant autobiography* **Clothes, Clothes, Clothes, Music, Music, Music, Boys, Boys, Boys**. *It's the finest evocation I have ever read of someone discovering their own musical voice and then making it heard, despite the sexism and elitism that she encountered on a daily basis.*

PLAYLIST:
Robert Wyatt - Shipbuilding
Graham Anthony Devine - Po de Mico (Itching Powder)
The Joy Formidable - Austere
Sweet Baboo - Cate's Song
Colorama - Too Much Data
Edwyn Collins - You'll Never Know
Jimi Hendrix - All Along The Watchtower
Pink Floyd - Lucifer Sam
Stereophonics - Local Boy In The Photograph
The Slits - Typical Girls
Viv Albertine - I Want More

3: <u>William Tyler On First Notes</u>

I grew up in Nannerch, Flintshire, a village with a population of fewer than 500 (certainly back when I lived there.) I learnt my first chords as part of a happy clappy, folky ensemble in a neighbour's house. We'd congregate every Saturday morning and strum through Beatles songs. My abiding memory of our very keen and affable teacher, Mr Willis-Culpitt, was his enthusiasm for Maxwell's Silver Hammer, as played on nine, out of tune, three quarter-size classical guitars; a predilection that redefines the word 'masochistic'.

I went from there to Sarah Jones, a more austere and traditional classical guitar teacher, who taught some phenomenal guitarists (including Ritzy Bryan and Graham Anthony Devine). I wasn't too enamoured with the requisite discipline of playing the same pieces over and over again and soon stopped turning up for lessons. I wish I'd stuck with them. I really do.

By this stage, rock 'n' roll had come calling. I had a Tokai Strat and a 10W practise amp that I used to cart into Back Alley Music in Mold, where the Chicagoan proprietor Gary would teach me JJ Cale songs and pentatonic scales.

These were the people who shone a light onto the many mysteries of the guitar I couldn't solve myself. But it was my own hunger and curiosity that drove me onwards, inexorably – in my case – towards failure and obscurity.

What did people who went on to become good and renowned at their instrument do differently? That is one of the key areas I wanted to explore with On Making Music.

Of course, I understand that there isn't one simple answer to this question. 'Good' and 'renown' are pretty subjective qualities. However some insight from people who have forged a life from music should prove valuable to those of you who want to make a life of your own through music.

I suspect there is no more magic involved in getting good than dedication and having the bloody mindedness to follow your instincts.

'Renown' is something we have less control over. Attaining renown can be a lot about the luck of where you come from and who you meet. Being good will help, though. You'll need to work out what 'good' means for you, whether it means being technically adept, finding your own sound, or – most probably – a combination of the two.

William Tyler's renown is definitely a combination of the two. He grew up in Nashville, Tennessee, fabled for being one of the most musically fertile cities on the planet. His adeptness at the guitar, and the sense of adventure that is key to his sound, earned him the opportunity to play with artists of the stature of Lambchop, Bonnie Prince Billy, Silver Jews and Candi Staton.

I first came across William, his troubadour spirit and remarkable solo music, when I compered and DJ'd on the Walled Garden Stage at Green Man Festival in deepest Mid Wales in August 2014.

I like to make sure I know something about the artists I introduce. Mostly this is so I don't play anything wildly inappropriate before they start their set. I bought William's Lost Colony E.P off iTunes and I was intrigued. 'Karussell', in particular, resonated with me, somehow evoking memories of undeviating highways I'd never travelled, underneath an endless sky, going somewhere – I don't know where – but wherever it is, there is hope and possibilities. 'Karussell' sounds like a lost Kraut masterpiece, something by Harmonia or Neu![1], being reinterpreted by the Allman Brothers and Brian Eno. It's wonder filled. We drove all the way to Green Man with it on loop. It's *great* driving music.

William Tyler played his set on the Sunday evening: one man with a guitar, a pedalboard and a battered valise of fascinating anecdotes managing to enchant a couple of thousand people. His music is evocative, expansive, intriguing... all of those flouncy adjectives you end up using when you don't have the vocabulary to encapsulate music that gets you here (the heart) and here (the head). He makes me want to buy myself a Tele and an amp and to resurrect my musical dreams again, if only for my own satisfaction.

I stood at the side of the stage musing as to what William's musical journey had been; how he had become this panchromatic rush of sound. I wondered if he'd tell me how he learnt to be as good as he is for my book On Making Music, which could do with a chapter to that effect.

Some days later I e-mailed William a request for an interview and he said 'yes'. You'd probably guessed that much from the chapter heading.

What are your earliest musical memories, William?

Going to shows with my parents, who were both involved in the music business in Nashville... seeing a lot of older guys with long hair and guitars traipsing in and out of the house at odd hours.

The first music I gravitated towards was classical, and I remember watching an old cartoon where the 'William Tell' overture played through the whole plot. I called my granddad, who worked with the symphony in Jackson, Mississippi , and hummed some of the melody to find out what the music was. He told me it was by Rossini and the next day my dad took me out to buy a record of his overtures. So that was the first record I ever bought.

Was making music a calling for you?

Probably, considering it was on both sides of my family. But to be honest until late in high school I wanted to be a history professor. I feel like now I am trying to reconcile those paths.

People assume that it's inevitable, almost, that someone from Nashville will be born with a natural affinity for music. Is it a particularly musically supportive area to grow up in? Has travelling so much in recent years underlined how atypical that is?

Of course, and a lot of it is just that so many people grow up in musical families. So I experienced a close proximity to it at a young age, and so did a lot of my friends who grew up there. I mean, it is a particularly fascinating place, a city of half a million people and a huge percentage of musicians and creatives. It's something I take for granted and traveling has reinforced that.

How did you learn the guitar? Were there teachers? Were the teachers instrumental (if you'll pardon the pun)? Or is the most important teacher always your own curiosity and hunger to make music?

I took lessons for a few years but a lot of what I know now was self taught. My first guitar teacher was a close family friend and is still a big influence. I think it's really important to have someone guiding you through those awkward first steps of finger positioning, learning scales, getting callouses, etc. But the fingerstyle stuff I basically taught myself.

I'm making assumptions here (having never, sadly, been to Nashville), but I imagine that your music-making evolved in an environment where there were a lot of other music-makers... is having friends to play with key too, do you think? Being able to watch other people play? Get inspired by them and allow them to be inspired by you? But also a healthy sense of competition.

A lot of competition but I mean, it's so humbling to live in a city like Nashville with so many remarkable guitar players...you can't have an ego about any of it, you just have to go head down and play your ass off and try to keep up. I think the attitude in Nashville, at least among the 'pickers', is very close to Zen-like: confident but humble, very inspiring.

Are you still learning? Is that fundamentally important? (to stay hungry and curious)

Every day. And yes, staying hungry and staying humble are key.

Have you any theories as to what it was that made you 'good', that enabled you to turn making music into your

life? Is it a gift? Dedication? Necessity?

Probably all of those...I realised pretty early on I wasn't as technically facile as a lot of other dudes I knew but I am super focused on getting better and practicing. I really believe in 'vibe' and melody and identity...some of my favourite guitar moments of all time were by people who couldn't necessarily shred in a 'wow' sort of way. I don't think that's what music has to be about all the time.

In the chapter preceding this one, Deke Leonard from Man regales us with an anecdote about Hendrix, how he had the guitar with him whatever else he was doing around his flat: sleeping, eating, smoking, on the toilet... does that picture ring true with you?

Definitely at times in my life. In general I prefer there to be a guitar close by at all times...or I get kind of anxious!

When did you become aware that you had your own sound, a sonic fingerprint that had developed through the experiences detailed above?

Probably about five years ago. I was reticent to share the music I was making with other folks but I could tell that it resonated and that was very validating. And then when I decided to focus on that and disassociate myself from other bands I was playing with at the time, it just had to be a leap of faith, spiritually and sonically.

Were you at all conscious of encouraging your own sound, being a little different, or was it less self conscious

than that?

I assumed there would be a lot of 'oh no not another John Fahey' backlash, but I sorta didn't care. I recorded 'Behold The Spirit' seriously not assuming that anyone would want to put it out, let alone like it. But I felt very proud of it and I wanted to share it.

How much was having your own sound, your own way of doing things, key to you working with the likes of Lambchop / Bonnie Prince Billy / Silver Jews etc.? Or, as an occasional guitar for hire, do you have to sacrifice your own sound for the good of the whole?

I'm a flexible player because of my history. I have a 'sound' but it can blend well with all sorts of artists. Being in other people's bands at a young age taught me a lot about how to play behind people and not on top of them…but when I play solo I have to reverse that.

It was very clear, playing records on the stage before you went on, that your love for music, and subsequent musical knowledge, is profound… recognising Gerry Rafferty from an obscure Stealer's Wheel track, a Freddie King recording and Bryan Ferry's version of What Goes On… how important is being a fan of music key to your own music? It might sound like a facile question… but I speak to a surprising number of artists who don't appear to listen to much beyond their own music.

Music gets me through the day.…I mean if I hear a song that I need to hear again, I will play it like fifty times in a row. Right now I am totally obsessed with this live version of "Fat Man in the Bathtub" by Little Feat from 1974. And for almost a week I have been listening to it five times a day. There is nothing like a song to get you by.

Who have been the key artists in shaping you as a music maker?

Eno, Miles Davis, Alex Chilton, Ben Chasny, Sandy Bull, Ry Cooder, Richard Thompson, Bill Frisell, Chet Atkins, Sonny Sharrock, The Byrds, Prince.

How open-minded are you about technology? Your one man show utilises loop pedals and effects pedals in ways I've never heard them used before… it's pretty mindblowing!

I am super open-minded, but my wallet has to be a little closed! You can go broke with pedals but it's never going to be boring.

Has the kind of technology I refer to above enabled you, from the point of view that you can tour anywhere, in one vehicle, but still make a big, rich, wonderful sound?

Yes, I mean, I would love to run two amps honestly! But that's even more gear to lug around. I love creating a big sound with one person. It's good theatre and there's a lot of power in it. It feels like being a preacher.

What's next for you?

Working on my first commissioned piece for Duke University which is going to be a multimedia piece involving my music and a collection of old Civil War–era photographs. After that, working on a new album for early next year.

Please do visit William's website http://williamtyler.net and immerse yourselves in his excellent catalogue of music. If you love music, and making music, as much as he clearly does, the odds of you making a fine and intriguing noise of your own will increase markedly.

[1]*'Karussell'* **sounds like a lost Kraut masterpiece, something by Harmonia or Neu!** - *It's only as I'm compiling the Spotify playlist for this chapter that I realise that Karussell is actually William's interpretation of a piece of music written by Michael Rother (a key member of both Harmonia and Neu!) This is why downloads should come with sleeve notes and music radio folk shouldn't be allowed to write anything, until they've listened to all recorded music, ever.*

PLAYLIST:

William Tyler - Lost Colony E.P

William Tyler - Blue Ash Montgomery

William Tyler - Impossible Truth

Little Feat - Fat Man In The Bathtub

Michael Rother - Karussell

4: <u>Carwyn Ellis On Reading Music</u>

In the T.V series, The Wire, the highest compliment members of Baltimore P.D can bestow on each other is that of 'natural police' (or 'po-lees' as it's pronounced in the Baltimore brogue). It's recognition that someone has the necessary instincts for the role, they're not too stiff from learning or adhering to rulebooks to get the job done. See episode 4 season 1, when Bunk and Jimmy read a crime scene for a perfect example of what 'natural po-lees' means. Do, however, approach that scene with caution if you have any degree of aversion to 'natural cussing'.

Throughout this book we touch upon how important instinct and the subconscious are in making music. Charlotte Church talks about how her music is inspired subliminally, without paying too much conscious attention to what she listens to. Ritzy from The Joy Formidable allows her subconscious to nurture a new song, rather than trying to force her ideas out. Martin Carr tells us that his mind is constantly ticking over songwriting ideas in the background as he goes about his daily routine. Andrew Falkous preferred the sound his guitar made, and the options it presented him, when he no idea how it was tuned because that lack of knowledge gave him the freedom to play, and create, instinctively.

It's the things that you can do subconsciously, enabled by having done them over and over and over again so that they become – almost – reflex mechanisms, or "second nature" as every football commentator likes to put it, that make you 'natural'. And 'natural' tends to be good and more convincing or engaging for the listener.

This notion of 'grace' is a central tenet to one of my favourite books, Philip Pullman's His Dark Materials. Lyra, the main character, is given a device that can divine the future. She's an adolescent girl with no bookish training, whatsoever, on the subject of how to read the 'alethiometer', but she learns through dedication, curiosity and struggle, that the best way to interpret it is to not overthink it, to let her mind settle and allow grace, or instinct, to take over.

It's an excellent analogy for learning, and playing, music.

Carwyn Ellis, founding member and chief songwriter for the very excellent Colorama, is 'natural music'. His band's albums are a celebration of joyous, unfettered musical creativity. Nothing sounds forced or awkward. On occasions, his music sounds crafted – but craft is defined by that moment when a learnt skill becomes intuitive. Many of Colorama's melodies have the grace and conviction of a world class ballerina. Conversely when things get dirty or funky, you can hear a band playing almost entirely on their instincts and urges.

What kind of teaching and learning brought him (and his excellent band) to this rarefied level of expression?

Well, I'm being somewhat disingenuous: I knew the answer before I asked the question… which is the major reason for making a point of levelling this particular question at Carwyn.

I know that he had a more formal musical training than many of his contemporaries. I know that he reads music and I know that he has done a significant amount of session work (a paid guitar or keyboard player for hire) in the past.

On occasion, the prejudice is that learning an instrument in a more rigorous, 'classical' fashion – via scales and the dots – suppresses natural instincts and turns the players into nothing more than expensive, flashy-fingered automatons. But there's none of that in Carwyn's playing, none whatsoever; nor is there in Ritzy Joy Formidable's or Georgia Ruth's (both of whom also had a classical background).

Punk was a phenomenal watershed in making music, and particularly the making of music, accessible and thrilling for everyone. However it's interesting, also, to recognise and celebrate the benefits that some graft and learning can bring you.

Carwyn, what are you earliest music-making memories? Was there an instrument in the house? Can you remember feeling a particular fascination with making a musical noise?

As far back as I can remember, the only real deep interest I've had has been in music, even before I was aware of what music actually was. My mother sang and played the organ, so right from the get go there was an organ in the house. I vaguely remember mucking about with it when I was tall enough to reach it. I think I've had a compulsion to make noise ever since I've known it existed.

Was there a formal / classical aspect to your musical education from early on?

Yes – from about the age of 8. My folks started me off with lessons at the local organ shop with a nice lady called Julie. We started on the 'Complete Organ Player' Songbooks – popular hits from yesteryear mostly. Not classical as such. I started having classical piano lessons proper when I'd finished the 'Complete Organ Player' books. I was about ten or eleven then I think.

Carwyn Ellis On Reading Music

One of the aspects of 'classical' lessons that can put people off is learning scales and arpeggios, was it onerous for you? Can you now measure and understand the benefits that those exercises gave you?

Not onerous as such, just boring. I definitely understand the benefits of these now though. Different instruments require different skills, but most instruments definitely benefit from a knowledge of where to put your fingers, and which fingers make the task more manageable. The idea being that the more you do these things, they become ingrained so that eventually, you won't have to think about them. That's usually the purpose of the exercises.

How much did the more formal aspects of your musical education run parallel with an interest in non-formal music? Was there ever a danger of one almost discounting the other?

I always enjoyed making things up on the organ or piano. I played the recorder, then the clarinet, and then the bassoon by the time I was eleven. But all of these, especially the latter three, relied upon some kind of written music. I picked up the electric guitar when I was 14, and taught myself entirely. From that point on, formal/classical music making became less fun for me. Fewer possibilities and less freedom. Ultimately this did nullify my desire to read music.

Have you encountered much inverted snobbery from other musicians? Perhaps a prejudice against some formal learning on the assumption that it is somehow un-rock 'n' roll or anti-intuitive?

No, not really. I've never felt the need to really show off on instruments, or to show other people up. I know I can hold my own. Sometimes, early on in bands, I would stop things if they were a bit out of tune. This would annoy the hell out of others, who rightly believed they weren't doing anything wrong. I learned to get over that. My problem, not theirs.

How 'difficult' was it to learn to read music and to understand music theory? Or is 'difficult' something of a misplaced prejudice?

I don't know – everyone's different. I personally found all that stuff easy to absorb and I wanted to know as much as possible. I would read theory and history books in my own time too. The best thing a teacher can do is enable you to teach yourself. Ultimately, 'theory' is just that – nothing is more useful than intuition, application or talent. These cannot be taught, only refined. This applies to all walks of life.

How much has understanding the above (reading music / musical theory) helped you to develop your own sound?

I've never thought about it, to be honest. I formally studied music about as much as I could stomach, and spent a long time un-learning things afterwards. Somewhere in between the learning and un-learning something must have happened! I've taught myself to play most of the instruments and music I play on a regular basis. For the most part, I consider myself to be self-taught.

Can a formal knowledge help when it comes to composition / writing your own music?

Sure, but there are programs that enable you to do that on a computer now, without having the formal skills.

Can a formal knowledge hinder when it comes to

composition / writing your own music?

If you learn exactly how to write like Bach, Beethoven or Brahms, chances are you'll wind up sounding like them. And if you listen to the Beatles, Byrds and Beach Boys all the time, you may well sound like them too. The word 'formal' to me suggests 'constraint'. It can hinder you if you are not aware of other possibilities. Knowledge can empower but can also restrict.

You have a wonderful grasp of timbre and texture, as evidenced on all of your albums... how much of that comes from listening to orchestrated / 'classical' music?

Thank you! Most of it comes from other people who've been influenced by orchestrated or classical music, I think. A lot of the orchestrated music I've heard regularly in my life is post-World War 2, namely on pop records from Sinatra onwards, or soundtracks to movies. Lately, I'm enjoying more abstract music I must admit – pieces rather than songs. But still from 1950 onwards I'd say.

Sometimes 'technique' can be rather undervalued by rock 'n' rollers... what are the benefits of having a good technique?

It enables you to show off. Or to avoid showing off. By showing off, I mean vulgar displays of technique lacking in style or substance. And some people will pay a lot of money to watch or listen to these. Each to their own.

How enabling has been being able to do session work (which I'm assuming was at least initially predicated on your being able to sight read etc.)? Did those sessions open up doors and make connections that have been valuable for your music?

It's been a lifeline for me. I've met great folks and had great times through doing session work. None of which, by the way, was predicated on being able to sight read. But it's been a big part of my career in music, and definitely opened doors for me. I've been lucky enough to have had the opportunities to work with people who've enriched my existence, socially and musically.

If it wasn't an ability to sight read that enabled you to do session work, how did you end up as a gun for hire?

Well, I've never really seen myself as a gun for hire! To me, a gun for hire is someone who will play with anyone for money. I won't. My career has to be musically interesting for me, and I will not knowingly work with assholes, or people whose music I don't respect.

I started out in bands, and through these, met other people – hung out, jammed etc. The first people who hired me were the North Mississippi Allstars. They were over from America on tour and we met at a party / jam in London. They then asked me to go on tour and record with them, I guess because of my ability to play. And to party! We never rehearsed. Whenever I play with them, we just go onstage and play. It's purely spontaneous. I know not many folks can do that. The next person to hire me was Noel Gallagher, and this (I think) is because he liked the Allstars, and Southern Fly, the band I was in previously, and I suppose he liked what I did. Most of the folks I've worked with have asked me to play with them because they've seen me play with other people. It's usually the best indicator.

PLAYLIST:
The Left Banke - Pretty Ballerina
Jim Sullivan - Rosey
Nico - The Fairest of the Seasons
The Rolling Stones - Lady Jane
Francoise Hardy - La Maison Ou J'ai Grandi

Carwyn Ellis On Reading Music

Nick Drake - Fly
Roy Budd - Diamonds
Joe Zawinul - A Soul Of A Village Pt. II
Michael Kiwanuka - Tell Me A Tale
The Magnetic Field - Interlude
Jesse Futurman - I Love You So
Colorama - Temari (2014), Good Music (2012), Llyfr Lliwio (2011), Box (2010), Magic Lantern Show (2009), Cookie Zoo (2008)

5: <u>Listening</u>

A love for music is the reason that we're all here, right? You might think that's a given but you'd be surprised at the amount of musicians, DJ's and journalists I have met over the years who give the impression that music is, almost, the least interesting aspect of what they do… a means to an end.

I wish I had the courage to name names but this book's intention isn't to cause bad feeling. I'll save that for the next book: *On Bad Feeling*. It'll be a sizeable tome.

Music attracts more hummingbirds than any other means of artistic expression. Hummingbirds want to look nice and to hover around all the right places, zipping about with the similarly bright-feathered and tiny-brained. They'll chirrup on about the musical nectar that's drawn them in but in a shallow and unconvincing manner.

Try not to be a hummingbird.

The albums that I wore out as I grew up were John Williams' 'Cavatina and Other Love Songs', Frankie Goes To Hollywood's 'Welcome To The Pleasuredome', U2's 'War', The Beatles 'Revolver', The Cure's 'Disintegration', the debut Stone Roses album, De La Soul's 'Three Feet High & Rising', The Pixies 'Doolittle', Ride's 'Nowhere' and the Boo Radleys' 'Giant Steps'. There were hundreds of other LP's I listened to but these were the ones I wore out and had to replace. Their patterns and dynamics are part of my DNA.

It's not a particularly broad church of listening but each of these albums led in different directions that widened my musical tastes. The Stone Roses led to Love; Giant Steps led to John Coltrane, The Turtles and King Tubby; De La Soul to

Listening

The Jungle Brothers and Public Enemy; The Beatles to Motown; U2 to Roxy Music and Talking Heads; Ride to My Bloody Valentine… and so on.

Create your own music web. Start off with the bands you like the most, learn what you can from them and then move on to their influences, and then their influences' influences, and so on. Follow the strands as far as they go until the artists you're led to stop making sense to you. It's an interesting way to seek musical inspiration, using artists that have something in common with each other and – in terms of spirit – you too.

Nowadays we have the majority of recorded musical history at our fingertips. Take advantage of this inspirational resource but do try to listen rather than just flicking through just because you can.

Every week I have in the region of 200 different musical submissions to consider for my radio show. Despite my best intentions, it's criminally easy to skip past something that doesn't immediately impress me.

Many of my favourite albums took a lot of listening to for them to reveal their glittering genius. Of the LP's I've listed above, if I listened then as peripatetically as I occasionally do now, I'd never have forged a love for Giant Steps, Disintegration, Doolittle or Nowhere.

Fundamentally I had to learn to love those albums because each of them cost £15. I couldn't afford to abandon them because they hadn't pleased me from the off. Similarly the imported R&B records that Mick Jagger was clutching at Dartford Station in 1961 when Keith Richards spotted him, would have cost a relative fortune. Every sound on those records would have been absorbed into Mick's psyche – even the ones that would have, initially, left him unmoved.

The best albums ask you to invest your time and belief in them. Their depths aren't apparent on first, second or third listens. You forge a relationship with them. Whatever is happening in your life at the time gets linked inextricably with the songs as they find their way into your heart, one by one.

Bear this in mind when you're digesting music. You will learn more from music if you tangle with it. Skate over the top and you'll learn nothing but surface. And great music is rarely just about surface. Think about how many people must have been bemused by The Velvet Underground & Nico, or Tusk, or The Stooges, or Highway 61 Revisited when they first heard them.

Siphon a few thousand tracks off a peer to peer network and there's no way you'll give any of those pieces of music the chance to show you more than their superficial strengths. They'll all become hummingbird feathers. The real inspiration is down there below the feathers, in the anatomy and – particularly – in whatever magic it is that gives great music a heartbeat.

Sometimes people listen to music narrowly because they find what they want early on. I spent six years in a band with two people who rarely listened to anything other than what they knew they already liked. The bass player liked his hardcore and The Jam, maybe some Ride if he was feeling adventurous. The drummer liked Rush.

Both of them would dispute my claim that they listened to music 'narrowly'. They certainly didn't *listen out* for music. They weren't adventurous, seeking out new sounds at every turn to be inspired by.

It meant that our shared musical vocabulary was limited. If we, as a band, tried to push beyond our retro-indie straitjacket we would fall on our faces.

Ask them to play something a bit Kraut and they'd have turned up to rehearsal in questionable uniforms.

We were doomed to failure because we didn't have

enough of a collective love for the magical force that we had pretensions to wield.

My advice is for you to listen to as much music as you can handle. I don't mean the sheer amount of music you listen to... I'm not suggesting you try to plough through one of those interminably prescriptive lists of the 1000 Albums You Must Listen To – On Pain Of Death – Before You Die, or anything.

When I say "as much music" as you can, I mean: surround yourself with music, make it as omnipresent in your life as air. Treat music well. Don't just visit when you want something. The relationship is reciprocal. The more you check out, the more you'll be able to put in. I know this sounds like facile bullshit but it's my experience.

On the subject of those lists, I believe that the cosy consensus as to what constitutes The Greatest Albums Of All Time is something worth challenging. Don't feel the need to subscribe to a previous generation's definition of greatness. Tens of thousands of bands have taken inspiration from Revolver, Pet Sounds, OK Computer, It Takes A Nation Of Millions..., etc. ad nauseum. Find your own touchstones. Don't be afraid to disagree with the shadows of rock's past. When rock 'n' roll first swept through, it had a year zero policy on trad jazz and the syrupy bobbysox pop that preceded it. Punk killed prog (at least, that was its avowal). Acid house wanted to stamp out guitars (until guitars embraced it – there's a lesson there, of sorts, too). So give yourself the freedom and the courage to show the patronising and stuffy musical establishment two fingers. One of the reasons music in 2014 is a little stale is that there's too much damn respect.

Remember that what you listen to is your own business. Your private listening world is entirely your own. You can listen to whoever the hell you like without having to admit to it in public.

These days you even have the internet to hide behind. I

remember feeling embarrassed going to buy Kylie Minogue's Better The Devil You Know in Liverpool in 1990. I avoided the local independent shop – the still excellent Probe Records – after hearing a member of staff ridicule a customer for asking for a Betty Boo album. Record shops, in those days when the battle lines between pop music and 'proper' music were more clearly defined, could be snobbier than the Queen's garden party, if the Queen had an original pressing of My Bloody Valentine's You Made Me Realise and had stopped listening to it because she thought it was the moment they'd sold out.

I bought the Kylie single in Woolworths, stowed it deep in my bag and only listened to it when my flatmates were out. I even hid it behind all the poor indie CD's of the day. Better the Devil You Know was a far better single than any of those sub-Stone Roses wannabes: do you remember Top or The High? No. And for good reason.

There's nowt so queer as cool... or worrying about whether what you're listening to is cool or not – which in itself is severely uncool. So best to forget about cool altogether and listen to whatever the hell you like.

I'm not suggesting that you need to be eclectic or catholic in your tastes, certainly not just for the sake of it. But do make an effort to listen beyond your immediate circle of influences to find any inspiration that is just over the horizon. Making this effort will enrich your music-making. The more music you're exposed to, the more you will find inspiration.

If you check out Toots & the Maytals it doesn't mean you need to shoe-horn a skank into your sound; Funkadelic needn't make you funky, and listening to Chic needn't imbue your music with Nile Rodgers'-isms – lots of minor 7ths and minor 9ths.

There are a multitude of inspirations to be taken from these wonderful artists, chief of which is the courage to be unique. Adopting the signatures of their sounds would be missing the point somewhat.

My experience is that random, shallow eclecticism is unsatisfying and just leads to people being influenced by the most obvious tropes of a genre.

I have rarely heard a ska punk band who sounded like they'd listened to any of the Skatalites or Laurel Aitken or Prince Buster. Obviously the further along the line an influence is taken, over a number of different generations of bands, the more diluted it becomes... or unrecognisable to its root source. That's fine, of course. Reverence is over-rated and stultifying but tokenism, or something that whiffs of tokenism, will irk more than just the purists.

Find music that you enjoy and – if you get stuck in a creative doldrum – remember the inspiration and wonder that is catalysed when you hear something you love for the first time.

The truly life-defining and inspirational sounds are, by definition, few and far between. My whole professional life has been predicated on hunting down those moments. As the Bible tells us, "seek and ye shall find", although it's unlikely that The Gospels were referring to inspirational Welsh demos on the Introducing Uploader or Soundcloud.

Finding new music to listen to isn't a solitary experience. No doubt you'll have friends who recommend stuff to you. Perhaps your favourite radio shows turn you on to brilliant music you hadn't heard before, old or new. Maybe you read one of the monthly music magazines, or feast on the multitude of music blogs out there.

When I was 18 years old and just starting out in a band, an older friend of mine made me a compilation tape. It had XTC, the Beach Boys, Jethro Tull, King Crimson, The Zombies, Killing Joke, The Undertones, The Turtles, Dave Brubeck, The Bonzo Dog Doo Dah Band, Tomorrow, Yello... all kinds of everything, woven together with a real love for music.

It was one of my key influences. And for those at the time who were suggesting that home taping was killing music, it led me to many 100's of pounds worth of music.

If you know someone who is a music hound, badger them to make you a compilation. They'll love the opportunity to dust down their favourite music and you get to benefit from their knowledge and trove of secret gems.

Having an awareness of contemporary music, either the music being released commercially or the music that is being made by your immediate peers, will give you a sense of what 'the audience' is interested in. Rock 'n' roll music is rarely made in isolation. Its history has been a series of chain reactions... one scene reacting to another and evolving their own musical answer to what preceded it. This isn't about jumping on bandwagons. If anything, it's about stripping the bandwagon and modding it to suit your own needs.

You'd be surprised by how many new artists claim to not listen to any new music.

The commonest error that I hear in songwriters who send their stuff to our show, is they don't listen to enough new music. I don't think songwriters should listen to music in order to copy it but you do need to be aware of what the undercurrents are if you're going to swim against the tide. You need to be in the same headspace as your audience. Even if you're going to make music that cuts across directly what's going on. Don't do it from a position of ignorance.

Tom Robinson, 6Music / songwriter

Listening

Be aware of what's going on in the current music scene if you want to be relevant as a recording artist in the recording industry.

Paul Draper, Mansun

Maybe you don't want to be relevant. Maybe the notion of being part of the 'recording industry' is the antithesis of the purity of your art. But *if* you want to sell records, or downloads, or whatever format music ends up on in the future, it's important to recognise the *industry* part of that statement; whether you run a DIY label or want to get signed to Sony.

Assuming, then, that you've immersed yourself in music and you've paid attention to what is going on around in the current musical landscape, what do you then do with these influences?

PLAYLIST:
John Williams - Cavatina
Frankie Goes To Hollywood - Welcome to the Pleasuredome (LP version)
U2   - Like A Song
The Cure - Plainsong
The Stone Roses - Waterfall
De La Soul - Change In Speak
Pixies - Wave of Mutilation
Jungle Brothers - Because I Got It Like That
Public Enemy - Rebel Without a Pause
Frank Wilson - Do I Love You?
Talking Heads - Love - Building On Fire
The Velvet Underground & Nico - Venus In Furs
Fleetwood Mac - Tusk
The Stooges - Penetration
The Small Faces - Tin Soldier
Badly Drawn Boy - Disillusion
Bob Dylan - Desolation Row
Kylie Minogue - Better The Devil You Know

Toots & the Maytals - Reggae Got Soul
Funkadelic - Who Says A Funk Band Can't Play Rock?
Chic - Everybody Dance
The Skatalites - Beardsman Ska
Prince Buster - Sister Big Stuff
Laurel Aitken - Shake
XTC - Dear God
The Beach Boys - Tears in the Morning
Jethro Tull - Fatman
King Crimson - I Talk to the Wind
The Zombies - Time of the Season
Killing Joke - Requiem
The Undertones - Beautiful Friend
Dave Brubeck - Unsquare Dance
The Bonzo Dog Band - The Intro & The Outro
Tomorrow - My White Bicycle
Yello - Oh Yeah
Tom Robinson - 2468 Motorway

6: <u>Influences</u>

It's OK to be influenced by someone. Just don't copy. If there's someone that you really love and you think that you could do what they do, but bring something new to it, then that's great. If there's someone that you really love and you just want to do exactly the same, it's boring. We've heard it all before.

Colin Newman, Wire / Githead

Never be too derivative of your favourite artists. They will have absorbed the influences that they liked but it would have manifested itself in something fresh and original.

It's inevitable to be derivative when you start out. I was. My early stuff was derivative and of the time but very quickly I discovered my own voice and I pushed myself. And you should push yourself too — to aim for the stars in everything you do: from your writing, to your singing, to your recording and to your playing. And you'll land some way short but you'll land in a place probably beyond where you ever thought you could be.

Paul Draper, Mansun

Our musical sensibility is like a baby. We should be mindful that what we feed it will have an effect on how it grows up. Feed it nothing but sugary crap and by the time it's an adult its teeth will have fallen out and it'll be bloated. Give it too much in the way of wholesome, fibrous stuff and it'll get flatulent, worthy and boring.

It's all about balance. 5-great-songs-a-day is the recommended amount, according to government

Influences

guidelines.

Whatever you feed the baby will shape the sounds it eventually makes for itself.

It's inevitable that our favourite sounds are going to influence our own music, especially – as Paul notes above – early on.

People start out derivative because they're still a product of the sounds that taught them the fundamental shapes of their chosen instrument. Bob Dylan digested folk music through his hero Woody Guthrie. The chord sequences, songs and vocal delivery went into Dylan by osmosis. His first album sounds like a proxy Guthrie. It wasn't until the second and third albums that we heard Dylan step out of the shadow of his hero.

This is a cyclical story repeated everywhere in popular music.

Paul Draper's two favourite artists are Prince and The Beatles. Whereas both went on to make some of the most brilliant and original music in the canon, both were also interesting, but recognisable, reflections of their influences on their earlier recordings: Prince in thrall to Stevie Wonder; The Beatles in the shadow of Little Richard, Chuck Berry, Buddy Holly and Motown.

There are very very few people who appear in the world fully-formed and original. Even Bowie – Davey Jones as he was billed on his earlier singles – had a false start as a modish pop star. Ziggy Stardust spent a lot of time fermenting in Bowie's head.

So don't pressurise yourself to bring something new to music from the beginning. Your initial aim is to make your music well and with conviction. But do keep an ear out for your own voice. Your own 'voice' isn't just the vocal, it is the expression of your own musical identity; your musical DNA fingerprint, if you like.

It'll be an indistinct smudge when you start out but it will be there. Sometimes it's in the things that you try to iron out when – for example – you're covering a song. If you find yourself thinking, "this'd be closer to the original if only I sang it a bit more like…" Stop there! Let yourself sing in your own voice. It may sound wrong, or jar at first, but it'll be more right than slavishly copying someone else.

Have the courage to be yourself! This particular maxim will echo throughout this book.

Escapism and pretending to be someone else are both part of the fun of rock 'n' roll – but make sure that there's enough of you glowing around the edges, an identifiable corona, so that you don't just become another jobbing plagiarist.

Your influences are stepping stones and the promised land of your own sound is the other side of the river. Spend too long on the stepping stones and you're likely to slip on one, fall in and drown yourself, never to be heard of again. But without the stepping stones, you're going nowhere.

Balance, you see – save your big splash for after you've got to the other side.

Of course, it's worth noting that music isn't the only influence on your songs. Music is the vehicle but it's what you experience in life, or your dreams, that determines the journey. Bands who overlook this fact, and only echo back sonic influences, risk being less than one dimensional.

We'll talk about how life and culture influence your writing in **Chapter 14:** *'Songwriting'*.

Finally and in short: be careful to use your musical influences in an interesting way. Try to take the things you love most about music and do something new with them and something *you* with them.

Influences

PLAYLIST:
Wire - Outdoor Miner
Woody Guthrie - Hard Travelin'
David Bowie - Heroes
The Beatles - While My Guitar Gently Weeps
Prince - Controversy
Little Richard - The Girl Can't Help It
Chuck Berry - No Particular Place To Go
Buddy Holly - Rave On
Davy Jones & The Lower Third - You've Got A Habit Of Leaving

7: <u>Charlotte Church On Listening</u>

Jet-lag can be a surreal experience irrespective of what you witness amidst the sleep-deprived confusion. I went to 2012's Focus Wales festival in Wrexham straight from the airport after ten days in the States on a tourbus. I was hallucinating curtains of light in the periphery of my vision and the floor of the venue listed on a rolling sea. Things felt weird.

Then, in a development that had my suspension of disbelief in imminent danger of crashing to the ground and morphing into a pirouetting pink elephant, one of the most recognisable women in the UK took to the stage in a gold sequin catsuit and started making music the like of which I'd never heard before. And I've heard a lot of music.

"That's Charlotte Church, that is," my brain was trying to tell me, but I couldn't square what I was hearing – reverberations of Talk Talk, Bjork, Grimes, even – with my expectations of what Charlotte would sound like on the basis of the accelerated evolution we'd all witnessed in the UK, of her from cherubic singer of arias to royalty, to pop vamp and (brilliant) chat show hostess, and then unwitting focus of a morally bankrupt, paparazzi scrum.

Even from the dipping prow of my jet-lagged ship I remember thinking that Charlotte was dead good. She was even better when I saw her in Manchester the following year, but by that point I'd heard the first three of her solo E.P's and had some idea of what to expect. Still, it was a magnificent and adventurous set. This time round, my expectations were turned upside down by a cover of Ultra Nate's 90's club classic, 'Free', which stuck because it was a joyful and unashamed celebration of pop music. Now, that doesn't happen often in the context of a leftfield music concert, trust me.

Too many 'artists' work really hard to give the impression that they don't give a fuck, but Charlotte's set that night was evidence that she really didn't give a fuck. She was, and is, only here making this music to please, to extend, and to express herself.

At about the same time, I interviewed Charlotte about her, then, new E.P 'Four'. She talked about the Green Man Festival she had just spent the weekend at, enthusing over the bands she'd seen, and the musical catalysts for the E.P were surprising (we bonded over Spirit of Eden) but hadn't been framed to impress or convince anyone of her artistic integrity.

I think she knows as well as anyone I've ever spoken to, that the only valid measure of artistic integrity is the one meted out by the artist themselves.

It struck me that Charlotte would be an excellent person to talk to about the subject of listening to music, and influences, and the notion central to the philosophy of this book, of 'being yourself'.

Is yours a musically fertile home? Would we hear a lot of music if we were we to visit the Church household?

There's hardly anything else, to be honest. Music is a constant presence. From the moment everybody's awake then either somebody's tinkering on the piano, whether it's Jonny (her partner and chief musical collaborator), or me, or one of the kids. There's lots of musical instruments just hanging about. Generally somebody's playing something or there's some music on. Lots of new music... especially in the mornings...

On Making Music

Why does new music work well in the mornings?

Oh, I don't know. Mainly because Jonny gets up and he listens to really abrasive music in the morning, like the most abrasive music he can get his hands on, which is sometimes quite challenging. So we tend to start the day with new music and then as the afternoon wears on we'll tend to listen to old favourites… some stuff from the 60's, 70's, 80's, 90's… whenever, really.

When you were growing up was there a lot of music around you? Of course, you were making music from an early age, weren't you?

I wasn't brought up around a lot of music, to be honest. All of my family used to listen to some seriously cheesy stuff. My aunty was a cabaret singer so she used to listen to a lot of 80's stuff that she used to love. They listened to musicals and Celine Dion and Barbara Streisand.

Did you get something positive out of that? Because 'cheesy' tends to mean something popular and sometimes, with the kind of show I do, it's easy to undermine popularity and think that it's a dirty thing…

Yes, absolutely. Well, I think there have been lots of things that have been popular that have also been great, but then I also think that there's a lot of things that have been popular that have been really shit. Sometimes quality is overlooked. I can't really deal with anything that's too cheesy unless it's properly kitsch cheesy.

When I was really young, 3 until 6, I absolutely loved Gloria Estefan and Billy Idol. I've no idea why. I've still got a bit of time for Gloria. My nana used to listen to a lot of opera. My bampy listened to a lot of blues and early rock 'n' roll… then, as you said, from the age of 12 I was working and on the road, and I had my own Walkman…

and so never had to listen to anyone else's choice of music ever again.

As an artist, do you actively seek sounds to be inspired by? Is that partly the reason you listen to music?

Subliminally, yes – but generally just for enjoyment.

That's an interesting distinction. When I'm listening to your four solo E.P's I can hear nuances of other people's music but nothing that comes across as remotely plagiaristic. However some bands I know, if asked a similar question, might be more forthcoming with an answer; may say, "oh we're influenced a lot by the early Clash" and they would sound very much like the early Clash. In other words, do you think that that has helped you, that the influences have come subliminally?

Yes, possibly. I also think that although our sound is, in places, quite sharp and particular, it's also sort of hazy and it's not necessarily all that focused and I think that nowadays, in order to push your music right to the forefront, you have to have a really strong aesthetic all the way around it. It's not just about the music, it's about the visuals that come with the music, it's about the fashion, everything that goes with it.

I suppose it has always been like that to an extent, but that's not really the way any of the band I was working with on those E.P's seemed to approach things. There isn't necessarily a strong aesthetic going through us, or joining us all together.

It's an amalgamation? I think that that has given you very much your own aesthetic.

Yes. It was just a bringing together of everybody's different influences. Because, as well, everybody in the band was so well-listened and so entrenched, wholly entrenched, in music of all sorts I think that all of the influences that came through were wide and varied and not necessarily focused on one genre or sound, where you could say, 'doesn't the guitar sound like this?', 'that melody reminded me of specifically this'. There was nothing distinct, but you can hear all of the band members' individual tastes in the music.

For me, listening to lots of music aids my creativity but then some days – and sometimes these days last for weeks – I'm just not very purple, if purple is creativity.

The book tries to not be sanctimonious and one of the things that it tries to encourage is for people to be themselves. Is that a part of your philosophy? One of things that you have, of course, is your remarkable voice, so you'll sound like yourself almost regardless of anything else...

I struggled with that in my teenage years, a bit. I wanted to conform a bit more and I wanted to make my voice conform a bit more. Then, as I got older... it wasn't even as if I fought against it, I just let it go.

For me, more so than being yourself, it's about being open. If you're working anywhere in the artistic field, if you're really open I think you improve your chances of being good.

Does that openness apply to inspiration from musical sources or does it apply to anything that might inspire a song?

Absolutely! Just open to everything, really, whether it be people, music, other art-forms, experiences, whatever.

I love reading the New Scientist and there's some interesting stuff in there, generally, about creativity and how that comes upon us. And a lot of the time it happens subliminally, it just gets into your psyche... a lot of the time you don't even think about it that much. An idea will just spark. I'm speaking so vaguely...

It's not a specific science, though, is it? I've had a lot of conversations about this for the book... and no one's specific because it's different for everyone. But for artists starting out, to understand that the process is quite nebulous, is empowering. Rather than sitting down worrying about creating, you can just go about your daily life with confidence that something creative and artistic will come from that.

There's two amazing things that I've seen in the past two years that have changed my opinion, quite a lot. One of them is James Murphy talking about failure, which really struck me. Basically he was saying that he had spent his time feeling self conscious about his abilities: he was a DJ, he was trying to do that but he felt like a massive bum and he wasn't getting anywhere. He was so scared of whatever he was doing not being good enough – things not working out, people not enjoying it or relating to it – that he was massively holding himself back the whole time and soon as he let go of that fear and thought "fuck it, what I create is what I create, there's nothing else I can do..." then everything started to happen for him. And he was a bit older at the time, which is always nice to see.

The other thing was a lecture by Sir Ken Robinson called 'The Changing Paradigms of Education' and I've banged on about this to a lot of different people. He talks about 'divergent thinking'. There was a longitudinal study of some children. The first time they tested them they were very little, 3 or 4 year olds in kindergarten. The majority of the kids scored at genius level at 'divergent thinking', which is an essential part of creativity. As these children became educated, they scored lower and lower for the same capability.

There's lots of things that could cause that, but Ken Robinson's theory as to why that's happened is that by that point they've become 'educated'. I find that really interesting, the fact that everybody has this capacity to be creative and mostly we lose it, and why is it?

Educationalists might say that they need something that's easier to measure. But it's sobering that we lose it, isn't it?

Yes. And the opportunity to think creatively is less now because of all of the different forums of entertainment we're subjected to constantly.

In light of that, and in this context of listening to music, do you make any effort to set aside specific listening time? To absorb music away from all of those multiple, potential distractions?

Not necessarily because all time is listening time. We have a lot of vinyl and I have a lovely set of decks. I was trying to learn to scratch DJ with a guy called Tom Clugston. That's a lovely listening experience because you do end up focusing more on sitting down and listening when you've got some vinyl on. I don't really set aside any particular time to listen because it's always happening.

What is next for you?

We're going to try a different approach for the next E.P, to keep things from getting tired. I'm going to try a few different projects under pseudonyms. Lots of ideas at the moment, but nothing is truly formed yet. I'm hoping to surprise a few people.

Are you considering working under pseudonyms because it's difficult to get people to accept your music on its own merits, rather than listen to it in the context of your history? My experience is that your music is accepted on its own merits, but my show – and its audience – are possibly an exception to the rule. However there is a lot of affection and enthusiasm for the four EP's so far...

Yes. It took a while to slowly change people's perceptions of what to expect. But I still don't think I'm quite there, yet. I'm almost at a place where my music would be accepted with an open mind if it was brought out under my own name. Also the way the music industry works nowadays, you can't just put all of your eggs in one basket.

Look at the way they do it in Iceland. I starting watching Screaming Masterpiece the other day, it's a documentary about how the music scene has evolved in Iceland over the years. The way it happens over there reminded me of the way that New Zealanders are about rugby. It's so ingrained into the population to do this one thing... I'd love to be able to be part of doing that, or creating that, in Wales.

There's this whole sense of friendship and family amongst musicians there. And like Iceland, we (Wales) are a small nation and we need to not be segregative and not be cliquey and to learn to help each other. And in that documentary they talk about sharing their instruments, and if somebody needs studio time they can get it. They share resources and a philosophy to propel each other and make music as important as it should be. And I think that here in Wales we have the talent and the capacity, and we're small enough, to do something similar.

And that could apply to a city or a smaller country

anywhere?

Yes.

A hugely positive and empowering note upon which to finish our conversation. Thank you Charlotte.

http://charlottechurchmusic.com

@charlottechurch

PLAYLIST:

Charlotte Church - Four E.P
Charlotte Church - Three E.P
Talk Talk - The Rainbow
Grimes - Go
Various - Screaming Masterpiece O.S.T

8: <u>Finding A Band</u>

The most famous rock 'n' roll meeting of all was at St. Peter's Garden Fete, Liverpool on July 6th 1957. A 15 year old Paul McCartney saw John Lennon's Quarrymen perform a rambunctious set for the parishioners. McCartney wanted a piece of that action and so introduced himself. He and Lennon shared a love for the same records. That's all the vocabulary you need when you're seeking out band members. McCartney was in.

Serendipity mightn't always bring you such good fortune, especially if you live in a rural area where there aren't a a lot of opportunities to meet – and weigh up – other musicians.

In their early press releases, Super Furry Animals claimed to have met on the roof of a train. Given the amount of very low, slate tunnels that Welsh trains have to pass through this is unlikely to have happened. In reality the various members of Super Furry Animals had been aware of each other for some time.

In Wales, entire families make an annual pilgrimage to the national Eisteddfod. The kids perform in musical competitions. The teens get their first rock 'n' roll experiences on the Maes B (a field dedicated to 'young people's music'). You'd soon learn to recognise the ones who had something to say with their playing. Bands would coalesce around the campfires as naturally as clouds empty themselves in the shadows of Snowdonia.

Nirvana's Kurt Cobain and Krist Novoselic were fortunate enough to have known each other at high school but they had protracted problems finding a long-term drummer, until – fortuitously – Dave Grohl was recommended to them prior to the recording of

Finding A Band

Nevermind.

One of my favourite bands, The Joy Formidable, hiccuped through a couple of name changes and line-ups until they found the perfect drummer for them. When they couldn't find musicians to play with in their immediate circle of acquaintances, they advertised in music shops and magazines, auditioning a long line of unsuitable candidates until Matt Thomas sat in the drum stool.

"He looked odd but played brilliantly," recounts Ritzy. "We gave him the gig and told him he wasn't allowed to cut his hair."

Finding the right people to play with is all about finding people who share your vision. It's not just about liking the same records. Great things can happen when musicians with different influences get together. The Clash encompassed rock 'n' roll, reggae and punk rock... different influences distilled through the passions of individual members.

And music isn't the only coalescing force. Many bands – Wire, XTC, Pulp, Roxy Music, Franz Ferdinand, The Mekons, Blur and a slew of others – formed at art college. Stick a bunch of hormonal teenagers with artistic pretensions in a student union together and anything can happen.

Sometimes a good anything.

Of course, you don't *have* to be in a band to make music, not at all. To some the notion of a band in 2014 is an anachronistic one, but woe betide anyone who predicts the death of a musical form or instrument. The most famous example of getting it wrong, in this regard, is Dick Rowe turning down The Beatles for Decca Records. He thought guitar music was a fad and that it would pass. That was in 1962.

Rowe did go on to sign The Rolling Stones, The Small

Faces, Tom Jones and a number of staggeringly successful artists to Decca, but he'll forever be remembered as the man who turned down The Beatles.

Bands are under a different kind of pressure now. The technology that new songwriters have access to – Garageband, loop stations, KAOS pads, and by god is this list going to date quickly! – means that individual writers can now realise their full, musical vision without feeling the need to collaborate with others.

Whereas I used to be swamped by band demos I now get hundreds of bedroom recordings from artists who have been able to record exactly what they wanted to, by themselves, restricted only by their own taste and talent. These music-makers are recording 'band-sounding' music without having to go to the inconvenience of finding themselves a band. What these bedroom singer-songwriters, who would hitherto have progressed to rehearsal rooms and bands, are potentially missing out on is the artistic push and pull that exists in a good band.

If you want to produce drama, spectacle, excitement and to have the freedom to break free and explode, achieving these things will be a challenge while welded to a loop station. They're useful music-making tools that have a place, but they're – perhaps – limited in their dramatic and musical scope. If you want more – if your musical dreams involve a more sophisticated thunder – then get out there, find people to play with.

Easier said than done, of course.

Before we get to some advice on how to find the right personnel, let's consider those of you who are solo artists and determined to remain so.

Being solo has advantages (you're entirely in charge of your artistic vision; you can travel more cheaply; you can play almost anywhere; you can only fall out with yourself and your own vision; you can take things entirely at your own pace; any renumeration earned will filter more directly to you) and disadvantages (you won't have anyone else's muse to feed off; it'll be more of a challenge to make your performances and recordings dynamic [generally, speaking]; there will be less of a sense of competition to motivate you.)

Solo artists are far from being the exception to the rule, of course, and this brings with it another potential disadvantage: it's difficult to make yourself stand out. If there are thousands of bands out there, there are tens of thousands of solo singer-songwriters / electronic producers. A quick survey of the current submissions on the BBC Introducing Uploader shows that 80% of the tracks submitted to my radio show this week come from solo artists. The majority of those are guitar playing singer / songwriters. One person is backed by a piano. The remainder of that 80% are solo electronic artists: trance, dubstep, techno and one hip hop track.

Bear in mind that I broadcast in Wales. It's not a country with a tradition of urban music. It's still surprising that only approximately 20% of the submissions come from bands. I think that fact is a lot to do with the band-in-a-computer software (Garageband and the like) we discussed above.

Some of the advantages of being a solo artist were excellently underlined by Badly Drawn Boy when I interviewed him right at the beginning of his musical career:

Because I'm on my own I can afford to work with anyone I want. Like working with DJ Shadow, different engineers, Andy Votel who I set a label up with... I do enjoy the variety of that approach but I'm conscious that I shouldn't be too eclectic.

Badly Drawn Boy

Basically as a solo artist you're free to go wherever the muse takes you but as Damon says, being too eclectic is a potential concern. Overcook it and you could obscure the thread of yourself that passes through your music and helps connect you to an audience. Not that confusing and challenging an audience isn't a good thing. To my mind, it is. All of those unsuspecting people who went out and bought Bob Dylan's Self Portrait or Lou Reed's Metal Machine Music may beg to differ.

This won't be the last we'll talk about solo artists in this book. Much of the band-orientated advice that's contained here is still relevant to you. I'll leave the last specific words, for now, to one of my favourite solo songwriters:

I'm just trying to serve the songs and my mood swings from year to year.

E, Eels.

As a solo artist you can be this free and philosophical about your music.

If you're looking for bandmates or collaborators, though, let's get back to considering where you may find them. A good place to start would be a local rehearsal facility, if there is one. Cardiff's Music Box rehearsal rooms are a real honeypot for local music-making folk and, on occasions, fortuitous meetings at Music Box have catalysed beautiful musical relationships:

I certainly know of plenty of people who have either formed a band or replaced / found a band member by meeting someone on the off-chance whilst they were here. I also know of plenty of people who have gotten gigs from meeting here, or who ended up with work as drivers, techs, sound engineers, producers etc. We certainly do our best to hook people up if asked.

Mark Foley, Music Box, Cardiff

Music loving people congregate in corners at schools, at gigs, in record shops, in nightclubs, music shops, bars and online in numerous groups and forums.

On the basis of the conversations I've had over the years, I'd say that the majority of bands have their roots in school / college bands. Ritzy from the Joy Formidable remembers being intrigued by her future bandmate, Rhydian Dafydd, during their time at Ysgol Maes Garmon in Mold, Flintshire.

I think I was drawn to Rhydian because he was very mysterious. When I joined Tricky Nixon as a guitarist, it was mainly because Rhydian was part of that group and my memory of him from school was that he was a very good guitarist, which I always admired. He was enigmatic and I remember him being a bit of a knobhead, really.

My abiding memory of him is he was quite cocky. I was intrigued to see if he'd mellowed. I do remember admiring him from a technical, musical point of view.

Ritzy Bryan, The Joy Formidable

Others (The Beatles and The Rolling Stones, as described earlier) formed as a result of happenchance – coincidental meetings that had huge reverberations for rock 'n' roll.

The lesson here is to keep your eyes and your ears open wherever you are.

And make yourself known and visible. This may run counter to your natural demeanour but music is filled with shy people who feel socially awkward. In essence, if you feel shy and like an outsider, finding other music-makers to hang out with and talk to is like joining a self-help group. Be reassured, if your music comes from an introverted place sharing it is a fine way to find empathetic people.

If you yearn to be in a band but you can't find people to make music with around you, try posting an ad in a local music shop. Most of them have noticeboards. Another option is to use the classifieds section in a music magazine or to register with one of the numerous Musicians Wanted websites.

How do you word your ad? Well, having read through hundreds of entries in various publications and music networks I'd recommend that you make your requirements detailed, specific and idiosyncratic enough to attract the attention of the kind of people you'd like to make music with.

'Guitarist seeks drummer and bass player to make music with' won't cut the proverbial mustard.

When Black Francis was advertising for a bass player to join the Pixies, he said he he was "seeking female bass player who likes Peter, Paul and Mary and Hüsker Dü." That odd combination stood out enough to attract the attention of Kim Deal who answered the ad, despite not actually being able to play the bass, and the rest – as they say – became history.

It's important to note that Francis' description wasn't too wide of the mark. Pixies did encompass the noise, focus and energy of Husker Dü together with a more melodic and harmonious sensibility you could attribute to Peter, Paul and Mary; although one more twisted and atonal than the folk trio would have recognised within themselves.

Finding A Band

What should you be looking for in potential bandmates? Well, as subjective as music itself is, the chemistry of what attracts one creative mind to another to make a great band is just as mysterious. People can spend less time finding potential husbands, wives and life-partners than they do bandmates. In some respects the requirements are the same: you're looking for people with whom you share a chemistry, who you feel a desire to mix your musical genes with, to give birth to sonic babies that you will then nurture through life.

So don't ignore your instincts or your heart. Find people you're attracted to musically. If there's a little bit of disagreement it can give you a creative advantage – a bonfire of a muse right at the heart of your band. Friction can be brilliant for groups. Many of the best bands are powered by creative partnerships that cycle between loving and hating each other: Dave and Ray Davies in The Kinks; Mike Love and Brian Wilson in The Beach Boys; Kim Deal and Black Francis; Jason Pierce and Sonic Boom; Lou Reed and John Cale... hell, Lou Reed and anyone...

Charismatic, artistic people have egos, and people with big egos are like magnets in a bag – half the time they'll be repelling each other, the rest of the time they'll be inseparable.

Sometimes – of course – especially given the subject matter, that mysterious force is sexual attraction. Having relationships with band members can bring with it a series of complicated tensions. Fleetwood Mac turned this to their advantage. The vitriol, jealousy and vengefulness that fuelled much of the songwriting on their albums post '76 created some of the biggest selling – and most radio-omnipresent – hits of all time. Abba, similarly, turned an un-romanticised and very autobiographical series of heartbreaks, into colossal successes.

It's a good idea to temper your expectations and requirements with pragmatism. That flaky-looking guy who

79

looks cool strumming his guitar in the common room, but who hardly ever turns up even to his favourite lessons, mightn't be worth the trouble.

Music attracts more poseurs – I think I rather euphemistically called them 'hummingbirds' earlier – than almost any other field of human endeavour. However people who are only interested in the romance and allure of being in a band, but who aren't prepared to put the very necessary work in, are likely to frustrate you.

Finding the right people to play with isn't easy, in terms of finding good, talented players with shit to say, but who also have the discipline to stick around. There are a lot of very flaky people around, you know? People who like the idea of being in bands but who never stick around.

That's the thing about music, it's not just about having something to say, great player, blah blah blah, it's actually also about putting some graft in and rehearsing and sticking together. People come and go all the time. It was like that for us for a few years.

Rhydian Dafydd, The Joy Formidable

Commitment is vital especially in the formative / early days. You can't legislate for people who lose their hunger, six albums in, when their third child is on the way. However if a band member keeps missing rehearsals, or can only be bothered to do a gig when there's a fee involved, they may need to be dropped. There are a few half-arsed band members who went on to become iconic, or influential. Sid Vicious, for example, didn't do much apart from look subversive enough to make middle England pee itself with fear. In most cases, a band member who makes it despite not pulling their weight musically was lucky enough to travel in the slipstream of a significant musical presence.

The absolute need for dedication has been echoed by many of the notable musicians I have interviewed over the years.

You must be ruthless in pursuit of your dream. Forget your friends and family because, if all goes well, you'll be too busy to see them.

You must be obsessive about music. You must live it and breathe it. To succeed you need perseverance, stamina and myopic dedication. If you're not totally committed you will not survive the hardships of life in a rock n roll band.

Deke Leonard, Man

That's quite a statement. It's worth reading a couple of times. I think that Deke is exaggerating somewhat to make his point. Music makers who I know, who become international touring artists, do have to compromise relationships with family and friends; that's an inevitable consequence of life on the road.

And to get to the point where they are "international touring artists", most of them have had to be myopic in their dedication to music.

Perhaps Deke isn't exaggerating after all?

On Making Music

Only work with people as talented as you. That's managers, accountants, roadies, other musicians, other writers. Don't include your friends or your lovers if they aren't as good as you are. It's a business. That's why it's called the 'music <u>business</u>'.

Kim Fowley, Impresario and record producer

Well not all of you reading this book will regard your music in such stark commercial terms. We'll get to the business side of things in due course. I do think that Kim's advice for you to try to only work with people as talented as you is as wise as it is to the point. Passengers weigh bands down. There are few things more likely to cause negative feelings in the band than having outsiders single out a member as a weak link. In the first band I was in, every gig was followed by a whispering campaign about our singer's 'weedy' voice. He was my best friend in the world. It didn't stop us, after 12 months of trying to coax him into singing better, from dropping him. I remember every detail of that conversation in a battered Citroen, parked up on a garage forecourt next to the Ruthin Castle pub in Mold, Wales. The guilt is amplified by the realisation, in hindsight, that that decision didn't do us any good in the end. These kind of decisions aren't easy to make. You can only be honest with yourself, and then between yourselves.

Deke used the word 'ruthless' above and it applies here. Don't be fooled by the aura of fuzzy romanticism and gang-like camaraderie that surrounds many bands. A lot of them – think of the way The Rolling Stones treated Ian Stewart and then Brian Jones – have mercilessly weeded out the deadwood before they got anywhere near recognition.

I know how dispassionate this sounds. Friendships are important – especially when you're trapped in rehearsal rooms and transit vans for hours upon hours – but a band founded on friendship alone is unlikely to find a significant audience for their music.

The greatest challenge for a band is finding a decent front person. Great, even just plain-good, vocalists are rarer than their instrumental equivalents. The history of unheard-of-bands is the story of the cocky mate with a bit of front who couldn't play an instrument, but who wanted to be in the band anyway, getting the gig as front-person by default. Fortunately the history of the greatest rock 'n' roll is the story of people who ended up in bands for the exact same reason, it's just that they had something in their voice that made other people want to listen to it. That's what you're listening out for when you're searching for a singer.

You now have your inspiration and some new bandmates – or collaborators – to make brilliant music with. But unless you're a solo artist who is happy with what's written on their birth certificate, you're going to need a name.

PLAYLIST:
Roxy Music - Editions of You
The Beatles - Money
Super Furry Animals - Crys Ti
Nirvana - Negative Creep
Eels - Last Stop: This Town
Lou Reed - Metal Machine Music, Part 1
Bob Dylan - Wigwam
Badly Drawn Boy - My Friend Cubilas
The Joy Formidable - Whirring
The Rolling Stones - Little Red Rooster
Pixies - Gigantic
The Kinks - Susannah's Still Alive
The Beach Boys - Surf's Up
Husker Du - Sorry Somehow
Peter, Paul and Mary - Where Have All The Flowers Gone?
Spacemen 3 - Revolution
The Velvet Underground - Sister Ray
Fleetwood Mac - Go Your Own Way
ABBA - The Winner Takes It All
Sid Vicious - My Way
Kim Fowley - The Trip

9: <u>She Makes War On Being Solo</u>

I have been promoting artists at my local venue, Telford's Warehouse in Chester, since 1997. There have been almost as many magical and unforgettable nights as there have been under-attended damp squibs, nights that burnt a hole deep into my bank account. Such is the fate of the part-time promoter.

I've stuck many hundreds of posters up in record shops, cafes, taxi offices, chippies and the occasional, broad-minded church hall; hundreds of thousands of flyers have been shoved through reluctant letter-boxes; tens of fingers have been chewed by slavering guard chihuahuas; countless soles have been worn down by the seemingly endless, pavement trudge... but – and it's a big, glorious, joyful 'but' – my soul has been raised up high on enough occasions for it all to have been worthwhile.

One of the most original and memorable artists that has blessed our stage with her inventive and excellent songs was She Makes War, a.k.a Laura Kidd. Laura struck me as the epitome of a 21st century troubadour. She had gathered enabling digital technology (a loop station and effects pedals) together with a grab bag of instruments and a brilliantly-wielded megaphone, to present her songs in a fresh and dynamic fashion.

My mum and dad, who were present at the show, still ask if the charming, charismatic woman with the tattoos, the marching drum and the bullhorn is going to be returning to bewitch us all again, sometime soon. More tellingly, they still listen to her CD regularly. And that's a fact, not a contrivance for the sake of this introduction.

She Makes War's songs are the key reason for her gigs to live long in the memory, but the uniqueness of what she does as a solo artist – meeting the challenges of surviving in the current economic (and cultural, with regards the decline of the traditional music industry) climate with ingenuity and resourcefulness – make her notable too.

So notable, in fact, that Laura is called upon on frequent occasions to deliver talks and workshops on being a DIY artist.

She is a songwriter, a multi-instrumentalist, a technician, a film-maker, her own record label and manager, a stylist, a peaceful provocateur and an uncompromising, erudite communicator. She harnesses all of the multifold potentials of social networking in a thoroughly creative and un-crass manner. Although there is something of the spirit of Crass about her, too.

As you can probably tell, I'm rather smitten by her enthusiasm and enterprise, but mostly those great, great songs.

It's a wonder she has the time to write and record them, given the other onerous responsibilities I imagine she has to keep on top of: booking her own gigs, planning travel and accommodation, scheduling recording sessions, handling accounts and paperwork, making sure there is enough money to pay the bills.

I don't want to over romanticise Laura's achievements. Many of us, me included, are self-employed and have to keep on top of an equivalent list of logistical challenges. Thing is, though, we don't also have to make time to capture our muse and nurture our creativity to keep the wheels turning round.

Who better, then, to talk to about transcending the challenges incumbent in being a solo, DIY artist? (Not that it's a competition, of course.)

At the core of She Makes War are your wonderful and original songs. When you have so much else to do, does writing and recording become a release and an escape, precious time to be valued and capitalised on?

Definitely. Creating music is supposed to be the core of the whole thing but there are lots of other activities that demand time and attention (maintaining a dialogue with my fans, vast amounts of admin, booking shows and travelling around playing them), and luckily I enjoy most of those too.

Do you set aside specific time to write and record? Do you think you have to be more organised because of the solo / DIY nature of what you do?

I do have to be more organised because I'm juggling a lot of things every day, and I also fill up a lot of my time with freelance work to pay the bills so it's tough to find the space to freely write and record. I also moved house two months ago so am still settling in, but my music space is ready to go now.

I'd like to be someone who wrote new stuff all the time but I have to book in days in my diary to make sure, and make hefty deadlines to keep to (the current one is that I have to have the album tracks written before my impending 6 week tour, then I have to make all my production notes while I'm on the road so my engineer is prepped for recording in December).

How much was the solo nature of She Makes War enabled by contemporary technology, loop stations & the like? Had you always envisioned She Makes War as a solo artistic pursuit?

In the dim and distant past She Makes War was supposed to be a band, but the other members weren't focused on it and left fairly quickly to do other things so I carried on solo. I'd never thought of being a solo artist before it was thrust upon me but it made so much sense and the creative freedom is really exciting.

I didn't really think about how I was going to do a live show until "Disarm" was finished at the end of 2009. Everything fell into place then. I'd started using a loop pedal that summer, inspired by my friends Lobelia and Steve Lawson, and the one-woman-band idea came about organically because I wanted to be able to have a physical dialogue with the audience by standing amongst them but needed to be heard over the loops. So I bought a megaphone and later on got a marching drum and foot tambourine.

Bands can rely upon dialogue, camaraderie, friction and competition to keep themselves motivated and inspired, is it at all a challenge to keep yourself going, when ultimately (and absolutely) you're your own fuel, your own engine and your own wheels?

It can feel like a very lonely path I'm on and sometimes that rises up and gets to me, yes. I'm a pretty happy person generally but I'm also extremely sensitive and definitely have a propensity to be derailed. There's been a lot of personal stuff going on over the last two years, hence me not having my third album written earlier, and I think if this project was a band it would have been easier to give it the time it needed. But then I'm pleased it's a solo project, it's more focused and meaningful in its message that way.

What are the positives of being a solo artist?

I always know when I'm available for rehearsals and gigs, it's cheaper to travel and find places to stay and I think there's a very pure, strong sentiment that comes across.

What are the challenges that are particular to being a solo artist?

Logistical things mainly, like having to get the gear to shows on my own on public transport. Touring around Germany on the train is really cool but I'm limited as to what I can take – I can't lug t-shirts around with me, which is a shame because it could be a really good way of funding the tour. In bigger venues I can't pack up after my set and run out to the merch desk in time to meet people just after I've played, which is usually the best time to say hello. There have been (thankfully a very few) occasions where people have been rude or inappropriate and that can be very isolating when you don't have anyone to back you up. I'm extremely careful with the situations I put myself in, but I still prefer to live life thinking the best of people.

You've also been an active member of a couple of bands... including being part of Viv Albertine's most recent touring band. Does the dynamic feel different? I imagine you can pick up enough inspiration working with someone like Viv to last a good, long while!

I love playing other people's music and helping them create the sound they want on stage, and I've been told by a few of the artists I've worked with that my presence gives them confidence. I've worked for a lot of bands over the years and have learned something from all of them, but my favourites were definitely Viv Albertine (for being utterly yourself with no fear), Erica Nockalls (for creating out-there musical landscapes) and Tricky (the king of atmosphere, and we went to some really amazing places to play shows).

When you're working and creating for yourself, you're entirely able to follow your own muse... do you think that that is helping to break new frontiers in music? You did something very interesting with a megaphone and a loop pedal when I saw you, and I'd never seen anything quite like that before! (or since).

It's definitely encouraged me to experiment with different ways of performing the songs, but I don't write with that in mind – I don't think I should limit what I'm doing in the studio because I can't play all the parts live. Limits are good anyway, they can make you much more creative. I also found Stewart Lee's book "How I Escaped My Certain Fate" a wonderful inspiration for performance, it really celebrates what you can achieve as one person with a microphone. Recently I was performing at Edinburgh Fringe and managed to meet him after one of his work in progress gigs and shyly tell him how much his book meant to me. That was nice.

What is the most important piece of wisdom you've picked up / taught yourself, with regards the use of social media?

I have a set of principles I try and follow which go something like this:

• be interesting (i.e. don't just shout about yourself)

• be positive (I don't like negativity and moaning online)

• maintain boundaries (I don't post very personal things online)

• respond to everyone (if appropriate)

• give back to the community (by responding to people's calls for help and connecting people when possible)

You have become something of a renowned speaker on digital autonomy and social networking, does that ever get in the way or overshadow the music? Or are the effects positive... helping you to spread the word about your music?

It's mostly very positive. I've met all sorts of interesting people that way and talking passionately on a subject is much more effective than just walking up to someone and asking them to listen to my music some time. They won't, usually.

On Making Music

I got worried recently that because people refer to me as the "Queen of DIY" etc (which is very lovely of them), if ever a great manager / indie label / agent heard about me they'd assume that I don't want any help, which isn't necessarily true. I'm interested in exploring all angles when it comes to growing my project, while maintaining the things that make it unique.

Sometimes I imagine it must be quite scary being a solo artist… not so much going on stage by yourself, but the fact that the buck stops with you. Does any negative criticism (that I'm sure is unfounded or misguided!) hurt you more than it would someone in a band, do you think? How much is that counter-balanced by the positives?

Because the feeling, theory and execution of what I do is very strong, I actually don't get too many stupid comments after playing, but once in a while some dickhead will come along and try to knock my confidence by acting like they know better, always without actually asking me what my intention was with the show. I choose to usually not play with a band, not just for financial reasons (I insist on paying musicians, or at least skill-swapping with them) but artistic ones too. So telling me immediately after I've sung and played my heart out at a show and come off stage that you'd "love to see me with a band", however well intentioned that may be, is not something I'll engage with.

I also got criticised recently by a man who actually enjoyed the music but didn't like the way I played my piano song. He came over to question me about it, leaned over and did a load of twiddly piano playing to impress me / make me feel shit about myself (who knows which). I'm hardened to these things now and laughed it off, politely but firmly making it clear I wasn't interested in discussing it.

I'm way too polite usually but have started to put boundaries around things a bit recently. I'm careful not to make anyone feel uncomfortable but I do try and stand up for myself in the moment rather than just accepting things and getting annoyed later on. I think most people are well meaning and don't realise the impact of what they say or do, and on the whole I don't have too many issues.

PLAYLIST:
She Makes War - Slow Puncture
She Makes War - Delete
She Makes War - Minefields
She Makes War - No Fireworks
Longpigs - Jesus Christ
Belly - Slow Dog
Radiohead - Pyramid Song
Elliott Smith - Coast To Coast
Sharon Van Etten - I Love You But I'm Lost
The Hysterical Injury - Maths
Wilco - I Am Trying To Break Your Heart
Emily Loizeau - L'Autre Bout Du Monde
Dixie Chicks - Not Ready To Make Nice
The Shins - New Slang
Ed Harcourt - Until Tomorrow Then
Blur - No Distance Left To Run
Elastica - My Sex
Echobelly - Dark Therapy
Viv Albertine - The False Heart
Birdeatsbaby - Ghosts
My Brightest Diamond - Gone Away

10: <u>Choosing A Name</u>

No band ever became famous simply because of their name. Although, somewhat ironically, the band that I was in did secure our management deal and a record release on the basis of what we'd called ourselves, not that it did us a huge amount of good. We were called The Immediate, after the Small Faces' post-Decca record label set up by Stones svengali Andrew Loog Oldham. One day, back in the swirling mists of the mid-90's, I received a phone call from a man with a Newport accent:

ME: Hello.

HIM: Are you in a band called The Immediate?

ME: I am. Why? Who's this?

HIM: My name's Alan Jones. I used to be in a band called Amen Corner. You may have heard of us. We were on the...

ME: Immediate record label!

HIM: Yes, I saw your band's name and thought I'd check you out.

The rest, I will say, wasn't history of note to anyone but me; not even Alan, because I suspect that all we did was burn a large hole in his beautifully tailored, moleskin pockets.

Generally, though, the name alone is unlikely to provide you with opportunities. However a bad name – one that's ill thought out – can definitely deter potentially

Choosing A Name

interested parties.

Somehow your name has to encapsulate your whole ethos in a few short words. If it is unimaginative, unwieldy, cheesy, derivative, hackneyed or bland, it will reflect badly on your music.

No pressure, then.

In my experience, and I've listened to demo tapes from thousands of artists over twenty years, a bad name tends to lead to bad music. Of course both are completely subjective judgements but this is the dog eat dog reality of the music industry, it's not a charity. The industry and the audience make snap, subjective decisions all the time. It's worth making the effort to load the dice in your favour as much as is possible.

Your band name is frequently people's first contact with you, whether it's a prospective audience member seeing your name on a gig listing; people mentioning your name in conversation; or the name is tagged on an .mp3 or scrawled on a jiffy bag.

People will make judgements based on your name whether you like it or not.

Admittedly when a band make remarkable music, a terrible name is quickly forgotten. The Beatles is a pretty crap name. I understand its etymology, sparked in Stuart Sutcliffe's mind by Marlon Brando's film The Wild One and then bastardised by John Lennon who wanted it to be redolent of the 'beat' music they were making. I just find it a singularly dull and reductive name – completely at odds with the melodic genius and invention of the band themselves, but there you go.

Over fifty years after they christened themselves The Beatles it is impossible to separate the name from their musical legacy.

You won't have that luxury when you're approaching

venues, radio stations, publications, labels etc. A name becomes less important as you progress. Once you've got people's attention, and hooked them in, it's more about the music. Seemingly peripheral concerns like your band name are important at the outset, though.

It's very interesting that Lennon 'branded' The Beatles so that people would recognise they were a beat band, at least initially. 'Branding' brings with it associations that may feel at odds with artistic integrity. However this is 'your' brand. You don't have to make any compromises, at all, with the name you choose, but it's a wise idea to consider your name from a number of different perspectives.

Like a brand, many artists choose names in a form or style that makes them immediately identifiable to a potential listener. Think of the long litany of pop punk / emo bands with long and portentous names: Funeral For A Friend, Bullet For My Valentine, My Chemical Romance, Taking Back Sunday. Think of all the 60's girl groups who ended their name with -ettes: The Marvelettes, The Velvelettes, The Ronettes, The Ikettes, The Chordettes. Then of all one word British bands who found prominence in the 1990's, in the wake of key albums by My Bloody Valentine and The Stone Roses: Ride, Pulp, Blur, Cud, (The) Verve, Suede, Oasis, Space, Shack et al.

Think of how heavy metal bands are duty bound to give themselves names that sound heavy: starting, of course, with Led Zeppelin... Deep Purple, Black Sabbath, Iron Maiden, Judas Priest, Motorhead, Saxon.

People package their bands with names in much the same way that retail companies brand and label their products. You won't find an aftershave called Lily of the Mist just as you wouldn't find a heavy metal band called Belle and Sebastian. These conventions haven't been written down anywhere – there is no legislature – they're just 'common sense', the norms of nomenclature.

Choosing A Name

As with any of the other advice in this book, I'd recommend that you familiarise yourself with the conventions and expectations, and then either adhere to them or buck them depending on what you want to achieve.

We'll deal with some of the considerations to take into account over the next few pages. Remember, this is only advice, it isn't a book of law.

To nail my colours to the mast, I love names that have a resonance for the music within: Super Furry Animals suggests something cutely epic, potentially dangerous and unpredictable; Stereolab evokes lab-coats and the BBC Radiophonic Workshop; Flaming Lips is a strikingly psychedelic and romantic image; Talking Heads infers a confusing, dadaist babble; Manic Street Preachers something filled with passion and polemic. I think these are great names. Mind you, I love these bands.

I have a shelf filled with thousands of CD's behind me (how quaint). I'll pick a few at random and we'll consider the qualities of the different band names (I'll ignore anything released under people's actual names) and some of the issues they raise. I do mean at random too. I have little choice. Since I ripped all of these CD's onto my hard drive, entropy has muddled any filing system I may have had, now long since forgotten.

First off the shelf is a CD single (Neil Jung – that'll be going on in a moment!) from Teenage Fanclub. To my mind, Teenage Fanclub is the perfect name for a band who so wonderfully evoke our earliest, bittersweet experiences of love and heartache.

It's a name that has an immediate musical resonance – and a resonance with the 60's and 70's bands who were their main inspiration (Big Star and The Beatles especially). In fact, the name rather cleverly pre-empts and disembowels any criticism the band might otherwise have drawn for being derivative or plagiaristic: they're 'fans', after all, and not pretending to be otherwise. And the word 'fanclub' reminds us of a time when fanzines, the Royal Mail, badges and photocopied newsletters were the main method of showing your allegiance for a group.

Teenage Fanclub immediately reminds us of our youth, of what could have been and – with the celebratory nature of the word 'fanclub' – what still could be. They're two words that are a perfect echo of the music.

Next off the shelf, 'Electric Warrior' by T-Rex. Perhaps more of the alphabetical order has survived than I first thought. This is interesting for different reasons. T-Rex, the biggest, fiercest carnivore that ever stalked the planet would seem like a good fit for the band who dominated the early 70's charts and brought massive glam riffs to the UK masses. However when they started out as a duo in the late 60's and went by the longer and more unwieldy name Tyrannosaurus Rex, they were plinking about delicately on an acoustic guitar, singing nonsense inspired by Tolkien over the top. Marc Bolan was tiny and elfin – it must have struck him as a very good joke to call his embryonic band Tyrannosaurus Rex.

Maybe it struck other people as a very good joke too. It's interesting that the band name got shorter as the they themselves got significantly louder.

This example rather undermines my earlier theory that a good name has to give you some idea of what the band sound like.

Damn you, random shelves!

Confounding, or inverting, expectations can also be an excellent way to intrigue an audience. Almost as if humans had brains and a sense of humour. Who knew?

Humour is, in my opinion, something to use sparingly. Other than Half Man Half Biscuit, who transcend all other considerations by virtue of being one of the finest bands the UK has ever produced[1], 'funny' band names too frequently need the inverted commas to underline the intention. After an initial guffaw, they become aluminium foil on a filling.

Sultans of Ping? Ned's Atomic Dustbin? No thanks. If Gorky's Zygotic Mynci was a parody of the latter, then good for them. At least Gorky's has some imagination to it and intimates something about their unhinged musical delights.

The next CD is a promo of a recent single from 'CHVRCHES'. That's not a typo. You still pronounce the name 'churches'.

The word 'churches' suggests something hallowed, ethereal and spiritual... traditional, even. Counterbalancing that is the replacement of the 'u' for a 'v' – surely more than just a clever graphical conceit? It contemporises the name and makes it unique. There's also something a little subversive about defacing a religious word.

One of the great benefits of bastardising such a common word is that – whilst memorable – it becomes unique to search engines making it much easier for interested people to find out about the band, as long as they remember to spell it with a 'v'.

This is a major consideration in 2014 and one that should not be skated over. Someone's curiosity after they hear a band on the radio, mentioned in conversation, or see their name on a gig-listing, is pretty transitory. If they can't find you quickly via a search engine, they may well give up. That's one potential customer for your music, your merchandise and your gigs lost.

Trust me, you don't want to be losing possible fans before they've even had a chance to sample your sounds.

Your favourite search engine can tell you within moments whether a band already share the name you're considering; a quick search will also tell you whether you'll be buried underneath millions of search results pertaining to the word(s) in your name. There is an excellent Welsh band called 'The Earth'. I've yet to see them listed on Google. They're buried beneath countless millions of results about, you know, the earth. Add 'band' as a search criteria and they're hidden beneath pages of results about Manfred Mann's Earth Band; another band called Earth; Earth, Wind and Fire... who is going to go to this effort?

Strikes me that it's an unnecessary amount of confusion and difficulty to cause your potential audience, however great your music, and however much you love the idea of being called 'The Earth'.

They're a great band, too. Which is the most important thing. But imagine if people were struggling to find their music online simply because they've chosen such an omnipresent word.

Another much more apparent problem is artists picking band names that are already in use. Frequently by tens of other bands in the UK and across the world. Over the last month I have received music submissions from bands called Empire, The Echoes, Ricochet, Howl, Crisis, Reef (I kid you not), Wolves (and there were already two bands in Wales called 'Wolves'), Little Bird (there are at least 5 different artists, internationally, called Little Bird)... there are more examples but I don't want to bludgeon you over the head to make an obvious point.

If a band pick a name that someone else is already using:

1) it's bad etiquette – if someone got there first, respect that precedence.

2) It suggests a lack of imagination, which doesn't bode well for the music.

3) It indicates a lack of vision / awareness – a laziness, even – that the band hasn't gone to the minimal trouble of finding out if anyone is using that name.

4) It risks causing confusion – people who invest time or money in a band's music don't want unnecessary frustrations put in the way of the band maximising their potential.

5) It makes it more difficult to secure memorable usernames and domain names on social networks – a key part of the promotional landscape nowadays.

For the last couple of years, an artist from France called 'The Keys' has relocated to – and been performing in – Wales. This has caused a lot of confusion. One of Wales' most enduring bands is called 'The Keys'. It's unnecessary to cause your audience – and their audience – confusion.

The Charlatans handled a similar situation in the U.S by adding the suffix 'UK' to their name when they were in the States but it's best to avoid those scenarios. To do so only requires a bit of forethought and the tiniest amount of research and effort.

I've found that a quick search for the band name you're considering with the word 'band' then 'musician' appended to it will let you know whether someone is operating under that name. I'd follow that up with a similar search on Facebook and in Spotify / the iTunes store. The names of these services may change as the years pass, but the principal remains the same. In the digital age you can easily discover whether someone else is already using a name you want. There's no need to duplicate. Pretending to yourself that you got there first is only storing up potential problems for the future. Lawsuits are a very expensive business.

We should go back to the shelves. Another two examples before we move on.

Ah, Funkadelic. I was hoping to pull a salutary 'bad' name off the shelf… maybe something by Coldplay or Mike and the Mechanics, both heinously bad names. Funkadelic, though, is a *genius* name. It sums up, in one word, the two poles of the band's sound: funk and psychedelic music. As a name it couldn't give you a more accurate idea of what to expect from the music. Plus it sounds cool. I'm not sure that other conflations of different genres would work as well – but they could lead you into some interesting sonic experiments: folkstep, dubcore, screamo 'n' western…

I'm not sure I want to hear any of those!

And finally… 'Homework' by Daft Punk. Hmm. I don't know how I feel about the name Daft Punk. I love their music… certainly this album was both commercially successful and hugely influential, but it's an odd name that doesn't fulfil any obvious criteria, other than being memorable. As criteria go, though, that might be the single most important one. 'Daft Punk' mightn't offer any clues, for the uninitiated, to the music they make, but people are unlikely to forget it as a phrase.

It's lucky we stumbled on this point towards the end of the chapter. It's probably the most important property of a good band name: to be memorable.

So how do you come up with a memorable name that fulfils all of the considerations that we've discussed so far? Band names have been inspired by music: Radiohead (Talking Heads song), Rolling Stones (blues lyric); by films: Duran Duran (from the film Barbarella); by books: The Go-Betweens, Marillion; by TV shows: The Prisoners…

In essence, by every aspect of life and culture. The key thing is to keep an ear out for a distinctive, memorable phrase; something that has a resonance to your music and something that hasn't been used before.

Scan the lyrics you've already written, even ones

you've discarded, to find an arresting combination of words. Christening yourselves with a name that has some organic connection to your music like this will work well.

Once you have found something that excites you, that you can imagine on album sleeves and gig posters, commit yourselves to it.

Don't sweat the small stuff, though. Your music is most important. A suitable name will grow out of your creativity, eventually, and finding a name will be much easier once you have an idea of how you will sound.

[1] **Half Man Half Biscuit** - *iconoclastic indie punks from Birkenhead in the UK. Influenced as much by British Folk Songs and damp Saturday afternoons watching Tranmere F.C. as they are by the Buzzcocks. The statement that they're the best band the UK has ever produced is contentious – but it's also true for me on at least three days of any given week.*

PLAYLIST:
Amen Corner - High In The Sky
The Ronettes - Be My Baby
Funeral For A Friend - Into Oblivion (Reunion)
Stereolab   - Ping Pong
Flaming Lips - Do You Realize?
Manic Street Preachers - If You Tolerate This Your Children Will Be Next
Teenage Fanclub - Neil Jung
T-Rex - Monolith
Half Man Half Biscuit - National Shite Day
Chvrches   - The Mother We Share
The Earth   - Baby Bones
Daft Punk - Da Funk

11: <u>Your Sound</u>

Be passionate about what you do. It should matter to you more than anything in the world. That you make a fantastic noise and you shouldn't give a damn what anybody else thinks.

Colin Newman, Wire

Good music is only the sonic celebration of a life lived hard. Which is kind of beautiful in and of itself. Life doesn't need to be celebrated, really; it stands on its own. We tend to race around shouting about things... we as a species, I mean, and music is one way we shout. We shout with architecture too, and science and lots of other things, but if music is your art-form, you can literally shout, which is fine.

Since a hard life isn't a pretty thing, good music isn't very pretty either. Beautiful is about the best you can hope for. And beautiful is sometimes really ugly.

Kristin Hersh, Throwing Muses / 50 Foot Wave

Strange to think that this thing we get so worked up about is just waves of energy vibrating our eardrums. Every sound we hear is the result of air molecules getting excited. What we're interested in here is how that molecular excitement is transferred to the brain and the heart, and why some music communicates to an audience while other music does not.

Sounding good helps. I don't mean fidelity – although that might be part of the equation. If you want people to love you and to invest their time and money in you, your music has to be interesting and convincing. You're asking a lot from your potential audience. If you want their interest, you will have to work hard to get it.

Sounding good is about a lot of different things: having memorable songs that people want to listen to; being well-rehearsed and knowing your music; having a consistent vision or aesthetic that an audience can invest in, and having the courage to be yourself.

Sounding good isn't determined by whatever technical talent you may or may not have::

Sometimes attitude can count equal to talent. You can have super talented musicians but they might forget how to feel something. You might get a kid come along who's full of beans and full of spirit and he's just as good as those.

Ian Brown, The Stone Roses

And sounding good isn't about intellectualising the whole process, over-thinking making music to the point that instinct gets lost. Sometimes the simplest philosophies work best:

We're just a band doing our thing. At the end of the day we're going to show other bands that you can write good classic songs like they did back then, years and years ago. There should be loads of bands doing it. And that's it.

Liam Gallagher, Oasis

Whatever (!) you think of Oasis' primary colours approach to finger-painting classic influences all over their music, it was phenomenally successful and made for some great records. "And that's it"… indeed.

However some music-makers are so in thrall to their influences that they allow them to dictate their entire sound. They don't bring anything of themselves to proceedings. Every big band ever has been followed by a slew of imitators who copied their haircuts, sonic palette, accents, even. Think of all of the plagiarists that Nirvana, The Stone Roses, Pavement, Oasis, The Libertines, The Arctic Monkeys at al begat.

Every town has their own version of the current en vogue band, but in that generic form none of those bands will go on to become anything other than big in their own back gardens. If you want more than a bit of local notoriety, aim far beyond your back garden and aim for a sound of your own.

Bandwagons pass through quickly and are soon replaced by a newer model and It's only the people who drive the bandwagon that get paid and lauded.

Nothing sounds passé quicker than a recording that echoes last year's zeitgeist. I almost drowned in the endless wave of Stereophonics-a-like demos that flooded through our letterbox in the late 90's. I understand music-makers getting drawn, subconsciously, to sounds that have a proven popularity with an audience. You may be lucky and be able to ride in on the coat-tails of a movement just as it's in its first flush of excitement and attention. The vast majority of people don't though: they stumble through the door clutching a banjo or a dubstep remix in 2014 and end up sounding more old hat than the rockabilly revival band who arrive at the same time.

Being good is useful, but being good and original will earn you an enduring audience, maybe even people who'd be prepared to release your music and invest in you.

Having a secondhand whiff to your music may, initially, get you gigs or a feature in the local paper but it's unlikely to make you memorable or distinctive enough to secure an audience's affection.

Of course, you're not here to pander to an audience; you're here to pander to yourself. If the music your heart moves you to make sounds like Duran Duran b-sides, then go for it. Derivative with heart is better than no heart at all.

A lot of great pop music is about opportunism. Being clever and cute with contemporary influences is the key. And timing is, in pop music terms, not just of the essence but the absolute essence itself.

Getting your timing right is about being able to pre-empt shifts and changes in music. You can only hone those perceptions by listening, acutely, to what's happening around you. Popular music's progression is about a little bit of thievery and a little bit of originality. The proportions of each aren't always clear. Too much of the former and you'll be derided as plagiarists. Too much of the latter, and it might be difficult to find an audience to help support and spread the word about your music.

It doesn't suit everyone to think so clinically about music, of course. Still, we have to acknowledge that some of the greatest records ever made – from the writing booths at the Brill Building to the legends clustered around the piano at Motown and Neptunes hot-wiring their imaginations to Pro Tools – were written by people who wanted to make hit singles and lots of money. Commercialism has been a clear motivating force for a lot of great music. And, it has to be said, an awful lot more soul-corroding shit.

Being yourself, in the escapist world of rock 'n' roll, doesn't have to mean being *yourself*. You can create a larger than life persona to channel your creative outpourings, as David Bowie and Lady Gaga have done. 'Being yourself' doesn't mean you have to sing about waiting for the spin cycle to finish on your laundry (but feel free to do so... looks like an excellent metaphor for something profound). Be whatever is true to you and your music.

I think we're only standing on the knee-caps of giants, we're not all the way up on the shoulders yet. The idea is to be yourself as much as you can, whatever that is.

E, Eels

I just blank it and do my own thing... nobody tells me what to do except for my own father, you know what I mean?

Ian Brown, The Stone Roses

'Being yourself' is a simple philosophy but what does it mean? Be true to the music *you* want to make. Take influence and inspiration from those around you but don't reshape yourself to the point where you're obscuring you. If your music changes with the seasons, cyclically trying to hook into whatever it is that's current, in a desperate attempt to find yourself an audience, you're trying too hard. Make a music that you believe in, first and foremost. Doing that with heart will endow your music with admirable qualities. You have a better chance of finding yourself an audience that way than by chasing someone else's tail.

I have been working with Marty Thau who brought the world the New York Dolls and Suicide. He told me something that has stuck with me ever since. And this really is wisdom. He said, "I've always believed there is a fine line between abstract and pure accessibility and that is what I've always looked for. An artist who can be abstract and conventional at the same time and – most importantly – reach people."

That's the magic we all seek. It's called originality. That's the starting point.

Jeremy Gluck, The Barracudas

I don't agree that it's the 'starting point'. Being original and accessible is the Holy Grail. However while you're still making 'mistakes' you probably have more potential to be original than when you attain competency. Being able to play generally means adhering to conventions, and conventions can defy originality.

The first couple of Happy Mondays albums are excellent examples of a band who couldn't play, in the traditional sense, cooking up a music that was entirely their own. They'd have attracted little interest if they'd been the slick Funkadelic-like band they aspired to. What was wrong made them right.

You'll be aware of the parts of your sound that aren't quite right. Perhaps you're reaching for something, a Prince-like falsetto or the scattergun energy of early Arctic Monkeys, but it's not coming out quite as you want. That not-quite-rightness could be the beginning of your sound.

Cherish and nurture the things that make you different.

Paul Draper from Mansun hated the sound of his own voice. He told me that when they were mixing their albums, he'd focus on the kick drum rather than listen to his vocal. I loved his vocals. He wanted to sing like Prince but felt lacking in comparison. To me, his voice is what made them special.

You don't have to be original but it helps. I don't subscribe – at all – to the belief that it's all been done before and that there are no original ideas or sounds left. We're unique. When we pick up a unique instrument and play it with our unique fingers or toes or larynx or brain, we're making a unique sound. The devil is in the detail and the detail is the source of wonder. People who make blithely reductive statements about music or art don't love or understand either.

If you open your heart and you allow your creativity to make music inspired by your own life – however mundane you may think it is – you will be an original artist.

Have the courage to make mistakes and the wisdom to learn what you can from them.

I think The Kinks are very courageous to make mistakes because we always tried new things, against our better judgements sometimes. We did a whole series of albums that were unrelated to the album before. We did Muswell Hillbillies that experimented with country music; then we did kind of a hard rock album - Give The People What They Want.... which was designed to be heard in a stadium.

I think sometimes The Kinks went too far in trying to be courageous. But it really is the only way to stay on top of your game as a writer because if you're bored as a writer, your audience will be bored. You've got to keep yourself sharp and I try to write a bit of a song every day.

Ray Davies, The Kinks

Ray's observation that being bored will make you boring is something to be aware of and challenge at every turn.

This book is somewhat hamstrung by the 'Why Don't You'-syndrome. Why Don't You was a popular kids TV show from the 70's through to the 90's. Its school holidays tagline was 'Why Don't You Just Switch Off Your Television

Set and Go and Do Something Less Boring Instead?'. Obviously if everyone followed that advice – to the letter – no one would have watched the show.

One of my key philosophies is that finding a good sound and being an interesting music-maker is a lot about doing rather than thinking about doing, yet I'm asking you to think about all of these aspects of your music. Don't forget that spirit and instinct play an important role in rock 'n' roll. The knowledge in this book should give you a better foundation upon which to express yourself instinctively. And have fun!

We lost the fun for a while! That's what it's meant to be about... I could be working in Kwik Save tomorrow but I'm in a band for God's sake. It's supposed to be a laugh!

Jimi Goodwin, Doves

Making good music is about having fun. Even if you're responsible for the darkest music imaginable, you can still have fun with it. Fun – a sense of wonder in what you're doing and a spirit in the way that it is performed or recorded – will make your music attractive, even if that music is a bloody two-fingers to the rest of the world.

Whatever you do, you're never going to win, so you might as well – I think, first and foremost – enjoy it.

Tjinder Singh, Cornershop

Well, that's quite a fatalistic approach... but a little fatalism and objectivity will stand us in very good stead for the imminent chapter on being your own worst critics. But first, let's hear from a man who's responsible for some of the most inventive and original sounding music it's ever been my pleasure to grill the airwaves with...

PLAYLIST:

Wire - Map Ref 41 Degrees N 93 Degrees W
Throwing Muses - Not Too Soon
Ian Brown - F.E.A.R
Oasis - Live Forever
Pavement - Shady Lane
The Shirelles - Will You Still Love Me Tomorrow?
Smokey Robinson & the Miracles - Tears of a Clown
Pharrell Williams - Happy
Lady Gaga - Born This Way
David Bowie - Moonage Daydream
The Barracudas - Summer Fun
Suicide - Ghost Rider
New York Dolls - Trash
Happy Mondays - 24hr Party People
The Kinks - Living on a Thin Line
The Doves - Catch The Sun

12: <u>Andrew Falkous On His Sound</u>

It takes something special for a CD-R to stand out in your memory, when you've received tens of thousands of the anonymous buggers over the course of your professional life. The reason this one stood out, initially, was because of the single word scrawled across its surface: 'BEST'.

Best what? CD-R? That was some hubris, was that, even in 1999 when the rest of the postbag was a slosh of sloppy seconds, stale with wannabe Coldplay and Stereophonics B.O.

It wasn't a great time to be receiving demos. Best sounded like slavering, addled, noise perverts in comparison.

What, though, did they mean by 'Best'? It's a word you can't ignore. It thrums with contradictory possibilities. It could have referred to their musical standing, or it could have been a tribute to The Beatles' rejected drummer. Or maybe we were supposed to be thinking about George; not impossibly-graceful-and-elusive-on-the-football-field-George, but George when he was pissed out of his head, dragging Miss Worlds through avalanches of breaking glass and entropic champagne waterfalls.

So many potential layers of meaning. And this was just the band's name, not even a full portion of their lyrical dupiaza.

Welcome to the early days of the certifiably unique, disturbingly febrile, cliche-goading world of Andrew Falkous and his verbal genius.

112

Best became mclusky and saved me from Starsailor and hoards of own brand Stereophonics-a-likes. I forged a love for them through the debut album I think they'd rather forget, through 'mclusky do dallas' (as good an album as any you'll hear), through 'The Difference Between Me and You Is That I'm Not on Fire', up until their rather acrid end.

I remember being very sad when I read their Dear John letter. There was still some hope, however: "there'll be more music soon, from all of us..."

Eventually, then, came Future of the Left. In a world filled with more disappointing second acts than mosquito larvae, Future of the Left became that rarest of entities... a new band who trumped the old, critically-lauded band's legacy. Again and again.

They're the most-played artist on my radio show. They're winners of that particular tin cup because of their continued, evolving originality and excellence. The proudest moment of my professional life was presenting them with the 2012 Welsh Music Prize for 'The Plot Against Common Sense'.

Every album adds much to their already bristling equation.

They're the only band I know where I can say, with conviction, that every new album is their best. They're not entirely indistinguishable from mclusky or, even, Best (that thought will horrify them, probably), they are just so much more.

Much of that is down to Falkous' determination and vision. So I asked him some questions about determination and vision.

How much has the sound of mclusky and Future of the Left been shaped by a determination to not sound like anyone else?

On Making Music

My deep desire has always been to make exactly the kind of music that I want to hear. Early on, it's clear to me, I wanted to be in the Pixies (a band of whom your readers are probably aware) but that developed, by the time of mclusky's second album, into wanting to be in the best band in the world. Note, I said 'wanting' (as opposed to 'being') and 'best' (as opposed to 'biggest'). If I'd heard what I wanted from other bands on anything approaching a consistent basis then I doubt I'd make music at all.

When you very first started out making music, who were the people you wanted to sound like before you had the confidence to be you? Assuming, of course, that you went through that stage.

I went through that stage, hard, in a state of mostly blissful ignorance. Pride brings the personality through, I would guess/expect. It's all very well playing at a band and recording a demo tape but when you sit down to listen is there a piece of it which is of you, that exists in the world because of the make-up of your particular cells or do you simply hear a functional collection of notes which exists only because there was nothing better to do at the time. Too many bands just exist.

At what point did you have the confidence to start sounding like yourself?

It just happened one day. Mostly, I still do. It's usually obvious when there's been an overreach or anomaly. Occasionally I pull a Colin Newman/Jello Biafra vocal impression out of my colon - I tell myself it's a kind of loving pastiche but really it's because my actual personality has failed me. Sometimes it's nice to take a holiday in somebody else's sound.

Andrew Falkous On His Sound

A good proportion of the identifiability of 'your sound' is due to your voice. Have you always sung in your own accent? A lot of people... too many... don't.

No, but embarrassment soon sorted that out. My accent is a complete mess at the best of times whether I'm singing or ordering a kebab. Sheffield people singing like Californians. New Yorkers appropriating Cockney. It's so CUTE.

Was the singular way that you string / tune your guitar a conscious effort to make your bands sound different?

At first it was because I had broken some strings and from that point two factors (poverty and laziness) intersected to mean that I didn't replace them. I wrote about four songs with a guitar-tuned to (jargon alert) fuck-knows-what because I didn't want to second guess what I was playing - I just fell in love with the sound, the tone of the strings flapping around and the genuine surprise I felt at almost every note. I'd been playing conventionally tuned guitars for a while and I'd become tired of knowing exactly what was going to happen before I'd even touched the strings.

I think of mclusky and Future of the Left as being two of the least generic bands I have heard, but you know your music's genetic map far better than I do. Are you more a sum of your influences than I give you credit for?

There's a stage of the sound writing process when songs can absolutely reflect their influences. Then, if they're any good, they change (often in relatively minor ways) and take on a completely different aspect. 'I don't know what you ketamine' on the last record is a perfect example of this. In that case, Jimmy's guitar was an almost alien element which made the normal, or at least relatively normal, interesting. To me, at least.

You don't collaborate with other people, or endorse official remixes or fuck about with the sanctity of what you have. Is that to keep the integrity of your band and your sound intact?

It works for some people. Me, not so much. I've never heard a remix or collaboration which excited me. What is a collaboration anyway? A half-arsed band? People who 'collaborate' are the kind of cunts who do 'projects'. Ugh. Projects. We got asked if Don Letts could talk over our music once on a Channel 4 Television show. We said no. It was a pretty easy decision to make. I wouldn't have cared if it was Chuck D or Greg Dulli. Still no. Let's do something properly or go home and have a bath.

You're not easily impressed by other music (compared to me, say). Does that make it harder to find musical inspiration?

Nah. When it does come, which is often enough to know I'm alive, it really hits. I envy your love of music. That's the truth.

Although the focus here is on you, your albums are collaborative, band creations. Is that also key to your music's originality? I imagine that Julia, Jimmy and Jack bringing their inspirations and ideas to the creative process helps to keep things fresh. It's not as if you all share the same influences, is it?

It's not. I mean, I head it up, but anybody is free to throw in things (and everybody does). The one thing we all agree on, I would think, is that the song itself has the ultimate power. Everybody is pretty good at controlling their egos and playing simply what is required - that wasn't necessarily the case in mclusky.

116

Although you work with a relatively limited sonic palette, every new album brings surprises, which are all the more effective because they don't rely on an orchestra of banjos. How much of that is a conscious philosophy? (Finding variety within limitations.)

It's not conscious at all just, I suppose, a natural human need for variety. Gimmicks usually end up sounding like gimmicks but hey - some people really like gimmicks.

Do you kill songs early on if they start to sound like someone else?

We might keep them back as a low-pressure, fun-to-play b-side. 'No Covers', the mclusky song, was identified as a Nirvana rip-off fairly early on, whilst 'fucked up runners' from the last record did a similar, albeit excessively poppy, job with the Shellac template. It's all good fun. They become … less art, if I may. More process. A document of people in a room rather than our earnest bloody everything.

I understand that, for the most part, you work quickly in the studio. Is that because the energy in a new song can dissipate if it's not captured quickly, and is that immediacy a key component to your sound?

Immediacy, yes, and the love of novelty. I'm very quick to praise new songs at the expense of the old, Julia is always pulling me up on it. We won't play a song for two weeks and I'll condemn it to history, and not a glorious one.

What is it that keeps you hungry to get better?

Being an intensely competitive wanker who rarely hears real things. Also, a great fear of something I can't ever put my finger on.

You've been working on some solo recordings, have you chosen a different palette of sounds to work with to distinguish those recordings from Future of the Left?

The means of working, at home on Logic, means less in the way of strange time signatures and more harmonies (I'm a fruity little harmony slut, you can find me in the phonebook under 'four-way'). Nothing is consciously different other than the music is made in a different room, at a different time of day and completely by myself. Also, I never have to feed cats during a regular band rehearsal and there's something intensely liberating about doing a vocal take whilst waiting for some vegetables to steam.

A good proportion of my vegetable steaming has been done listening to mclusky and Future of the Left. It's a musical accompaniment that keeps the broccoli al dente, which is just how I like it. There isn't anything other than thrilling listening to be had from Andrew's back catalogue. You can find them via the usual download / streaming outlets. There are also excellent vinyl pressings of all of the albums, and many of the singles, if you can find them.

Keep an eye (and an ear) on http://futureoftheleft.net for news of upcoming Future of the Leftreleases. Follow Andrew Falkous on Twitter @shit_rock

The back catalogue now includes Andrew's excellent one-man-band album release, 'i am scared of everything that isn't me' (under the name Christian Fitness). Find out more details here: http://christianfitness.bandcamp.com

PLAYLIST:
mclusky - Without MSG I Am Nothing
mclusky - What We've Learned

Future of the Left - adeadenemyalwayssmellsgood
Future of the Left - Manchasm
Future of the Left - Arming Eritrea
Future of the Left - You Need Satan
Future of the Left - Notes On Achieving Orbit
Future of the Left - Donny of the Decks
Future of the Left - French Lessons
Future of the Left - Singing Of Bonesaws
Dead Kennedys - Holiday In Cambodia
Wire - French Film Blurred
Public Enemy - Welcome to the Terrordome
Afghan Whigs - My Enemy
Shellac - Canaveral
christian fitness - soft power itches

13: <u>Be Your Own Worst</u> <u>Critics</u>

It's art. Don't ignore the fact that it's art, don't pretend it's something else, you should be doing it for its own sake not for anybody else's sake.

Colin Newman, Wire / Githead

Greatness, spirit – these things are not mediocre and mediocrity is to be avoided at all costs. Greatness or bust must be our watchword as artists. There's nothing else worth aiming for.

Jeremy Gluck, The Barracudas

Finding an audience for your music – beyond immediate friends and family – is not easy. There is more competition out there for people's attention, support and money than ever before: immersive video games, the internet, satellite TV. You're also competing with rock's past. A large proportion of radio and streaming services are founded on 'oldies' – songs that people already know they love. Familiar artists of yesteryear do remarkably well on revival tours and, if people can't see the original, there is a choice of amusingly-named tribute bands.

You will want to be able to elbow your way through this ever-growing throng to get yourself heard.

Artistic movements aren't immortal. Rock 'n' roll has been with us since the mid 50's. It's of pensionable age. What keeps it going is its startling capacity to evolve and outmanoeuvre stagnancy – which is where you come in.

Rest assured, if you're making brilliant music people will trip over themselves to support you. There is a multitude out there – many more than ever before – actively seeking music to broadcast, blog about and release. They have articles, broadcast hours and release schedules to fill. They need you but only if you're good.

The sobering reality for you is that however many people and services there are hungry for exciting new music to support, they are dwarfed by the number of aspiring artists.

My radio show is dedicated to playing new Welsh artists, yet I still only play roughly 10–15% of the music that is submitted to me. Maintaining a high quality threshold, even in a country as small as Wales (population 3 million), isn't difficult because there are so many people making music out there. And aiming for a high quality threshold is vital if I want to appeal to an audience beyond the artists I'm featuring on any given show.

I played 2194 different artists on my radio show between January 2011 and June 2014. The majority of these would be 'bedroom' artists – people whose music-making autonomy has been enabled by the digital revolution. Relatively cheap computing technology and music software have democratised music-making to a startling degree. Wherever you are in the world, there will be fellow music-makers around you seeking an audience. It's a more competitive environment – in terms of the green shoots of your music being able to reach the sustenance of an audience, or media support, or a record label – than ever before.

Of course, you can create music just for you own enjoyment. I love to do this myself. There's a great purity to that philosophy. However I suspect that if you've gone to the trouble of reading this far, your ambitions extend beyond your own headphones.

Fortunately achieving wider-reaching ambitions can

start right inside those headphones.

The key piece of advice that I want to impress on you *in this whole book* is to **be your own worst critics.** It's in bold type to press the point home. I'd have it printed in MASSIVE NEON LIGHTS if that were affordable / possible.

I've probably listened to more demos than anyone else in the UK. I've heard every stratum of quality from the awe-inspiringly sublime to the heinously awful. I am frequently astounded by what some people deem suitable for broadcast. Listening to a dictaphone recording of someone doing a Celine Dion cover in a utility room (not a fabricated example) – with a tumble dryer in the background – fully expecting me to play it on the radio, I wonder if 'we' are getting the message across clearly enough. And I wonder what on earth that person hears when they listen back to their recording.

Listening back to it critically, it would be obvious even to a doornail with a penchant for Celine Dion covers that it's not suitable for broadcast. Clearly this is an extreme example but it is in an excellent example of how unfathomably wrong some music submissions can be.

To complicate matters further, if the 'Celine Dion backed by Tumble Dryer' recording had come from one of Wales' more esoteric labels, and had revelled in its own ironic post-modernism, I may have played it. Context is pretty important too. One man's turd on a stick is another man's thrilling deconstruction of the mores of Modern Art.

I do not expect high fidelity recordings from everyone, by any means. I've played dictaphone recordings of some artists (notably Irma Vep) that are some of my favourite songs of all time but that's a rare example of where the talent transcends the limitations of the technology, or makes a merit of it (excellently written songs, recorded with great immediacy and little over consideration).

For Irma Vep, and the likes of Daniel Johnston, a

spontaneous and honest recording is more important than fidelity. It is part of the artist's philosophy and aesthetic. However when I get a dictaphone recording from a screamo band recorded in their front room and the accompanying email says: "We don't have a microphone or PA so the singer had to stand by the recorder and shout..." well, I'm thinking before I've even clicked 'play' that it's not going to be broadcastable. Call it intuition or evidence of a sixth sense. In that example (not as rare as you would imagine) the recording sounded like blocks of out of tune slate being tipped into a bucket of cold vomit. Now I know that there are people who would claim to like that sort of thing, but it's not for me, sorry.

Neither would it be suitable for the majority of labels, blogs, magazines. One bad recording can taint your name and your reputation. We'll talk more about this in **Chapter 29:** *'The Perfect Demo'.*

Having set our parameters, let's talk more specifically about what I mean when I say "be your own worst critic".

Try and force yourself to listen to your recording as if it had come from a complete stranger. This is very hard to do. It's like asking someone with a car on their foot to pretend the limb belongs to someone else but it's this kind of objectivity that is essential if you want to (truly) judge the merits of your work.

When you're caught up in the dizzy rush of creating something of your own, you lose much of your ability to judge whether it is any good or not. I know this from personal experience. The first demo I recorded was a ham-fisted cover version of The Cult's Love Removal Machine. We'd recorded it in a day at Rick Astley's demo studio in Widnes. The drums were the best bit. The guitars were a little out of tune. The bass sounded like it had been played on an elastic band submerged in a slurry pit. My guitar solo was Billy Duffy being chased out of Dodge by a crowd pelting him with bum notes. The vocal – pegged on in the last ten minutes of the session – would have earned itself a TV slot at an early X Factor audition, for all the wrong reasons.

Yet, once we got home from the studio I listened to nothing else for weeks. It was me and my best mates, for crying out loud! (And crying out loud was what my mum and dad were doing the 6,000th time they'd heard Paul maul the opening line.) I couldn't hear any of the fatally obvious flaws (that it's a cover version of The Cult being the most glaring). My ears forgave them. I listened to it aspirationally, filling in all the gaps, smoothing out the awfulness.

What I should have done was listen to it and judge it dispassionately next to the original. That's what I should have done.

Being your own worst critic means acknowledging every flaw and weakness in your recording, because the dispassionate, objective listener who isn't you, your Nain or your bestest mate, will hear them writ loud, trust me.

Good to great bands don't let anyone hear their music until it has passed their own exacting standards.

Being a perfectionist needn't ruin the immediacy of rock 'n' roll. It's all about you having high standards and pride in what you do. Make it the best you possibly can before you send it to anyone. It will improve your chances markedly... and (importantly) not just with me. I'm making all the demands here, but this advice will serve you well whoever you're sending your music to.

'Perfectionism' doesn't mean identifying the faults in a recording but submitting it anyway, with an email riddled with provisos and excuses: "the singer had a sore throat that day and a vicious iguana had stolen all of the keyboard player's white keys. The next recordings we do will definitely sound better than these."

124

Don't send them then! Making anyone feel that you're sending them your second best will cast your recordings into the Recycle Bin as quickly as if you have a singing voice like an out of tune Joe Pasquale.

BE YOUR OWN WORST CRITIC. Get it tattooed somewhere convenient but unlikely to be seen by the public. (The drummer is a good place.)

Please note that I'm not suggesting you try to second guess or analyse yourselves at every stage of the creative process. Create unselfconsciously. Bring your critical faculties to the fore when you've drawn the initial, inspirational strands together: when you've finished writing a song, say; or when you're considering what to record; or during the mixing process of a recording session.

Being too analytical in the early moments of creativity will stifle your flow and make you self-conscious. Learn when, and how, to turn the unforgiving, critical spotlight on, and when to leave it off.

Sometimes when you're writing, a half-baked idea will transform into something more beautiful and inspirational. Give yourself – and those early, stumbling steps towards a song – the chance to evolve into something spectacular.

However once you've worked through an idea, explored it from every angle and finished shaping it, be unstinting with your criticism.

It will serve you well. Especially during recording and mixing.

Here's an incomplete list of the kind of things I hear all the time that relegate submissions to my 'Rejected' folder: unnecessarily out of tune instruments; unnecessarily out of tune vocal (even just a single phrase); timing problems; clichéd lyrics; unimaginative, preset sounds (electronic music); self indulgence (too long, yawn-inducing solos); a failure to apply the essential adage: 'don't bore us, get to the chorus!' – even if you don't have choruses; dullness (but if your music is dull, you never know it); lots of swearing (not a quality issue, I just can't play music with swearing in it); heard-it-all-before-a-million-times-and-done-better-ness; missing spark.

See the **Chapter 37:** *'Reasons For Rejection'* for a full, unexpurgated list.

A lot of people lose their critical faculties when it comes to their own music. It's a strange phenomenon.

I know from personal experience that bands spend a lot of time sat around in cafes and pubs aggrandising themselves. You do need a certain amount of bullishness if you want to succeed in the music industry but it's imperative you don't get caught in a feedback loop and end up believing your own bravado at the expense of the objective realities of your music.

Remember it's in your vested interest to believe in your music but it's not in anyone else's. If you're having to twist people's arms all the time you're missing something fundamental about your music.

Be your own worst critic and you may discover what it is.

PLAYLIST:
Irma Vep - One Eye On Everything
Daniel Johnston - Love Wheel
Daniel Johnston - Ain't No Woman Gonna Make A George Jones Out Of Me
The Cult - Love Removal Machine

14: <u>Songwriting</u>

When I'm asked how I go about writing a song – what comes first, the music or the lyrics, what inspires me and so on – it's always a difficult question because there's no precise method to it. I'll start with the music and hopefully something will come to mind lyrically, just some mumbling along with the chord sequence. But the songs I'm happiest with are the ones I could sit down and explain exactly what each line was about.

Jim Bob, Carter the Unstoppable Sex Machine

It's the fag-end of October 2013 as I start to write this chapter of the book. I've just presented the Welsh Music Prize at a ceremony attended by many of my music-making heroes, where I made a speech to mark the 20th anniversary of my BBC Radio Wales new music show. I fretted over what I should say. It's hard to get up in front of the true magicians of this industry and feel that you can entertain them. So I focused on that magical element in what they do and the awe that it inspires in we non-musical, muggle folk.

Because it is magic. Great music-makers create something out of nothing. They emit a sonic vibration that can move hearts wherever the music is heard. Even Brian Cox and his quantum physics can't do that.

These waves of sound can turn rain into poetry; heartbreak into hope; loneliness into empathy; dead-ends into dreams; hardship into defiance; anger into energy.

Humankind is capable of no more magical a feat.

And the phosphorescing core of that magic is in the

128

songwriting process. That's where everything that we've talked about so far – influences, philosophies, sounds, skills, instincts, collaborations and imaginations – are smelted together in ways that we only fractionally understand.

If we only "fractionally understand" them, what's the point in offering advice on their mysteries?

You don't have to understand this magic to be able to perform it. In fact, trying to *understand* it – and over-analysing its constituent elements – is likely to nullify the magic itself. Grace and instinct play an important role in any form of creativity.

Learn enough to be able to make music without having to think so much that you drown out the truth in your heart.

Because there is so much advice to give on this subject, it will be split across a few chapters. This chapter is about songwriting in general: the advantages of writing your own songs; the key philosophies; how to recognise a 'good' song; where to find inspiration; how important instinct and grace are to the process and the absolute, fundamental importance of *being yourself*. This credo has equal importance throughout this book to *be your own worst critic*.

The subject of lyric writing is partitioned off to the next-but-one chapter so that this chapter doesn't become too long and unwieldy. Music and lyrics hold equal importance in my mind. There are no hard fast rules as to which should come first. The advice from these chapters is intended to run in parallel, not in sequence.

For the sake of these chapters, a 'song' is any piece of music that you write regardless of whether it has lyrics or not.

Why go to the effort of writing songs? I'm hoping that

this most rhetorical of questions sounds to you as stupid as me asking 'why go to the effort of breathing?'. This book is for original music-makers. Writing songs is, to my mind, what it is all about. Don't let X Factor's karaoke shit-storm fool you into thinking otherwise.

Make sure you have 25 good radio songs and a major label will sign you. If you don't have 25 good radio songs – which equals a 5 year record deal at 5 songs per year – then make sure you tour a lot. Because there's another saying: bands that don't get record contracts break up; bands or solo artists who have recording contracts, but records that don't sell, they break up; who doesn't break up? Answer: the ones that get on the radio are the ones that the most people hear the most often.

Kim Fowley, Record Producer

Kim Fowley's assertions may seem to belong to a golden age, long since past. Record companies and their contracts no longer dictate whether your music is successful or not (which, for a long time, was the measure of an artist's success or failure). However regardless of the shape of the industry, songs are your currency, of that there is no doubt.

If you're spending all your time hustling for gigs, rehearsing for gigs, playing gigs, you're kind of missing the point. Because the thing that's going to take you to the next level is, really, a killer song and the only way you get to the killer songs, is by writing rubbish ones. So you have to be able to write 10 songs a month, or something, of which 9 are going to be rubbish, to get to the 10th one. So, write a great deal more than you think you need to.

Tom Robinson, songwriter / 6Music DJ

As Tom points out above, writing a "killer" song will open up more doors for you than anything else. Focus your limited energies and time on getting that right *first*. Great gigs and great records follow great songs. It's not a chicken and egg situation.

So what makes a song 'great'?

In a world where Celine Dion will never have to work again but Future of the Left's Andrew Falkous has to take temp work to keep a roof over his head, it's obvious that there is a wide variety of opinion on this subject. Good isn't always popular and popular isn't always good.

A great pop song is something that holds the listener's interest. So, initially that would be the way you've written the song – the melody and the lyric – and then production becomes quite important and arrangement. It's a process of not letting the listener get bored. A pop song is quite a short medium — it's not a symphony so you have to say a lot in a short time.

Clive Langer, Record Producer (Madness / Elvis Costello / The Teardrop Explodes / Dexys Midnight Runners)

Clive Langer's assertion that a good song holds the listener's "interest" and doesn't allow them to "get bored" is useful but still subjective. In a world of leisure activities that range from train-spotting to free-running, gradations of boredom are as varied as tastes in music.

Many of the finest songwriters I have met have a very low boredom threshold. If they manage to finish a song it's generally a mark that it's a good one. If you're struggling to finish writing a song ask yourself bluntly whether it's because it's boring you or become a chore. If the answer is 'yes', it's likely to bore an audience too. Ditch it. If there's a good idea in there – a lyric or a riff you're proud of and want to hang on to – it's likely to resurface elsewhere, perhaps in a better and more usable form.

Frequently songwriters are Dr Frankensteins, resurrecting ideas and stitching them together to bring life to something new. Don't fret over a great, new idea that won't work itself into a song immediately. The more you try to shoehorn an idea into a composition, regardless of whether it is adding something to the whole, the more you'll change the composition's shape and the less attractive it is likely to be.

A key thing is to define for yourself what a good song means to you and your music. Frequently this will bear some relationship to the norms of what is widely perceived as good music – i.e. having a quality or qualities that would compel someone to listen to it again and again. It's important while doing this that you don't delude yourself. 'Be your own worst critic'. If there are obvious failings in a song – if it aspires to being tuneful, say, but the melody is moribund or it purports to rely on volume but has all the power of blowing through a used tissue against a broken-toothed comb – it will not be 'good'.

If you find that you're filling in the spaces, making excuses for elements of the song, then it is not 'good'.

I listen to tens, sometimes hundreds, of demos every week from artists whose quality control is so out of kilter with the rest of listener-kind that it can only be a product of their own delusion. Yes music is subjective but that doesn't mean there is no such thing as bad music. You loving your own music unreservedly and uncritically won't make it good. Other people loving your music can, though.

Having said that, one of the finest and most original songwriters that America has produced in the last quarter of a century makes an argument for creating in your own bathysphere, disconnected from other people's expectations:

When you play music it helps to imagine that no one will ever hear it, which might very well be the case. And it'll make your songs better. There's nothing like working in a vacuum to keep you unselfconscious. Which in turn will keep you un-whiney. Which is good. And un-flirty. And un-ego trippy. And working in a vacuum will keep you un-rich too – which is good, because rich people don't live hard. That's why rock stars are so whiney. And ego trippy and flirty.

Kristin Hersh, Throwing Muses / 50 Foot Wave

Kristin's songs are singularly un-flirty, un-ego trippy and unselfconscious. It's what gives her work a freshness and originality that sets it apart from the majority of rock 'n' roll's canon.

Try to fathom whether you're in this to play the game, to indulge in a rock 'n' roll fantasy, or in this to be yourself. This can be the baseline for your writing and it may be worth referring to if you lose sight or inspiration as you go on.

As Tom stated earlier – and it's a piece of wisdom echoed by many songwriters – not every song you write will be a great one. You will need to write a lot to hone your craft and to increase your chances of composing something brilliant.

When I was writing songs I would write loads and loads of stuff until something decent fell out. And I discovered that every three songs that I wrote, there would be something in one of them that appealed to my gut instinct. It was usually a great melodic movement. The lyrics and the production you can work on but a great melody is the thing that is very difficult to capture.

In terms of the mechanics of songwriting, from my point of view it's not a mystical thing where you're a conduit for something greater, so to speak — but it's more like a craft where you learn the skills to put songs together.

Paul Draper, Mansun

And, again, the notion that songwriting is a 'craft':

Work at your craft. Songwriting is paramount. If you don't write your own songs then you are doomed to end up in a covers band with plenty of local gigs but no prospects whatsoever. Study your favourite songs. How they're constructed, what goes where, how are the lyrics framed for maximum effect.

Learn the tricks of the trade.

Deke Leonard

What are those 'tricks of the trade'? Well, that very much depends on the kind of music you make.

The Beatles learnt a lot about song form – verses, choruses, middle eights, key changes – from the standards that made up the bulk of their set when they paid their dues in Hamburg and at The Cavern.

It's easy for me to get sniffy about songwriting courses – or scriptwriting courses or creative writing courses – but it does seem that we're socialised into certain expectations about the journey a song (or script or novel) will take us on. I don't like to look at something that I regard as magical in such a reductive and pragmatic way but having an intuition as to how the structure of a song can improve its effectiveness is important.

If you've written a verse and a chorus (or a chorus, then a verse, if that way round works better for the song) that you're excited by, but you don't know how to then elevate it to the next level, to keep the song interesting as it progresses for you or your listeners, a key change can be your friend, or space for a solo. A lot of the dynamics of a song are refined in its arrangement, production and recording – but getting the foundation and the structure right from the start will serve the song well.

Having said that, I don't believe that you should be too reverent in the writing of your songs. You don't have to join a songwriting guild and pass exams. Rock 'n' roll is supposed to bend and break the rules, not adhere to its own prescriptive, new set. Whatever music you make, whether it's supposed to be insurrectionary and unsettle the status quo or fall nicely in line with the great songwriters of music's past, practising what you do, and what you write, can only make you better.

Write, write and, then, write a little bit more.

So, you know the importance of writing your own songs, you're thrilled by the possibilities but daunted by the idea of making something good that stands up against what has gone before and that will be fair testament to you. Where do you start? How do you begin to pull together the strands that will make something magical from the void?

Firstly, give yourself the time and space to write. One of the myths about music-making is that to be receptive to your muse you have to be tuned into it 24 hours a day, that any other work or distraction will diminish your artistic effectiveness. In my experience, that's utter bullshit. I subscribed to that point of view for five years, secreting myself into a freezing rehearsal room in a dead-end town. I made my best friends hate me as I spent hour-upon-hour chasing my muse to fruitless effect.

I should have been out there experiencing life. That would have given me all of the muse I needed.

Secondly, try not to over-think the process. When I was that young man with songwriting ambitions I read an endless stream of biographies about Ray Davies, The Beatles and Brian Wilson. I wanted to write songs better than theirs but I was paralysed by a surgical understanding, derived from the innumerable interviews and biographies I had read, of the greatness of the work of those artists. I was the reserve team ballboy allowed on the pitch with the Premier League first team – too terrified to express myself in case I made a mistake.

Few of the music biographies I have read detail the creative process. I hadn't understood that many of my favourite artists created instinctively and hadn't, necessarily, worried about the mathematics or architecture of what they were producing, at least not early in the writing process.

If you sit there and fret over every chord change, or every subsequent note in a melodic phrase, your music will most likely be stilted. If you just let yourself go, accept that whilst writing you'll make mistakes and missteps most of the time, but on occasion also stumble across something natural and sublime, your compositions are more likely to flow.

Listeners are drawn towards pieces that sound natural. Awkwardness is generally off-putting.

You can't really think about it too much else you'll never come away with anything. I think variety and different types of approaches to songs is always a good thing because it keeps you on your toes. Just express yourself. I think that's a good thing for any human being to be doing.

Tjinder Singh, Cornershop

If you're in a creative doldrum, suffering from the dreaded 'writer's block', sparking your muse can be difficult. One potential route towards inspiration is to keep your approach to writing fresh. Give your fingers and your imagination the opportunity to stumble across something different. Don't always let your fingers reach for the obvious chord. Try a different tuning (guitar) or a different sound (keyboards). If you usually start the process instrumentally, try starting with a lyric instead. Or composing a cappella. There are a multitude of different ways to generate that initial spark.

I also try and make a point of, if I feel like picking up the guitar I make myself go over to a different instrument, because I think if you go to an instrument that feels familiar to you you're liable to put your hands where they feel comfortable and write something that you've written before. If I want to go over to the guitar I'll go over to the autoharp instead and write it there to get something fresh.

E, Eels

Giving yourself the freedom to mess about, to *play*, is key. If you get anxious about the creative process, or too self conscious, your well of ideas is likely to be dry. In fact, get too wound up and the well will be difficult to locate. Give yourself the freedom and the space to have serendipitous 'accidents'. If there's a chord, a button, or an effect, or a tuning, or a preset that you haven't explored – or that you've maybe discounted – have the foresight and wherewithal to try it, whatever it is, to explore beyond the boundaries of what you know works.

If you think of your music as a map, it's always the mysterious, uncharted areas at the edge of your known world that hold the most allure and mystery. Traipse over the same ground again and again and you'll bore yourselves as much as you end up boring your listeners.

If nothing is forthcoming – go for a walk; read a book; watch a film; listen to whatever your current musical touchstones are. When The Joy Formidable were writing their (phenomenal, to my ears) debut album, periods of frustration, writers block and conflict were alleviated by walks in the hills that proved to be one of the chief sonic muses for that album.

So don't be afraid to walk away. It'll give you perspective and a chance for your creative muscles to recover. It's not an accurate, anatomical analogy – your creativity doesn't come from a muscle, but a harassed, aching mind is unlikely to be a fertile breeding ground for good ideas.

Do make it easy to catch ideas when they come to you. Snatches of melody, lyrical phrases, will visit when you least expect them. Keep a notepad, a dictaphone or – these days – a mobile phone with a simple voice recorder close at hand at all times.

Last week I decided to start writing using a little Walkman dictaphone, and that's really helped because I just pick up a guitar dead quick if I get an idea, bang it down without vocals, maybe just humming a melody and sometimes I can record two or three songs in one night.

It makes them sound more cohesive together. The flow and cohesion comes from not labouring the ideas too much.

Badly Drawn Boy

Approach your writing as fearlessly as possible. Your

best chance of making an indelible mark in the world of music is to be yourself. You are unique. The more you there is in the formula, the more intriguing and compelling a prospect your music will be.

Songwriting isn't an exact science. There are a multitude of different philosophies and approaches. I hope this chapter has given you some inspiration as to the infinite possibilities. In the next chapter we will hear from one of my favourite songwriters, Martin Carr. After we've heard about his experiences of writing songs, we'll focus on a more specific aspect of songwriting: the lyrics.

PLAYLIST:

Carter The Unstoppable Sex Machine - The Only Living Boy In New Cross
B. Bumble & the Stingers - Nut Rocker
The Runaways - Cherry Bomb
Dexy's Midnight Runners - There There My Dear
Teardrop Explodes - Treason
Madness - It Must Be Love
50ft Wave - Clara Bow
Mansun - Wide Open Space
The Kinks - Shangri-La
The Beatles - If I Fell
The Beach Boys - Don't Worry Baby
The Joy Formidable - Wolf' Law
Eels - Last Stop: This Town
Badly Drawn Boy - Disillusion
Cornershop - People Power

15: <u>Martin Carr On Songwriting</u>

Dan was the singer and I was the guitarist. We were best friends. We lived together on Ullett Rd. in Liverpool and our hunger for music was voracious and far-ranging. We were great white sharks hunting for good vibrations in any waters. We'd play records, tapes and CD's through the night, contemplating a chess board, getting psychedelic, huddled around our portable gas heater.

The romance is only kicking in now i'm thinking about it almost twenty-five years later.

We smoked foraged dog-ends, drank bottles of Thunderbird Blue Label, gave each other scabies, sometimes had to break the ice on the loo to take a piss. It wasn't romantic at the time, trust me.

The music we listened to had mostly been inspired by tapes made by our friend back home, Richard Holland: King Crimson, Python Lee Jackson, Cat Stevens, PP Arnold, Killing Joke, Julian Cope, XTC, The Beach Boys, Jethro Tull, The Zombies, Love, Dave Brubeck, Tomorrow, Peter Green-era Fleetwood Mac, The Undertones, Argent, The Kinks, The Creatures… they were fucking astonishing compilations. As key to my being here waffling all this as anything. As everything, in fact.

We liked some of the bands we saw in town or at The Tivoli back home: Ride, Lush, Swervedriver, The Real People. None of them appeased our appetite for something as multi-dimensional as those compilation tapes, though. Well, maybe one band.

I'd bought Ichabod & I (1990), The Boo Radley's debut

album, from Crocodile Records in Mold. I liked the name of the band. To Kill A Mockingbird was my joint 4th favourite book of all time. The album sounded like wet farts through distortion boxes. It wasn't very good.

I didn't hold musical grudges back then. I can't have done because I remember adoring their Every Heaven E.P (1991). The Finest Kiss felt like weeping over a lost, first love. I had no idea how in thrall the band were to My Bloody Valentine or Dinosaur Jr. I wouldn't have cared. I adored it. I still do.

I remember liking their second album, Everything's Alright Forever. It impressed me with its scope and trumpets.

"We could do with more scope and trumpets, Dan..."

"Scope and trumpets... yeah... pass the bong."

It's alright. I didn't inhale.

I'd try and spot them when we were out and about in Liverpool, in Planet X or Chaucers, The Cosmos or Casablancas, Macs or Mardi Gras. Thing is, I didn't have a clue what they looked like. A bald one, a black one, a beanpole and a hairy one. Unless they were all there, en masse, playing Does This Hurt?, I wouldn't have stood a chance.

A warm affection turned into something close to an obsession when they released Lazarus in 1993. By then I'd moved back home and we'd dumped Dan from the band. I listened to Lazarus over and over again. It shared a similarly explorative philosophy to Screamadelica... dubby bass lines, unexpected developments, scope and trumpets.

The subsequent album, Giant Steps, is one of those that

shaped me the most. Like Rich Holland's compilation tapes, Dave Haslam's DJ set when the Stone Roses played the Empress Ballroom in Blackpool and Mark Radcliffe's Out On Blue 6 radio show, it puffed my mind and my musical imagination out in a thousand different directions.

I would highlight the artists and records that Martin and singer, Sice, would name as influences in their interviews in the music press and go out and buy them: records by The Turtles, King Tubby, John Coltrane, Love, Public Enemy.

Unlike some of their contemporaries, they didn't come across as twats. They came across as fans, fans who'd made a gloriously, rickety, ambitious album that was reaching for sounds out the very top of the heavens, perched on nothing more than a few step-ladders teetering on crackly amplifiers and a pile of very well-thumbed records. But I loved that: trying to build symphonies out of spit and a fuzzbox. And, of course, scope and trumpets.

I saw them at Glastonbury in 1994 and I met Martin Carr for the first time. I bought him a Guinness and I interviewed him. He was lovely despite not getting me that Guinness back.

This pattern has repeated itself ever since.

I think Martin has some of the finest musical instincts of any human being I've ever met. Or heard.

The Boo Radleys made 3 Top 20 albums (including a number 1 album with 'Wake Up!') and 7 Top 40 singles. Wake Up Boo! broke the Top 10 in 1995 and has been comped onto as many 'Greatest Indie Hits EVER' albums as 'There She Goes'.

It was everywhere in the summer of '95: car stereos, caffs, hairdressers, supermarkets, indie discos, T.V. My bass player's best mate, Crag, thought "you can't blame me now for the death of summer" was the stupidest lyric he'd ever heard. My daughter Ava says it's her favourite of the multitude of songs I force her to listen to on long car journeys.

It divides opinion as surely as it imprints itself on your conscience after a single listen. It's melody rabies. Pop genius.

After The Boo Radleys faded out, Martin went hard left into electronic music (as bravecaptain) then, eventually, returned as a solo songwriter. His 2009 album 'Ye Gods & Little Fishes' is as beautiful as it was over-looked. His new (as I write this in September 2014) album, 'The Breaks', is a revelation.

Ladies and gentlemen, Martin Carr...

Was songwriting a calling for you? I grew up (musically-speaking) reading interviews with you and Sice where it was clear you were in love with pop music, the stories, the images and the songs themselves: was music 'just' a vehicle to be part of that story, initially at least?

When I finally got around to learning a few guitar chords (14/15) I immediately started to write songs. There were two reasons for this. The first was that I couldn't work out how to play other people's songs just by listening to them and, secondly, I instinctively knew that if you were going to be in a band and get famous then you did it with your own songs. It didn't occur to me that the people I saw on the telly and heard on the radio might have had their songs written by someone else.

I can still remember the first song I wrote, a rather downbeat waltz about me not staying with a lover and telling her to leave, very confusing. I had never had a girlfriend at that point so I was still unsure how it worked. All I knew was at one point, somebody would have to go and it was probably going to be me.

On Making Music

Me and Sice started writing songs at the same time. He would come round to mine and we would go to separate rooms and pretend to write songs that we had already written earlier in the day, then we would play them to one another. His songs always sounded like songs in that they had a verse and bridges and a strong chorus and sometimes a middle bit. They were good songs and I can still sing them now.

Mine were a bit weird and formless and I was really into Dylan so I was writing about Russians and paranoia and stuff I had no real insight into. This was the mid-eighties though, Reagan and Yeltsin and Two Tribes, so all that Cold War stuff was still valid but I remember my dad giving me one of the few bits of good advice he ever gave me upon hearing that song; he said "write about what you know, write about yourself". Unfortunately it would be another seven years before I did that and I wish I'd started then.

Songs are diaries, signposts and memories. They tell us about ourselves long after we've forgotten who we were when we wrote them.

We didn't form a band for a few years and our first gig was mainly Sice songs, I think. He was the main writer until around 1988 when we got into Dinosaur Jr and My Bloody Valentine's new direction and suddenly I found a sound to write songs around. I'm still not sure how that works exactly but I wrote everything after that. I had a clear direction. Before that we had no idea what kind of music we wanted to make, neither of us could play guitar that well, we liked such a diverse range of styles but despite this we knew something was going to happen.

I heard Jack Dee on the radio last week talking about this feeling of destiny he had even at his lowest points, well for us it was the same. We knew we were shit and that we had no direction and no plan but we were pretty cocky. There was no question of us doing anything else.

My songs were still about love problems but you would

never have guessed. The language was oblique and the worst kind of mid-60's Dylan doggerel that had none of his wit or scope.

The song that changed all that was 'Lazarus'. I didn't write that until 1992 but that was when I started writing with more, maybe too much, honesty and I was writing about my private life which unfortunately included other people's private lives and I took it too far the other way.

How much of your success as a songwriter was down to hard work, how much down to inspiration?

I think my successes were a combination of both but then I started to rely too much on inspiration. It had all seemed so easy that I forgot about the work we had put in the shitty jobs we had done in order to hire vans and buy gear, and the nights in writing songs while everyone else was out living it up. I stopped working hard in the late nineties I was drinking and drugging heavily and by 2005 I was finished.

I believe in the muse, I believe you have to protect and attend to it; the harder you work at it the better you are. Once you are out of the period – I would put it at your mid-twenties, when inspiration peaks – you have to put the hours in. You have to write ten bad songs to write a good one, a hundred to write a great one.

What, for you, makes a great song?

I can't define that, it can come from anywhere. It can be played on any instrument or no instrument, in any style. They just get you. The best ones take a few listens to unfold and reveal themselves to you, they speak to you, know you. Music and songs exist in another dimension.

Do you have a song that you're particularly proud of, where you nailed it? If you do, which one and why is it your favourite?

There aren't many of my songs that I'm happy with, two or three maybe and they're mostly ones that make me feel how I felt when I wrote them. It's usually the lyric that lets them down, I find it really hard work and sometimes I take the easy way out. You can't do that, you will always regret it.

'Wake Up Boo!' was a big success, a bona fide hit single – did you write it with that express intention? Was it clear from its inception that it would be popular? What, do you think, made it a hit?

We had done Giant Steps and we were a big, just-outside-the-top-40, indie band and that wasn't enough for me. I wanted to be on Top of the Pops and be on Radio 1 all day and do something that my aunts and uncles and people I went to school and people I had worked with, something that they would hear. I only wanted to do it once and then get back to doing what we were doing, but there is no going back from something like that. I didn't know that then.

I wrote the chorus first, in a small crappy flat in Preston, and once I had that I worked really hard at the arrangement, harder than I've ever worked on a song. Conversely I took no time at all on the lyrics. It beggars belief how useless they are. We did a version of it and decided between us and with Creation that it wasn't right, which shows how seriously we were taking it. So we did it again and we did it properly.

I wish I had written brass parts down, I sent the players the track and vague instructions and was horrified when they turned up and played what to me sounded like the Jimmy Young theme tune. It was cheerful which was not what I wanted at all, so I flattened as many of the notes as I could but it was too late, we had run out of time.

I remember the week before it came out, someone at the top of Creation saying that they couldn't sleep, that if that wasn't going to be a hit then they didn't know what would be. Even so, I don't think any of us could have foretold its longevity.

In your experience, do the best songs come quickly, or do you whittle them out over weeks? Or - as I suspect - is it a combination of the two and difficult to generalise?

I tend to write in bits, I've always got four or five on the go. Sometimes they appear fully-formed and then it takes weeks for you to believe that its come from you. Eight out of ten times it's 'Abracadabra' by The Steve Miller Band. Sometimes they come while you're out walking, or listening to something, or when you can hear snatches of music from a distant building. I have to have a notebook and recording device on me at all times, these inspirations are fleeting.

Are you a disciplined writer? Will you set aside certain hours in the day for writing? Or is it more random than that?

I have to be doing something. It's not even second nature, it's far more innate. Whatever I'm doing, I'm doing that. People laugh when you tell them that but, somewhere in my head, I'm working and sometimes it can be very frustrating if I can't get away and think clearly.

Is 'randomness', a certain amount of anarchy, key to the spirit of rock 'n' roll, do you think?

Randomness comes with performance when writing, rehearsing or recording. You play a wrong chord or sing the wrong thing in the wrong place, whatever, and it might change everything so you give thanks and move on, but it's just an accident. You can't force it.

"There are no morals in songwriting. It's mostly about theft with a bit of 'you' sprinkled over the top." Discuss.

Only a person who has never heard any music can write music that isn't influenced by any other and it would be interesting to hear what that would be like. Sometimes you take a mood or a chord progression, a harmony, a beat... but it's unforgivable to leave a trace and there is no excuse for writing something that sounds like its been copied directly from something else.

What fires your muse? Has it changed over the centuries?

Money and revenge.

How important is the music you hear in catalysing the music you make?

I go through periods of not listening to music at all, but I can't really tally that with any phase in my writing cycles. As I said earlier, anything can influence a song you're writing or kickstart an idea. Sometimes, if you're stuck it's good to stick the radio on and listen to a random selection of music that might give you the idea that will get you out of the hole you're in.

You've gone through fallow periods where you've changed tack completely, switching from electric guitar to a completely electronic approach, then to acoustic guitar…

were those seismic shifts about boredom / changing the landscape completely to find inspiration -- and did that approach work?

Around 1994/5 I stopped liking most of the music that I heard on the radio and I started buying old dub records and new electronic records like Squarepusher and Aphex Twin as well really digging the Wu Tang stuff, in particular the Genius / GZA record 'Liquid Swords'. I had no interest in Britpop but I didn't consider reinventing the band as I should have done. The other members were happy doing what they were doing and we'd stopped hanging out and listening to music together.

I was drinking and hanging out on the scene instead of taking what I did seriously and meditating on new directions. We did C'mon Kids and I thought it was something different, but it was only if you compared it to other indie rock bands. My music bored me and by the time we came to record Kingsize the songs had no direction and there was no enthusiasm from the band or the label or the audience. I blew it. I blew it big time.

And even after that, when I couldn't switch the radio on in case I heard Travis or the Stereophonics or Jet, I didn't pursue the sound that was in my head, a kind of Kid 606 / Beach Boys thing. Most people didn't know what you were talking about if you mentioned Kid606 or Doseone in 1999/2000 and I went back to writing songs that were getting more boring and nobody was interested in them because I wasn't interested in them. A song displays the love and care that has gone into writing it, you can always tell when something is half-arsed.

I then made three albums where I tried to marry electronica and songwriting, not putting wussy little beats behind a tune but trying to integrate the two into something exciting but the budgets had gone and I was doing it at home on computer speakers and sonically the records were poor. I was still writing songs but eventually they dried up in 2006. I had started going to the computer first instead of the guitar or the piano and I forgot how to do it. The label dropped me and I was left with no management or band or anything for the first time since I started and I was depressed. I tried to write songs every day for months but nothing came, not one song and I just quit.

I suffered from a bad back in 2001/02, very painful and I remember going to the chiropractor who had to do that thing where they crack your neck at the base of your skull - it's hard to relax when you know that's going to happen, so she would say 'wiggle your toes' and I would wiggle them and she would crack my neck. because I was focusing on my toes my neck relaxed and that's what happened with my songwriting.

For two years I did something else, I bought a camera, learned how to use Photoshop and ended up doing illustration work for The Times but I still played my guitar every day and taught myself a finger picking pattern which, as I should have known, started me writing songs again. If you're stuck do something new, put a capo on, learn a new chord, play the piano – it makes a difference.

I managed to write enough songs for an album which came out in 2009 and since then I've worked myself back up to a level of writing that I'm almost happy with but it's taken nearly ten years to get to this point. The muse needs tending or it will go elsewhere and it may never come back. I'm pathetically grateful that it did because the songs I write now might not sell thousands but they feed my need to write them. I need to write as much as I need food and water and the output, which to the audience is the whole point, is secondary to the creative process. I love writing melodies, I love hearing the structure work itself out through me.

Are you consciously aware of songwriting conventions /

structures, or does each song feel out its own shape as you develop it?

Not really. I know what a bridge and a verse and a chorus is but I don't feel obliged to use them for the sake of it. I've just recorded an album that has very traditional song structures because that was what I had decided to do and I paid a lot of attention to it, but I have songs that are quite formless and the work there is keeping them interesting to myself and to the listener. The songs write themselves. I know that sounds corny but it's like when a writer says that their characters start talking to each other, the song is there, you just keep playing until it takes its intended shape, like a sculptor chipping away at a lump of stone.

Can an idea you initially feel a little ambivalent about still flower into a great song? Is it important to keep your most withering critical faculties on a back shelf, early in the songwriting process?

Sometimes you can record a song that you're not sure about and the recording, the musicians, elevate the song into its true self but this won't happen with a bad song. Sometimes the recording reveals that the song wasn't much in the first place and you should ditch it despite it being something that you thought was great. Both happened to me during the recording of my current album.

Writers, of all different disciplines, hate the question: "where do your ideas come from?" Is that because you'd rather not risk over analysing what comes instinctively? I precipitated a very long bout of insomnia when I was in my early 20's wondering about how, exactly, I fell asleep.

I don't know where they come from. It is a gift, if you want to talk in those terms, but you have to be open and receptive to them, you have to recognise them when they appear and that means working. But working can mean daydreaming, laying on your back on the floor of a quiet sunlit room, walking, sitting in the park, sleeping, all of these are an important part of creating and are what I miss most about my pre- fatherhood days. It is work, it's the most enjoyable, satisfying work but it is work and it's hard. Of course people think it's a doss but when you have this kind of magic under control, who cares what people think?

You said you weren't sure that a book like this would help an artist, certainly with regards something as esoteric as songwriting. What did you mean?

An artist has all the tools inside them. There are no manuals. Some people must go through life not even realising that they can do this but if you're lucky enough to find it, you don't have to look any further.

Hear Martin's new music at:

http://sonnyboy.bandcamp.com

The Boo Radleys' albums are available via iTunes and Amazon. Giant Steps is a flawed masterpiece. The flaws are one of the many things that make it great. Martin is good for a round of drinks, too – my claim otherwise was a little poetic license. Or 'a lie' as they call 'em in court.

"Barney and me…"

PLAYLIST:
The Boo Radleys - The Finest Kiss
The Boo Radleys - Wake Up Boo!
The Boo Radleys - Lazarus
Martin Carr - The Santa Fe Skyway
Python Lee Jackson - In A Broken Dream
Fleetwood Mac - Man Of The World
Argent - Hold Your Head Up
The Creatures - Right Now

Ride - Seagull
Love - Maybe The People Would Be The Times Or Between Clark And Hilldale
John Coltrane - Spiral
The Turtles - Happy Together
King Tubby - King Tubby Meets The Rockers Uptown
My Bloody Valentine - You Made Me Realise
Dinosaur Jr - Freak Scene
Swervedriver - Duel
The Real People - I Can't Wait
Squarepusher - Tommib
Aphex Twin - 54 Cymru Beats
GZA - Liquid Swords
Kid606 - Dodgy
The Boo Radleys - Barney And Me...
Martin Carr - Santa Fe Skyway

16: <u>Lyrics</u>

A great piece of music with a honking bad lyric may as well have a tone deaf parrot with laryngitis squawking 'this song is shit, this song is shit' over the top of it. A bad lyric is like a pubic hair floating on the top of an otherwise delicious consommé: it can ruin everything. The only way to fix it is to remove it completely, preferably out of sight and before you serve up…

At least, that's what I'd like to preach here. I'm not sure how I can vouch for the truthfulness of that first paragraph when one of my favourite recordings of all time is The Kingsmen's 'Louie Louie', a recording with lyrics so unintelligible, the F.B.I. spent thousands of dollars trying to fathom its meaning, lest it was leading America's youth into a heaving cesspit of hedonism and debauchery.

A song, then, doesn't need a great lyric for it to be a hit, at least not in the poetic sense. A great lyric can be something that's as dumb as monkeys on tricycles. Something simple, but memorable, is more likely to capture the general public's attention, but if you have artistic pretensions that extend beyond popularity, your lyrics are as precious a part of your self expression as the music itself.

It's worth tempering such a lofty notion with the realisation that, for many people, a lyric is but one ingredient in the main dish, and not the one that has most baring on whether they fall for a song, or not. Again, it's about context. A dumb pop song sparkles all the more gaudily with a dumb lyric, but stick a dumb lyric over the top of a magnum opus of pretentiousness and it'll sit wrong and be unconvincing.

Incidentally, I love dumb pop. It takes a very sharp

lyrical mind to write a great, dumb pop song. Dumb is by no means a criticism.

Bad lyrics tend to be unmemorable and bland, inconsequential verbals that carry the melody with all the imagination and enthusiasm of a dog walker ferrying turds in a plastic bag.

A great piece of music with a great lyric is The Holy Grail. "I may not always love you..." think about the boundless wonders that follow that opening line, the utterly perfect synthesis of music from the innermost vaults of the heart married to a lyric so yearning, ardent and truthful that its sentiments attain universality. That song is one of the wonders of human achievement, to my mind. Up there with the nylon string guitar, Julianne Moore, Shakespeare, the Apollo Moon Landings and chocolate fudge cake.

This is what you're aiming for: as perfect and chiming a synergy between your lyric and your music as is possible.

Fortunately that synergy is there innate within you. Speak the truth in your heart, that comes from your own eyes, through your songs and you will be a good lyricist, simple as that.

Don't try to wear someone else's idioms or lyrical style, they won't fit and your lyrics will be unconvincing as a result.

A lot of the songwriting greats refuse to discuss their lyrics with any degree of specificity – it destroys the magic, don't you know? This shouldn't stop you from listening to their work and trying to fathom what it is about their lyrics that is fascinating, or moving, or worthy of acclaim.

As with everything that we have discussed so far, there are no rules. School's out. You can do whatever you please.

This chapter is hamstrung by the popularity of great lyrics. Music publishers know just how valuable an iconic lyrical phrase can be. If I were to quote Dylan, Reed, Smith, Morrissey, Ryder, Mitchell et al to support any of the advice shared below, it would cost me thousands of pounds for permission to do so. So, I'll refer you to songs as examples but I'm afraid that you'll have to absorb the specifics yourself – which is no bad thing, as the relationship between the lyric and the music – the way that they intertwine, compliment and highlight each other – is absolutely fundamental to a successful song.

When you're analysing lyrics, try to do it within the context of the whole song. Those great lyrics by the likes of Bob Marley, John Lennon, Patti Smith or The Smiths, that get quoted frequently and lionised on posters and t-shirts and the like would never have been heard if they'd been dropped into a slurry pit of a piece of music.

A great lyric on top of a moribund piece of music still makes for a moribund song.

The reverse isn't necessarily true (this isn't algebra!): a moribund lyric doesn't always ruin a great piece of music... it just seems like a wasted opportunity.

One of my favourite lyricists is Nigel Blackwell from Half Man Half Biscuit[1]. He's T.S. Eliot, if T.S. Eliot had gone to the University of Saturday Afternoon Footie and Weekday Evening Soap Operas, instead of Harvard, Oxbridge and the Sorbonne (as Eliot did). Blackwell's lyrics are rich with wit, pathos, vitriol and an unshowy, everyman intellect, somewhere betwixt and between Viz and The Wasteland.

And Half Man Half Biscuit have much better tunes than T.S. Eliot.

This is the first verse from the song 'Depressed Beyond Tablets', from their excellent 2005 album Achtung Bono:

156

Lyrics

I walk caverns and abysmals

That I hope you never dream of.

I search around for exits,

But I'm doubting if there ever was an entrance,

In the first place.

©Half Man Half Biscuit / Nigel Blackwell

I can't think of another song that evokes depression so acutely, and without a whiff of self pity or melodrama. A line from later in the song, *"Your optimism strikes me like junk mail addressed to the dead"* is as hilarious as it is profound and sad.

Half Man Half Biscuit's catalogue is a trove of fine songs. What elevates those songs to greatness is Blackwell's polymathic and spongelike brain, his wit and his courage. I do think it takes a certain type of courage to sing about a subject like depression, especially when so many other lyricists are happy to dole out nice rhymes and platitudes. It's not battlefield courage, but I wouldn't fancy being the one towing the caravan if Nigel *was* stuck in a Bottleneck At Capel Curig. He cycles a lot. That'd hone anyone's potential for psychopathy.

One of Nigel's great qualities as a lyricist is the free-ranging intelligence of his words. It's clear he's well-read, but he's not bookish about it. He can include literary allusions and historical allegories in the same breath as observations about sports presenters, people working in 24hr garages or actresses in long-cancelled soap operas.

And his words could be looked back on in centuries to come as chronicles of our times. Future historians or folk singers (because Half Man Half Biscuit's songs are folk songs) would get a better sense of 21st century, British life from '90 Bisodol (Crimond)' (their most recent album as I write this) than they would from Muse or Bastille, say.

That's not a fair comparison.

I will sleep better, though, knowing that somewhere in this book I have highlighted Half Man Half Biscuit's lyrical genius in contrast to those bands' bombastic, yawing, meaninglessness.

You do not have to be literary, in an academic sense, to write great lyrics, not by any means. Here's a quick, rather random, list of renowned songwriters who did or didn't study literature at degree level:

Studied Literature: Lou Reed, Leonard Cohen, Thom Yorke, Paul Simon, James Murphy, Nick Drake, Georgia Ruth, Ritzy Bryan.

Didn't Study Literature: Bob Dylan, Patti Smith, Marvin Gaye, Shaun Ryder, Bruce Springsteen, Joni Mitchell, Carole King, Morrissey, Chuck D, Nick Cave, PJ Harvey, Elliott Smith, Amy Winehouse, Laura Marling, Smokey Robinson, Black Francis, Rakim, Lennon / McCartney, Alex Turner (although he intended to study English), Gruff Rhys, Andrew Falkous, Jarvis Cocker, Joe Strummer, Brian Wilson.

There are notable, eloquent and poetic writers in both (somewhat arbitrary) camps. Don't feel as though language, and particularly poetic language, is the domain of an academic elite. Language is there to have fun with, to express yourself with, it is your tool. However do not treat language with too much respect: treat it reverently and it is less likely to ring with you-ness. You need that you-ness to stand out and make your songs fascinating enough to revisit.

If at any point you constrain yourself to fit in – whether lyrically or musically – you'll be missing the point; or at least you will be if you have pretensions to make your own mark in music.

Do have the confidence to write originally. Writing original lyrics – doing your utmost to bring new poetry to timeless emotions – is essential if you want your work to have currency. Anything else is just filling in blanks and hoping that an audience won't be discerning enough to notice.

The Beatles deliberately kept the words to their early songs simple and universal. It's a matter of fact that many kids, throughout the world, learnt their first English words from Beatles records. Read Ernest Hemingway, John Steinbeck or George Orwell to learn how the simplest, most un-flowery language can be used to express the complexities of the human condition most vividly.

Then think on the simple genius of the phrase 'Hard Day's Night' and how combining simple language and idiom can create a phrase that is both simple to understand and original and arresting.

Ian Brown also recognised the universality of a simple lyric:

I was deliberately brief with my lyrics on the album, there's certain phrases that get repeated and I deliberately did that for the people who buy my records that don't speak English. I get a lot of letters from people who say they've learnt English from a Stone Roses LP, or they've tried to.

My girl's Mexican and I've been to Mexico about ten times with people who don't speak English, or only speak a little English, so I've consciously tried to make my lyrics brief so that non-English speaking people can understand them.

Ian Brown, The Stone Roses

Some of the truths you want to fill your songs with, or the language you want to use, will be unpalatable to others. I don't think you should compromise your lyrics for the sake of radio play, for example. Having said that, in the very conservative times that we're living through as I write this, it would be wise to understand that BBC Introducing and other OFCOM-regulated radio stations will not play anything with swearing or questionable content in it. Radio stations have different standards and watersheds than TV stations. Hearing 'fuck' at 9pm on BBC 2 doesn't mean you'll hear 'fuck' at 9pm on BBC Radio 2.

Go to the OFCOM website, or make a direct enquiry to the station you're targeting, if you need clarification.

An unnecessary restriction? I think so, but as a radio presenter I have to adhere to the broadcasting standards set for me. I like having a house and food to eat. No one who isn't directly involved with your music will risk their livelihood for your art.

If you have what you regard as a 'killer radio song' but it has swearing in it, produce a radio edit. Don't bleep the offending word(s) – that sounds too intrusive. The best strategies are to either change the offending word(s) to something less offensive (as Radiohead did with Creep... "so fucking special" to "so very special"), to edit the word(s) out or to reverse them, making them unintelligible.

Weigh up which is the best strategy for you and your song.

Finding something to write about is the hardest aspect of songwriting, for me. I don't want to write just for the sake of it. I definitely need some kind of a muse to write a song. Whether it's a concept, like the album that I wrote about a troubled school... once I had the fairly simple idea of a school and its orchestra, the whole album followed pretty easy and quickly. There was suddenly a load of teachers and different pupils and their experiences to write about.

Jim Bob, Carter The Unstoppable Sex Machine

So, where can you find inspiration for your lyrics? Jim Bob, above, found a concept inspirational. If you engage with life, keeps your eyes and ears open, read, absorb whatever it is that is going on around you, you will find inspiration. This doesn't mean you need to go inter-railing or self consciously thrust yourself into new 'inspirational' environments, for the sake of it.

Be sensitive to your emotions. Remember the things that are provocative to you. Find interesting ways, whether through imagery or direct language, to share those things. Songwriting is all about sharing your point of view in as compelling a way as possible.

You may feel particularly strongly about someone or something. Whatever it is you feel strongly about, write about those things: whether it's sex, love, cake, trains, politics, hedgehogs…

For other sources of inspiration, read what you can. After seeing an early version of this chapter where it was somewhat glossed over, Andrew Falkous stressed to me how important he thought reading should be to an aspiring writer. And guess what… if you're a lyricist, you're a writer. Get the absinthe out, the crumpled jacket and suck the end of that pencil. Or laptop. You're probably better off sucking a pencil.

Stephen King makes the same point in his book On Writing. It's difficult to imagine that anyone would consider writing words, without reading being the tinder.

If your life is too busy for reading, do what Falkous and King do and immerse yourself in audiobooks. That way, you can 'read' when you're washing up, or driving, going for a run.

And listen to the lyrics in the songs around you, have an ear open – at all times – to the rhythm of language. Because much as you may think – as some writers do – that this is an exercise in vocabulary, successful lyric writing Is more to do with the rhythm of language than how impressive, or big, or self consciously poetic those lyrics may be.

Listen to Springsteen, Dylan or Costello. They're the masters of understanding the rhythm of language and how complex, arresting, poetic lyrical phrases can flow with beauty and conviction throughout their songs.

I'm particularly in awe of the lyrics to Bob Dylan's Tangled Up In Blue: an astonishing chronicle of ill-fated love, life and peregrination. Nothing is stated explicitly. Dylan's love is subjugated by life's trials. The romance that drives the song is neither romantic nor idealistic: two people kept apart by the rigours of life, painted in striking images. It's a riddle with a thousand truths in it that we can all relate to, regardless of whether we've been to Delacroix or out West.

There's a great, jousting pathos and resignedness to the lyric that's reflected in the rolling chords and peripatetic rhythm. It's a remarkable feat of songwriting: a song to live with that will reveal new truths as your own emotional landscape rolls by and changes.

Lyric writing is fundamentally different to writing music. Your musical palette is somewhat restricted to the range of the instruments you use. A guitar in standard tuning spans 3 and a 1/2 octaves, or thereabouts. The English language, as one example, contains approximately a quarter of a *million* words. You have such bewildering scope to say interesting, original things in your lyrics. In 2014, indulging in 'fire', 'higher', 'desire' cliches is plain lazy.

This doesn't mean that you can't write about love, for example. Don't feel as though certain subject matters are off limits because other songwriters have harvested the same fields. Your challenge is to do it with freshness, from a new perspective. This is easier than it sounds, if you're honest and reflect the world around you.

Your life and your outlook are unique. The stew of experiences that has been bubbling away in your life so far is utterly original to you: the places you've visited, the people you've known, the things they've said, the passions you've developed.

The most interesting lyricists are the ones that walk to their own beat along a path they've chosen for themselves. Copying Lou Reed, Prince, Kate Bush, or Alex Turner will not imbue you with their innate coolness. Each of those artists... every artist that has any enduring music legacy whatsoever, had the courage to *be themselves*.

If I had to give a piece of advice to aspiring songwriters I'd say experience life and write about that. I'm not suggesting walking the streets alone in the dark, waving £10 notes, until your muse quite literally strikes you, but write about something different. Write about something that no one else is writing about.

Jim Bob, Carter The Unstoppable Sex Machine

You may have had a fascination with fossils when you were growing up. I did. OK, so palaeontology isn't a renowned wellspring of rock 'n' roll inspiration. My point is that any subject that hasn't already been subsumed into rock's lexicon provides new opportunities for your lyrics. Say you wrote a song comparing your love for someone to the eternity of an ammonite preserved in limestone for hundreds of millions of years, that would bring a freshness to the hoary old "I'll love you forever"-lines that pepper other people's songs.

If you work in a warehouse and you've fallen for a forklift driver, write about that! Love doesn't just strike when someone walks in a room, or past you on a street, or when you see them dancing in a red dress (as a large number of popular songs would have us believe). Reflect that in your songs.

I think it stems back to the fact that I had a lot of free time when I was living in Sheffield.

For instance, it could apply to this room at the moment. I'm in this room in London, talking to you down the wire, it's a very blank room and within a few minutes I will have left it, but say somebody made a mistake and I was stuck in here for 5 years – or something – I would probably have to construct some kind of mini universe of my own in here and I'd probably find out some interesting things... like count how many screws there were in the equipment.

I try to put lots of details into our songs because I think the little, small details which sometimes might seem insignificant at the time are always the things that bring a memory alive, that trigger it off. They're the things that you can't imagine, you had to have been there and seen those things. That gives it a certain authenticity.

Jarvis Cocker, Pulp

Be true to yourself and the details of your life. The truer you are about your experiences, the more real your songs will be. If people can relate to the truth in your songs it will embed them in their hearts.

Equally people who aren't familiar with the environment you're singing about – whether it's a council estate in Sheffield or a beautiful hilltop in North Wales – will revel in the newness of the scenarios you describe, as if you're a magical travel agent; that is if you imbue your lyrics with truth and detail.

Great songs are, frequently, a sonic reflection of the writer's surroundings or memories. Think of the London Carnaby St. / Mod bands of the 60's - The Small Faces, The Who, The Kinks; the slew of raw garage bands who came out of Detroit in the early years of the new millennium; Sheffield's experimental synth bands of the late 70's who came to define a whole new genre; East and West coast gangsta rap. All of those different sounds were echoes, sonically and lyrically, of the environments they were created in.

Try to do this. A sense of place gives songs gravity and truth.

Escapism is one of the great qualities of rock 'n' roll. But if you're going to live out a fantasy in your lyrics make it convincing.

Don't write anything by half measures. Have the courage to challenge lyrical conventions. Don't be constrained by what you think fits in. Lyrical phrases that may sound silly, initially, because they're rhymes or images that no one else has used, about subjects that haven't been sung about before, can give your songs an originality and freshness that will set them apart.

Julian Cope, Half Man Half Biscuit, Joni Mitchell, Kate Bush, Kelis, Lady Gaga, Pavement, The Kinks, Pixies are some of the artists who wrote lyrics inspired by subjects that had never, hitherto, been part of the rock 'n' roll curriculum: ecology, restless legs, coyotes, gender roles, milkshake, the paparazzi, not getting your haircut, Waterloo Bridge, environmentalism via Hebrew numerology.

The possibilities are as limitless as your imaginative horizons. Exciting, no?

It may also help to imagine who you're addressing your song to. Sometimes it'll be obvious: whoever is the object of your affection, or who has broken your heart. Other times it may be less clear.

In general, as a songwriter, my only advice to anybody who's writing something for someone else to listen to, is some advice I was given by a TV producer when I was presenting The Booktower – a children's TV programme about books: "when you read the story, don't think of millions of kids out there watching the television, just picture a child you know and read the story to that child."

And I thought, "that's a fantastic piece of advice" and it crosses over into songwriting. Imagine someone you know and you're singing that song to that one person. And if it means something to that one person it's going to mean something to lots of people, but only one at a time.

Neil Innes, Bonzo Dog Doo Dah Band / The Rutles

One final thing to pay attention to: your song title is the shop front for your song. If you have a boring title, the likelihood is that the song will be mundane as well.

Give a song an arresting or original title and people are more likely to check it out… especially as a lot of music discovery in the digital age is done by scrolling through song titles. It doesn't have to be Don't Eat The Yellow Snow-daft (Frank Zappa – there are a whole host of oddly-titled songs in his back catalogue.) Try and make it m e m o r a b l e o r n o t i c e a b l e .
Yet another song called 'Fire' is unlikely to set the world ablaze.

However, call the song 'Yet Another Song Called Fire' or 'I Set The World Ablaze' or any of a multitude of other derivatives, and your effort to makes the title interesting is

Lyrics

more likely to reap dividends.

These chapters on songwriting are probably the most important, but nebulous, in this book. It's difficult to write about something with authority that I have no recognised ability to do myself. However I do have an absolute love for brilliant songs. Millions upon millions of people do. Those of you who are artists get to soundtrack our lives, if you write well. What an immeasurable honour that is.

A simple distillation of these chapters is: *have the courage to be yourself.* Don't forget it. The truer you are to your self, the easier it will be to deal with, or entirely ignore, other people's reactions to your music.

[1]**One of my favourite lyricists is Nigel Blackwell from Half Man Half Biscuit** - *Andrew Falkous, Ray Davies, Ritzy Bryan, Smokey Robinson, Black Francis, Gruff Rhys, Elliott Smith, Georgia Ruth are most of the others. It isn't a competition, is it?*

PLAYLIST:
The Kingsmen - Louie Louie
The Beach Boys - God Only Knows
Lou Reed - Last Great American Whale
Patti Smith - Land
Morrissey - Everyday Is Like Sunday
Joni Mitchell - Edith and the Kingpin
Half Man Half Biscuit - Depressed Beyond Tablets
Radiohead - Creep
Bruce Springsteen - Badlands
Elvis Costello - Tokyo Storm Warning
Bob Dylan - Tangled Up In Blue
Kate Bush - The Man With The Child In His Eyes
The Who - The Kids Are Alright
The White Stripes - Hello Operator
The Gories - Nitroglycerine
Cabaret Voltaire - Nag Nag Nag
Human League - Being Boiled
NWA - Fuck Tha Police
Tupac Shakur - Keep Ya Head Up
Dr Dre - Nuthin But A G Thang

Grandmaster Flash - The Message
Nas - N.Y. State of Mind
Wu-Tang Clan - Method Man
Julian Cope - Safesurfer
Joni Mitchell - Coyote
Half Man Half Biscuit - Restless Legs
Kelis - Milkshake
Lady Gaga - Paparazzi
Pavement - Cut Your Hair
Pixies - Monkey Gone To Heaven
Frank Zappa - Don't Eat The Yellow Snow

17: <u>Georgia Ruth On Lyric Writing</u>

It had been a soul-sapping, damp, grey flannel of a Saturday at the fade out of 2007. My football team had been beaten. I think I'd missed yet another family day out, chained to my computer, hunting far and wide for music to fill the yawing, three hour gulf of airtime that loomed the following night.

Clearly my martyr complex was having a right rumtime with me. I remember how sorry I was feeling for myself with a rare clarity (and a not-so-rare feeling of embarrassment) because of what happened next.

My laptop dinged, which was unusual post-midnight at the weekend. After all, other people were out having bright-eyed fun, not in with their arm around a bloody MacBook.

"Who's e-mailing me at this time? Oh brilliant, another demo… probably someone doing a crap Bon Iver impersonation. Or a Jay Z wannabe from Tredegar, replete with de rigeur, unconvincing 'hood accent. Hmm, it's someone called Georgia Ruth Williams… is she the one who does the unaccompanied Celine Dion covers?"

My expectations couldn't have been much lower as I downloaded the .mp3 and waited for it to play…

When you're tasked with finding new music, a good proportion of the time you're filling in blanks, smoothing out rough edges, listening in hope but with cynically low expectations.

Mostly you're wasting your time. The majority of music you hear is drivel and you feel guilty for thinking that.

170

These are other people's dreams, after all, even if they are out of tune dreams, or dreams that so want to sound like Funeral For A Friend (this was 2007, remember) you can hear the music makers' own personalities evaporating in the background, sacrificed to the clicky, double kick drum and screamo-to-sugar-sweet vocal paradigm.

The moments when you hear something – someone – truly remarkable are few and very far between. So rare, in fact, that you end up doing a double-take, assume that someone's winding you up and has just mailed you something off an obscure, classic album to test you, to try and trip you up.

But Georgia Ruth Williams sounded like no one I'd heard before. Even now, 7 years on, with that very recording looping in my headphones, bringing a moistening of joy to my eyeballs, I can't tell you exactly how or why it filled my head and my heart with wonder, like no other demo had before or has since.

Perhaps it was the simple, economic beauty of the song and the performance. The arpeggios on the harp are hypnotic and irresistible, like the intro to ABBA's 'S.O.S' (see the forthcoming chapter on 'Arrangement'). Georgia's voice sounded as lovelorn and plaintive as I felt. The lyrics resonated so perfectly with the notes and the tone of the piece, I didn't have to be distracted by them…

Islands, castles, pebbles, puddles, lakes, ripples, fish, fins, currents, tides…

I've listened to 'Ocean' hundreds of times in the subsequent years. I still couldn't sing the song back to you. The lyrics are the heart of the song, but we don't need to bare a heart or know its architecture to be moved by it.

In that three minutes, 'Ocean' became my Teenage Kicks… not that I'm trying to elevate myself to John Peel status, or – indeed – have Georgia's music compared to The Undertones. What I mean is this: if someone asked me to play one piece of music to sum up what I've spent the last 20 years doing, it would be 'Ocean'.

So in that respect, it *is* my Teenage Kicks.

If you punk rock kids, having listened to it, are tittering at the back… munch on this: it's as punk a recording as any I've ever played on my show[1]. Fact squared.

'Ocean' didn't feature on her debut album. I suspect that Georgia feels she has written better songs and I'd agree with her if it hadn't been for how and when that song arrived in my life.

I learnt a lot from 'Ocean'. It renewed my flagging belief in the potential of an unsolicited demo… and I remind myself of the experience recounted above whenever I feel my expectations diminishing and cynicism comes calling.

Subsequent to (but not as a result of) that play on my show, Georgia played many of the UK's foremost festivals (Glastonbury, Green Man) recorded a unique, beautiful and atmospheric debut album ('Week of Pines' - Welsh Music Prize winner 2013); collaborated with Manic Street Preachers; has been lauded by some of the UK's most influential writers and broadcasters, and has become, I think – and I'm not alone – a lyricist of great skill, originality and, on occasion, humour. I mention 'humour' because the way I've described her music, revered it with my huff and hyperbole, might give you the impression that it's dour or worthy. It is neither of those things, in excelsis.

Georgia's lyrical sensibility formed in a camper van-shaped crucible that rolled along the B-roads around Aberystwyth ringing with her parents' tapes: Bob Dylan, Joan Baez, Paul Simon, Joni Mitchell et al. She heard and sang traditional Welsh folk songs in school. Her contemporary listening includes Bill Callahan, Rufus and Martha Wainwright, A.A. Bondy… and whatever's on the radio or the jukebox in the pub in Caernarfon. It's a fascinating and uncontrived mixture of the traditional, the poetic, the pretentious and the pop.

All of these things, and her own great songs, make Georgia an excellent person to talk to about lyric writing.

I'd like to start off talking a little bit about language itself... because one of the things I take from your songs is very much a love for, and an understanding of, language. Where does that come from?

I guess the obvious answer is that I studied English Literature for 3 years as part of my degree. Over that time I went through something of a warping process. I began with a feeling that the English language was something that I was very fond of and loved... I'd read a lot at home and written the odd thing. And after going to Cambridge and 3 years of intense analysis and digging and ponderous, lengthy examinations of literature, I got to a point where language felt weird and I didn't enjoy it. I felt that I'd been interrogating and excavating language for years and it really took writing my own stuff, then, to combat that and to realise that language is something very precious and personal.

Did you start to apply the critical tools you picked up in university to your favourite lyricists or were they somehow immune, or protected, from how mundane language had otherwise become to you?

They were, they transcended it. I'd listen to music when I was studying and it would still be in its own sphere. The words in those songs remained uncontaminated by all this over-thinking. That must have been quite important to me, looking back. Novels I had to read – I say "had to" as if it was terrible thing I had to do – but I'd read through these books and they were so heavily-annotated that I couldn't move for notes and references. Thankfully that approach didn't make me think like that about the records I love.

Obviously I have opinions on people's lyrics, one way or the other, but I think there's a safety in music. You're more able to say things. It's almost like the music around you is cushioning any potential criticism. I've always felt that, that there's a freedom that comes with writing music lyrics that you don't get when you're writing poetry or prose. The very essence of poetry and prose is that the words are what you're claiming to be best at. Whereas with music, there's a forgivingness there, maybe. You can be forgiven for getting it wrong and have more freedom to do what you want. That freedom's enabled by the music being there, so the focus isn't all on the words, and I don't think it should all be on the words.

Was that something that's borne out by your own personal experience? The songs that you love... that you you heard when you were a child and grew to love, did your appreciation of the words come later after you'd been attracted by the melodies and arrangements?

I think so. I remember having this conversation with my mum. I must have still been at school and I was listening to something – I really can't remember what it was – and I was saying "I love the words to this" and my mum said, "that's weird, because I never listen to lyrics!" I couldn't believe it! How can you not listen to the lyrics of a song?

She still maintains to this day that she can't hear lyrics in a song. I ask her how she gets the pathos, or the anger, or any of the energy of the song. And she conceded that she must take the lyrics in, subconsciously, but because they're carried along by the music, not the other way round. Or they're so innate to the music that she doesn't need to isolate the words.

I like that, but I'm not sure that I listen to music in that way.

My experience, as a Welsh learner with rudimentary understanding of Welsh, is that I can – generally – interpret a song's lyrical and emotional content just from listening to the song. When I hear a translation of the lyrics, it's quite accurate. Is that the mark of a great lyric? A symbiosis between the music and the lyric?

A lot of the time, but part of me loves songs that don't sound like the words, so there's that gulf between what's being said and the music. I think the Velvets used to do that really well, you'd have what sounded almost sweet and then these shocking, sadomasochistic words and you'd have to go back and listen again to double check you hadn't misheard them.

I like that technique. It's not something that I'd necessarily use myself because I'm more about matching what I write about with the general tone of the music.

Because you have something of an analytical, studied approach to language, do you have to make an effort to be more instinctive with your lyrics, to let the emotions out?

I tend to approach the lyrics in two ways. Usually I'm very conscious and considered in what I'm writing. The obvious exception to that rule was 'Dovecote' from 'Week of Pines'. With that song, I just sang over some chords and whatever came out, I kept. It was really liberating and part of me wondered why I hadn't done it before.

I'd be lying if I said I didn't then adjust some of this stream of consciousness to be a bit more cohesive, but largely what came out in that song was all unfiltered.

I have a voice recorder on my phone and I just sang. I was left with these quite troubling words and I thought, "Hmm, OK! So that's what my subconscious has decided to vomit, today."

Usually I would try and revise that, or hone and arrange it, but at that point in time it felt like the right thing to do was to leave it as it was. Funnily enough, when I listen back to the album now, from the point of view of having played those songs an awful lot over the last 12 months since the album came out and being a little bit exhausted by them, and having reached the state where I don't really want to listen to my own words anymore, the one track that I can still listen to and be vaguely perplexed and intrigued by is Dovecote. I don't know what the process was. I still don't know what the process was. There's still quite a lot of mystery there for me, in the sense that I didn't consciously write it.

I've never tried that since. I'm scared by what might come out.

I know that you grew up hearing Bob Dylan, Joan Baez and Paul Simon, they are regarded – and quite rightly – as remarkable lyricists, was is inevitable, then, that lyrics would be important to you and to your songs?

I guess. I felt like there might be an expectation for the lyrics to be at least OK because of that history and the fact that some people knew that I'd studied literature. If I didn't put time and thought into the lyrics it might look a bit odd. But the fact that I'd studied literature doesn't mean that my lyrics would be any better.

I studied literature, too. I know a lot of people who come out of the process with a real pseud-ishness to what they write. I don't think your lyrics have suffered from that. You'll use words and turns of phrase, unashamedly, that other people don't, I've always loved that – but I've never got the sense that there was anything pseudo-intellectual

about your lyrics.

I'd hope not! It's something that I hate in writing, too. Don't get me wrong, I do quite like pretentiousness. I think pretentiousness is actually quite important. Richard James (founder member of Gorky's Zygotic Mynci, excellent solo artist) talked about this recently, saying that he preferred pretentiousness over cynicism any day of the week, and I thought, "so do I!" because at least there's a playfulness when you're pretentious.

Having said that, I would hope that I wasn't bringing pseudo-academia into it. I really try not to.

For me, music was the alternative. It was a retreat from all of that.

There's always been that thought in my head that I might write a book. And I think that if I did write a book, that part of my brain – the more academic part, maybe – would come back in force.

With music I don't worry about that. I derive a lot of comfort and pleasure from writing lyrics.

Do you think, then, that they come from different parts of the brain, or your psyche, to the bookish knowledge, as it were?

Yes, probably. There's that aspect of how other people perceive your lyrics. I have this conversation with my parents where they'll say "there's quite a lot of violence in your lyrics, George... are you all right?" And I hadn't really realised that, but yes, actually, it's true! I don't know what part of me that comes from.

I also feel like, really, you could analyse and talk for years about lyric writing and essentially it doesn't matter. Lyrics can be shit but the song can still work.

I personally don't think that there should be too much importance placed in lyrics because it's different strokes for different folks, isn't it?

You're familiar with traditional Welsh songs and these lyrics have endured over the centuries. Are there qualities within those lyrics that you've absorbed into your songs?

I was talking to someone about this. What I haven't said here, yet, is that my style of writing English lyrics is entirely dependent on the fact that I'm bilingual, in that I'm a Welsh speaker. A lot of the turns of phrase I use in my English writing are, probably without me realising, derived from Welsh. So, funnily enough, a lot of my Welsh language influence comes out in my English writing.

When it comes to writing in Welsh, that's a totally different part of my brain, definitely, because I have to think about it more.

The folk songs are quite enduring and the images just work.

Is it the imagery or just the universality of the emotions that has made them endure... love, pain, death, loss... it's the human condition, isn't it?

Only in so much as any other form of artistic expression also reflects the human condition. I don't glorify folk songs like that, I think they're just songs. I honestly don't think about it. I certainly don't think about it in terms of lyrics. I think about them in terms of the images that they use and motifs. I think motifs are the things that excite me about folk songs.

One of the things that Week of Pines has is a consistency of imagery... is that important to you, a cohesion between

the atmosphere of the recordings and the lyrics?

I like the idea that each album, or each record – not just mine, I'm talking about any record, apart from Best Of collections or artfully-curated Late Night Tale compilations – I've always felt that each one should be a little microcosmos and if you were to enter in, you are to enter in for the full hour and then you'll be cast out.

Ultimately I like there to be a world that is going to keep me safe for the running time of that record and the best way that that happens, usually, is when there's some theme or tangible thing that makes it cohesive. Whether the lyrics do that, I don't know… you could be very thematic and conceptual. I don't mean concept albums…

It's something that comes out in analysis, afterwards. The books that I've read about Bob Dylan, for example… I don't know how disingenuous he's being, a lot of the time he claims he's not paying a huge amount of attention to the words that he writes… and then those words went out and were analysed to the nth degree by a number of pseudo-intellectuals and *they* discovered, or applied, the patterns within his lyrics, after the fact. That kind of lyrical imagery is maybe something the listener gets, certain words ring true or resonate throughout your songs, for the individual listener, but maybe without intention.

It's hard for me to know. It's really hard for me to say because, to me, 'Week of Pines' still feels like quite a random collection of songs. All they share in common is the time they were written and the time they were recorded. But, of course, it would be silly to say that the lyrics weren't in some way related to each other. I suppose you go through phases of thinking, and being inspired by what you've been reading. I'm trying to think what I was reading when I was writing Week of Pines, and I can't remember… probably Heat magazine.

I can identify a different style in those songs from what I'm writing now… and if I think about what I'm reading now, I can see some influence and think 'Oooh, yeah – I've moved onto a new phase.'

I was very surprised to hear that Bones (from Georgia's debut E.P. proper, In Luna, on Recordiau Gwymon) **was about your time working in a ticket office on the London Underground. This despite the fact that I was familiar with that part of your story and the fact that the recording starts with the sound of a tube train! How many more clues did I need? Maybe my idiocy can be explained by the rather fragmentary nature of your lyrics. Is that deliberate so that people can read themselves into the songs?**

No, not really. I leave them quite vague enough. I don't think you should explain things away. People have said to me that they've heard different things in the songs that I never realised were in there, and that's amazing. That's the best thing that can happen with your songs because if all you get back from people who listen to your music is what you think you put in, you can never be surprised. If you leave it just vague enough, there's always a chance that you'll be surprised by what people hear in it.

That's gratifying. It keeps things exciting for you because you may discover things in the lyrics that you hadn't even realised you'd put in them.

With Bones, it was about working in an underground vault, which did feel a bit like a coffin. It was more, I guess, about living in London and being a little bit lost. I'd gone to London ostensibly to "make my name" and it just wasn't working for me. I was having not nice brushes with the industry and was really at that stage where I didn't know who I was and what I was doing. I suppose it was a song about needing to just feel something, trying to get back to who I was. How naff does that sound?

Not naff at all, because that's what I heard in Bones and empathised with. It's interesting that songs take on a life of their own when they leave the hands of the writer.

How important is the rhythm of the lyrics to you. I don't think I know anyone who manages to squeeze as many syllables into a song (occasionally, that is) without it sounding claustrophobic...

I don't think I do! It's something I don't think about too much. I really don't know. The music and the words have different rhythms in counterpoint to each other and part of the game is trying to get one to interlink with the other.

A lot of the lyrics I hear don't have that counterpoint, they're welded religiously to the beat. It gets really boring and predictable...

I quite like songs that are welded, sometimes. It just a different method of expression. It doesn't necessarily work for me, but I think some of the best pop songs have that welded quality that isn't airy and isn't too gossamer, which is sometimes something that I struggle with, trying to get the words to actually work with the music. I don't think it's one rule fits all, really.

One of the things that I've found writing this book is that it's important to avoid giving the impression that there is One Right Way that everyone must follow...

The thing that I would say is this: a songwriter shouldn't worry or ask themselves the question, is some over-thinker going to come along now and scrutinise my work and draw conclusions about me and my capability based on my words?

You should just… well, there is no should. That's the great thing about writing your own songs… it's your outlet, it's for you to dictate, not for someone else to dictate how they should be.

If someone criticises you, and says, I don't know, that the rhythm of the words doesn't quite work in the song… it doesn't matter. It really doesn't matter.

That's the main thing. The only way that you're going to find any lyrical voice, really, is to be left to find it for yourself, and to not feel like you need to be copying someone who has been admired.

I have a perfect example. I was talking to Iwan (from the excellent Cowbois Rhos Botwnnog) the other day, and we worked out that most male songwriters between the ages of 40 and 70 have at one point in their lives, on at least one record, done what they think is 'A Dylan'.

What they've done is they've talked about a medieval court, and they've introduced a jester, and there's a fallen women who's flaky and has been disposed in a corner, and there's been talk of a lute and a merchant.

And these faux Dylan songs are just shit. Springsteen did it badly. Townes Van Zandt did it really badly. The thing is, if you listen to a 'Best Of…' of Springsteen or Van Zandt, those songs stick out like horrible sore thumbs, amongst what that particular songwriter does so much better, when they're being themselves.

Never feel that you need to mimic in order to express yourself better.

Obviously, take inspiration… but don't let it take you over, or obscure you.

Good lyricists are the ones who find their own way, aren't they?

They are. I think the worst thing people can be prescriptive about is the lyrics. There's so much snobbery. And so much circle-jerking about songwriting. Ultimately just chill out, and say what you want to say.

Georgia Ruth's debut album 'Week of Pines' is available from all the usual outlets on Recordiau Gwymon, and I can't recommend it highly enough. You can follow Georgia on Twitter @georgiaruth and visit her website:

http://georgiaruth.co.uk

I'm off to ask my mum what "circle-jerking" means... that's a new phrase, to me.

[1]**it's as punk a recording as any I've ever played on my show** - *where punk = having the courage to be yourself, entirely, and the wherewithal and motivation to do what you believe in, regardless of the prevailing zeitgeist.*

PLAYLIST:
Georgia Ruth - Ocean
Georgia Ruth - Week Of Pines
Georgia Ruth - Dovecote
Georgia Ruth - Bones
Joan Baez - Silver Dagger
Paul Simon - Diamonds On The Soles Of Her Shoes
Bob Dylan - Baby Stop Crying
Richard James - When You See Me (In The Pouring Rain)
Cowbois Rhos Botwnnog - Ceffylau A'r Drannau

18: <u>The Joy Formidable On Songwriting</u>

On Making Music originated as a book I had started writing about my favourite group.

The Joy Formidable are from Mold in North Wales. They have released two albums, both of which I adore. The Big Roar is the one I want to be buried with, playing on an eternal loop from a well-charged .mp3 player, if it's too impractical to arrange for an extension lead and Technics deck in my impressive, granite tomb.

A morbid thought, perhaps, but an honest one. Please take note, next of kin.

They've built a significant audience in the United States and Europe to compliment a loyal and discerning following here in the UK. They've never so much as shifted a single strand of hair to try and appease the deliriously shallow UK music press or radio playlisters. They're committed to following their own instincts and what they believe to be right. Great music, superlative live experiences, and a band worthy of our ardour are the results of their integrity and inspiration.

They're also funny as fuck and the least likely people to take themselves too seriously, in public at least. They can leave that, and the pseud-ish theorising, to me.

I love this band's music with the soppy unquestioning heart of a fanboy. I also think that theirs is a fascinating story, which is why I started to write that book about them. Interviews were conducted, a shape for the book was formulated, research was done, some chapters were written… but then the band went away and toured for a year.

Bloody bands! Going about their business as if that's more important than my magnum opus.

I spent a few days twiddling my thumbs. Then my fingers. Then my thumbs again, and I decided I would put the interviews I had already conducted with Rhydian and Ritzy to good use, and make hay while the sun shone on the writing routine I had (finally) managed to discipline into myself.

On Making Music grew out of that decision. It's their fault that you're reading this. Try to not hold it against them.

Ironically the quotes that I harvested from those initial interviews didn't entirely fit the tone of this book. So the first edition of On Making Music, which was inspired by The Joy Formidable, had very little Joy Formidable in it. It was something I was aware of very early on. The absence of their insight was a glaring hole that bothered me to the point that I found it difficult to promote the book. It was like trying to sell jigsaws door-to-door that I knew were missing some of the key pieces.

See, I know many of The Joy Formidable's qualities as artists and human beings. They embody that rare combination of originality of vision and tenacity. If this book can encourage either in its readers, it will justify its existence and your time in its company.

One of the lesser reasons that they occupy the loftiest position in my musical heart is to do with the fact that we share a hometown. I can hear home in their music: the natural grandeur, the elements, the awe and beauty.

I also hear poetry and truth in their lyrics. That's why their two albums so far were a salvation when I had tribulations in my personal life. In particular 'Tendons' and 'Silent Treatment' from their 2nd album, Wolf's Law, could have been written about my own personal circumstances.

Obviously I was reading between the lines, hanging my life onto their words, but that's what great songwriters give you the scope to do. And that's why I'm now addressing that glaring hole in the first edition of the book by talking to Rhydian and Ritzy about songwriting.

Do you both have different approaches to writing?

Rhydian: *I think we definitely have different approaches at times.*

Ritzy: *Would you, Rhydian, say that you have one particular way that you prefer? Because mine is probably just on an acoustic guitar. That's usually my go-to, in terms of starting a song off.*

Rhydian: *And you sometimes have lyrics that start the writing of a song, don't you? And then work the music around the lyrics, whereas I tend to do less of that, maybe let the music come first. I like to start with different things. Usually it's a guitar, of some sort.*

How much has this evolved over the years? If you look back at how you started writing songs would the way that you write now still be recognisably similar?

Rhydian: *Quite similar. I think. That core thing of writing with one instrument, which tends to be a guitar but can be a piano, remains the same. You're covering all bases with melody, rhythmic accompaniment and your voice. That hasn't changed much. But I think it is important to put yourself in different contexts to keep yourself challenged. That's a conscious thing.*

Ritzy: *I think that as the band's evolved we can be more dynamic within that simple framework. Even though a* *single instrument might be the starting point, as you're writing you're aware that it's just a stop-gap. The guitar might not even feature in the final version of that song, it's just a tool to help you create. In your imagination you can hear the drums, you can hear the piano, and the other instrumentation. So, for me, the guitar is the quickest and most spontaneous way towards that.*

The guitar's something you can travel with too, you can keep it to hand, by your bedside, for whenever an idea comes to you.

As the band has moved along I've started feeling that I didn't want to be limited by the one instrument. So as I'm writing on that one level, I'm thinking a lot more dynamically outside of the original starting point.

You've said something similar to me about 'The Turnaround' (from the album Wolf's Law). **It's an emotive, acoustic led song, but you had all of the orchestrated lines in your head when you were writing it, didn't you?**

Ritzy: *Yes, I definitely knew that I wanted it to sound big and orchestral. And yes, it did start on acoustic guitar, but I never wanted it to stay like that.*

Rhydian: *Now I think about it, my approach to writing probably has changed since we began. I started off in the bedroom with a guitar, then doing my own demos on a 4-track, then moved onto the computer and multitrack recording... and doing hundreds and hundreds and hundreds of songs. I've done it to the point that I can now hear other instruments in the arrangement in my imagination, like different layers.*

Ritzy: *That is very much Rhydian's approach: to get the idea and to track and demo it all quickly.*

Rhydian: *When I'm writing now I can hear multi-layers as we go along and I can hardly keep up with myself and the* *ideas that come. I wish I had an orchestra at my disposal, all the time!*

I think that what has helped was doing so much demoing in college. Hearing the possibilities is second nature, now.

I'm interested in what you mean by 'challenging yourself'. Does that mean picking up a guitar, say, but not reaching for an obvious chord or trying a different tuning?

Rhydian: *Maybe challenge isn't the right word because that sounds too much like you're pushing, and I don't mean it like that. It's things that invigorate you, like I'm hearing this particular rhythm… say, the sound of drops coming from my tap (laughs)… and you can be inspired by something that mundane. You're starting from a different place. In retrospect I think it's good to have different things inspiring you but you're not always thinking about it consciously.*

When I interviewed Charlotte Church I was telling her how 'be yourself' was the key philosophy for this book, but she thinks that being open is at least as valid a perspective… open, not just to musical ideas, but to anything. Would that have a resonance with you? Being receptive rather than forcing something out…

Ritzy: *I don't know. I'm not a purist, in that sense. I don't completely believe that if something doesn't come straight away then it wasn't a good idea to begin with. There are certain songs that you write that don't happen in one sitting and sometimes they do need a bit of eeking out and a bit more reflection. That doesn't necessarily mean that they're forced. They may just be pushing you in a different way or taking you out of your comfort zone.*

Maybe it's something that needs the imagination of the band as well. Sometimes it's not until you get into a room together that the idea for a song starts to make more sense.

188

We've definitely found that recording this album.

Rhydian: *Some songs are partly based on improvisation and being in the moment. There's one song, in particular, we've done multiple versions of, until now that we're happy with it.*

So sometimes an idea can come along that's a bit of an ugly duckling, but you can hear that it has the potential to turn into a swan?

Rhydian: *Yes. You know that, fundamentally, it's a great melody, a great song, but it doesn't sound quite right and needs some work.*

Ritzy: *Those are the moments when I really appreciate having another set of ears I can trust...*

Rhydian: *Same here, definitely.*

Ritzy: *You can really wrangle through something, but get to the point where you can't improve it or make it work. Sometimes, if it's your own seed and you lose your way with it, it certainly helps to get it back on track with somebody you trust.*

When you bring your ideas to each other, is it simply a case of amalgamating them or is there a different chemistry at work? A natural politics between you that allows things that could otherwise be quite territorial to work together.

Rhydian: *That aspect is really interesting, when you share something with someone else. You need to trust each other, for someone to be the dictator, sometimes, and on other occasions to step back. I suppose it's how much you believe in a particular idea. It's democratic at times, but can also be utterly despotic. The only way you deal with* *that is by trusting each other and, even though we trust each other absolutely, it's still difficult. We have massive arguments, sometimes.*

Ritzy: *We've started having them a bit less and I think that that's because… I don't know… it is that element of trust. If, for instance, I come to Rhydian with an idea on acoustic guitar, there is sort of an intuitive disclaimer between us that says, "this isn't really how it's going to sound at the end, but this is it in its simplest form…" For you to play that to someone else asks for quite a bit of imagination.*

And courage?

Ritzy: *Yes. I suppose that that is where the belief comes in. I'm a believer that if you play something on an acoustic guitar and it's emotive and you can stand behind it…*

Rhydian: *… that it should work.*

Ritzy: *Yeah, but not everybody would get it. With Rhydian, there's definitely that ability where he can imagine the bigger picture, whereas I might have that one vision for it. I play it to him and I can feel all of his creative juices and his imagination working on it as well. I think that that's really exciting, when you actually take the original, simple idea to the band you can bring all of those elements together.*

We used to clash a lot more when we first started writing together probably because we were still figuring each other out, over-compensating a little bit.

Rhydian: *We're obviously both strong-minded. With time has come trust and understanding that we write in different ways and maybe not everything we write works for the band… and that's fine, you know?*

Let's talk about two similar situations that your writing

grew through before you were working together. I know that you, Ritzy, immersed yourself in writing songs when you worked in Washington DC after finishing university, as a way to deal with a challenging period in your life. And similarly you, Rhydian, were writing and recording continuously when you were studying music in Wolverhampton, then Salford. You both spent an awful lot of time writing, without the express intention of refining your skills... do you think improvement and ability were the overall effects of those many, many hours you ended up dedicating to writing?

Rhydian: *Yes, absolutely – and also when we did come together, writing with each other at such an intensity took it to another level again. But yes, especially on the recording side for me, I was on a course where we were doing things like 'aural perception skills'. Those years, especially when I was in university, were absolutely integral. I wrote about 1000 songs. That's not always a good thing, of course. It depends what you take from it. It wasn't just crapping out an endless line of rubbish songs that weren't improving.*

Ritzy: *For me it has been more of a gradual thing. I've been writing since I was really young, on some level. I think I was writing songs from about 6 years old. Some of my finest work! "Going down the field to eat rabbit stew..." ha ha!*

I haven't always been prolific, either. Starting very young and being consistent with it, and having a lot of music in your life, is just as relevant as how much you're writing. And I don't mean sitting there and going on a crash course to see how many albums you can listen to in a week.

If music is part of your upbringing – there was so much music being played on the record player in this house when I was growing up – then that contributes to your music knowledge as much as writing a lot does.

I don't even know how I got to where I am as a songwriter. I can't explain why I know things or feel things or like certain changes, it's not necessarily from doing lots of writing, I can tell that it comes from my make up, how much music I've listened to.

One of the things I love about your band is that you wear your influences very lightly. You're foremost in the equation with subtle influences in the background. I make that observation because these days it tends to be the other way round, maybe because people don't spend as much time developing their own sound, they send their first demos in to BBC Introducing, say, and the next minute they're on the radio. So that period you had to go through of years developing out of the spotlight is rarer these days.

Rhydian: *It's that thing about sharing, isn't it? It's so easy to share on Facebook, Soundcloud and the like. It depends on what you want your music to be: is it about capturing a moment in time or is it something that you really work towards and chisel it all the way, so it's a perfect thing that you've sculpted over time? I think there's a place for both.*

Is there a place that you go, a mindset or in the real world, to find inspiration and write? Or is it simply a question of making space in a day to actually do some writing?

Ritzy: *I think that initial moment of hearing a melody, feeling something, wanting to pick up the guitar, that can happen very much at random. You can be sat here watching TV, eating, reading... we can be in a room recording something entirely different together... and an idea will come so I'll go into a quiet corner and start working on it.*

That first initial moment can be very random. Then for me, after that, it's very much about driving with the idea.

Literally driving, sometimes. There's something about not being static. Sometimes when you write and you're static, it's harder to get the idea out, a danger of overthinking it.

I find it easier, a lot of the time, if I've had an idea to follow wherever it might take me while I'm out walking or driving.

Rhydian: *It's about letting it work its way out of the background. It'll go stagnant if you think too hard about it.*

Ritzy: *You go into the walk or the drive with the initial idea, maybe humming it or turning over a lyrical idea. It's not a conscious step, though. I don't get an idea here and think, "I'd better go for a drive!" But almost every song I've ever written has had that moment... starting somewhere static but then teasing parts of the rest of it out while I'm on the move.*

Do you, Rhydian, work similarly to that?

Rhydian: *I think there are two different things. One is the musical aspect, that can be very random. I have ideas all the time, that's never a problem.*

Depends on what your music is, I suppose. If it's very lyrically-based, in terms of being a storyteller and what you want to say with the words is really important, that doesn't come like that (snaps fingers). That shit you have to really work on. You can jam with the phonetics, work out the rhythm of the lyrics, but then adding meaning and capturing something that you want to say, that – for me – tends to be less random.

There's lots of different levels to this process, aren't there? When I asked you earlier what you've learnt since you started, maybe it's that... where and how to encourage your ideas; the best way to subconsciously draw them out and then consciously fill in the details?

Rhydian: *Yes. There's a discipline in letting go, as well. From knowing that if you just get on with living, and feeling things, and keep writing but not pushing it, then eventually it will come. I think that's really important. You never want to push it too much.*

Ritzy: *I'm really relaxed when I'm writing a song. I really don't give a fuck whether I finish it, or not.*

Rhydian: *You do some of your writing in the bath, don't you?*

Ritzy: *Ha! Yes. I haven't had a properly relaxing bath for years!*

Rhydian: *When we're writing, we can be pushing too hard to get an idea out or formed, and nothing's happening, then Ritzy goes for a bath and rushes back after a while, "I've got it! I know what to do!"*

Ritzy: *The amount of times I've come into the room wrapped in a towel, with a damp notebook: "Quick, fire up the studio! I've got an idea!" I've always been relaxed about songwriting. I don't feel any haste. I have the attitude that if it's going to come, it'll come, whether it takes a day, a week, a month…*

Do you, then, have a lot of fragments that you carry round with you? Riffs that you haven't used, lines for lyrics, scraps of melody…

Ritzy: *Yes, a few, but I don't like to work on too many things at once. A couple at a time, maybe, but that's the limit for me.*

I'm talking about the seedling ideas for a song. It could be quite a long process but generally things will form quite quickly. I sometimes think that that is partly us jigging each other on, in the right way.

194

I've been surprised at how much you manage to do on the road. When I interviewed you before Wolf's Law came out you told me about writing Tendons in a two-bit motel room somewhere... so clearly you write on the road, too... is it a way to fill all of those empty hours of travelling with something constructive? In other words, does the lifestyle actually contribute towards you being good writers?

Ritzy: *When I'm on the road, it is one of the ways that I like to fill my day: sat backstage, or in a hotel, with a guitar.*

The routine keeps you quite fired up. There's a lot of repetition on tour, so it's good to spend some time thinking outside the songs in your set-list. Not with a view to writing something you could play that night! But it's also good to consider what you have in your repertoire that you can put in the set, and how to incorporate them, to keep things fresh.

I keep myself busy thinking like that when we're touring because there's a repetition to fight against, creatively.

Is it the same for you Rhydian?

Rhydian: *Erm. Well, I'm not as focused when we're touring. Not like that. I may have had a drink the night before. But when I've had a drink, ideas can come more quickly...*

Ritzy: *It's just that they're all shit. That's what you don't realise!*

Rhydian: *(laughs) Coming up with ideas has never been a problem wherever we are. In those initial stages I don't like to be too judgemental. I just really love the whole process of creating something out of nothing. It doesn't really matter if it's a good idea or a bad idea, I just do it. And then you can judge it when you've finished, see what's* *come out. Wherever I am, I like to do that.*

There's a lot of honesty in your songs, from a lyrical point of view. You've sung about the break up of your romantic relationship together, for example. It's not obvious because of the poetry and the symbolism in your songs. But it's there and it feels important. Is that honesty a philosophy?

Ritzy: *I think there's probably two things at work. It depends on where the song has started from. Some of the songs on the album we're working on now, and on Wolf's Law, came literally, as words first. Wolf's Law, for example, was a poem originally. I wrote it like a poem. Perhaps I took a little bit more time in the way I crafted the words. But what was driving the composition of the music was this absolute, complete understanding of what the beginning the middle and the end of the poem were. There's utter honesty, then, when you approach a song like that because you're very clear about the story that you want to tell, or the emotion that you want to convey with that set of words. You're not going to allow the music to compromise the words.*

I was wondering if it worked the other way round, too... specifically with a song like The Greatest Light Is The Greatest Shade. That piece of music, the arrangement and the production, I find incredibly moving; then the lyrics, again, are incredibly moving. Some bands might have the emotive quality in the music but might back away from being so honest – about break ups and hurt – in the lyrics. There is an integrity there between the music and the lyric. I don't hear that a lot in successful music... there can be a disconnect between the big stadium-filling sound of Muse, or Bastille, or Mumford and Sons and their lyrical content.

196

Rhydian: *I know exactly what you mean. I suppose it's the modern tic. We've somehow got to a place where we think that it's almost too much, too uncool, to emote or be revealing lyrically. But all the great artists have done that, to my mind. There aren't many artists who can do that and make the music work and it all to be listenable. I suppose that's where the fine line is between what is great and what is cheesy.*

Almost an embarrassment to be honest about the way you're feeling, in a song...

Ritzy: *I think that that song, The Greatest Light..., is an interesting example to choose in that context because my recollection is that I'd gone out until late. Rhydian had been in all day and all night, working on this piece of music, writing the parts and arranging it. It had melodies but no lyrics. By then he was boggle-eyed because he'd literally been working on this thing all day, and I was so moved and excited by this piece of music that I went, "My turn! Out the way!", and I think we finished it that evening: lyrically, everything. It was very fresh. I just walked into Rhydian's world and did it. There was no over-thinking. It just resonated with me. I went with my instincts and followed the emotional lead of what hearing that piece of music made me feel, what it evoked in me lyrically.*

That song is different to most of the other ones where there's more interweaving between the two of us, going back to sections, reworking things, building the lyrics.

What are the tools of the trade, with regards writing?

Ritzy: *A bath! Maybe some nice bubbles.*

(Laughs) Apart from the guitar, or the instrument you're

writing on, what do you use to capture your ideas? Do you carry a notebook and a voice recorder (on your phone) around with you all the time. Or are you like Van from Catfish & The Bottlemen (see Chapter 35: Catfish & the Bottlemen On Getting Gigs) and John Lennon before him, in that you trust to an idea only being good enough if you can remember it the next day?

Ritzy: *I'd be fucked if I worked like that! My memory's so all over the place, I don't think my retaining an idea or, more to the point, forgetting it would be any indication as to how good that idea is. I try to transcribe it on some level, or record it, or something. I go to sleep and by the time I get back to thinking about writing, I've had hundreds of other ideas and they all become distorted…*

Rhydian: *Most of the ideas, from my side, for this album went onto my phone. I'd just sing into it.*

You work a lot off vocal lines, don't you… Tendons started off acapella…

Rhydian: *And a lot of ideas on the guitar captured on the phone, too. Anything that's to hand.*

What about lyrical ideas… do you walk around with a notepad with you at all times?

Ritzy: *Well, I'm in a bit of a mess for this album. Because we've been so prolific writing for this record, I started off with a notebook, filled that… got another one. Lost the first notebook, and then got another one in case I lost the second one. So I've got about six notebooks for this latest record and I can't remember where anything is in any of them! Six really dense notebooks, so if we're partway through something and I'm trying to find a fragment or an idea that I know was really good, I have to trawl through six books of fragmented ideas. Still, though, I'm mostly a* *big fan of still having things on paper.*

Rhydian: *Most of what I do is on my phone. They can get nicked, can't they? Or break. So I would recommend writing them down too!*

Is there any other, final advice that you'd offer to someone writing and creating?

Rhydian: *It depends on what kind of writer you want to be. I suppose I'd say get yourself out there. Trying different things can help you realise what you want to do. Collaborating with people is a great idea. One of the things that's overlooked is that writing's not all about technical aspects: what to play and how to play it. You can do simple, obvious things to help yourself. For example, make sure, say, you read a lot if you're a lyricist. If you want to write, then write and, actually, write a lot.*

At the end of the day it's about living. Make sure you get life experience. If you shut yourself away maybe you're limiting what will inspire you and what you can say through that.

Of course, it works for different people in different ways. It's difficult if you say 'DO THIS' or 'DO THAT' because songwriters have to feel and do things in their own way, not as they may be told to do them.

Some of the technical, theoretical aspects are important. If you work with lots of different instruments and sounds, you work out what they can do and how they can best give voice to the ideas you have in your head.

What advice would you offer Ritzy?

Ritzy: *Dunno. I fucking hate giving advice, to be honest. Only from the point of view that it's so different for every* *band. I think that the main thing is to do it when you feel like it, don't force it, don't overthink it, don't go into it with some preconception of the way that you want to write, or what you think you should write, because you'll probably end up sounding shite and like someone else.*

Rhydian: *I think you've got to be open but also to trust your instincts and I think that's an incredibly difficult balance to have. That 'thing' that people are supposedly looking for in artists, is what their soul is, their unique thing, and that can sometimes get watered down if you listen to too much advice. You have to look within too, you know.*

The Joy Formidable are currently (at the time of writing, October 2014) neck deep in the recording of their third album in the hills outside Mold. They are also running a limited edition singles club called 'Aruthrol', releasing a series of vinyl 7"s that feature one of their exclusive new Welsh language songs as well as showcasing a recording from an upcoming Welsh artist on the flipside.

More information can be found here:

http://thejoyformidable.com

PLAYLIST:
The Joy Formidable - The Big Roar (2011), Wolf's Law (2013), Aruthrol 7" singles club (2014)

19: <u>Band Practise</u>

Rock 'n' roll is meant to be insouciant and effortless... at least that's the way it should come across on stage. It takes a lot of effort to get to that point, though. Much of that effort is exerted during band practice. It's all well and good practising so that you're note perfect when you're by yourself but the real magic happens when a band practises together.

When you're playing together, if you're listening to the whole rather than just your part, you'll hear spaces and opportunities within a piece of music opened up and created by your bandmates' imaginations. You will hear elements that you wouldn't have envisaged yourself, that will push you and the music further.

If you're in a good band and you're prepared to put the graft in, that is.

However bands can prevaricate like no other creative entity. Writing this book has given me insight into how difficult it can be, even working on my own, to discipline myself to create something every day. Multiply that potential for distraction by the amount of other band members and it's a wonder that anything ever gets written or recorded.

Potential distractions are legion in the digital age, especially if you're an autonomous / D.I.Y. Band managing your own affairs who feel as though they need to be on the end of a phone, or there to monitor e-mail and social networks.

Set aside specific times during the week for writing and rehearsing. At those times turn your phones and social networks off. Creating and maintaining your music is the priority. A gig offer, or a label enquiring as to whether you'd like to release something through them, will wait for a couple of hours.

Structuring your music time doesn't mean that you aren't free to capture the muse whenever it strikes. Nor does it mean that you're making rock 'n' roll as regimented as an office job or a tedious college course. This is what you love to do the most or you wouldn't be reading this book. Giving yourself a framework in which to create and practise your music, a certain amount of discipline, isn't against the spirit of rock 'n' roll. It will help you to refine your creativity. And it may even help legitimise what you do to the people you may feel most answerable to. Even Iggy Pop's parents probably hassled him about getting a 'proper job'.

Oh, and stay out of the pub or the local caff when you know you should be rehearsing or doing something musically creative.

We used to meet in the pub every day and plan world domination. This plan would also include more meetings at the pub. We would invariably get drunk and talk about how great we were if only we could get round to rehearsing more.

Richard Parfitt, 60ft Dolls

All bands are great at talking about making music and planning world domination. I bet even the Velvet Underground huddled around a solitary coffee for whole afternoons in a Chelsea diner, shrouded in cigarette smoke, cooking up their manifesto – no doubt hoping that Warhol would stroll in and pay the bill.

Executing these caffeine-hatched plans (or whichever stimulant fires your minds) is the real challenge.

Hard work isn't something that non-music making folk need associate with rock 'n' roll. Neither should they. Knowing how long Springsteen and the E Street Band slaved over his anthemic paean to escapism, Born To Run, would, after all, diminish its escapist qualities.

But hard work is what's required.

If you're doing it right, though, it will rarely feel like work.

Mark Foley co-runs Music Box, a renowned rehearsal suite and studio facility in Cardiff. He's seen the benefits that hard work can bring to bands, even if they rarely talk about it:

The old practice makes perfect thing comes to mind here. You're absolutely right that bands try to play it cool but all the bands that come here, that sound the most together and sorted, are the ones that rehearse regularly and put thought into it.

It does depend what kind of band it is though. You can have a bunch of session guys turning up to play for someone and they can just turn it on when ever they want. However, that comes with a lot of work that they will do privately before turning up to work with the artist.

In answer to your question there is a direct correlation between hard work and good results.

Music Box Rehearsal Rooms & Studio, Cardiff

When I started out in a band, we used to 'play some music' or – if we were within earshot of girls, 'practice' – at the local youth club. Pity those poor kids playing table tennis to Tash Gorse and I murdering The Cult at a volume that would deafen thunder. We'd started off rehearsing in his tiny bedroom on Stanley St. in Mold. To give Tash his due, he had made an effort to soundproof the room. There were egg boxes glued to the walls and the ceiling and, allegedly, some underlay between the boxes and the plaster but Tash liked to hit his drums hard... *really* hard! 30 seconds into Love Removal Machine and half the egg boxes had fallen onto the floor and the woman from two doors down in the terrace was banging on the front door because all of the ornaments had fallen off her mantelpiece.

Despite the logistical challenges of trying to find somewhere to practise, an all-encompassing desire to make music drove us on... more accurately it drove our parents all over northeast Wales on their precious weekends: to the back-room of a pub called the Ponderosa in Buckley; Gwernymynydd Village Hall; Shaun Delaney's mum's front room; Paul Oppenheim's dad's garage; heck – sometimes, even – school. It didn't ever seem like an inconvenience; we just wanted to play. We were so hungry for that buzz of volume, sounds, camaraderie and sense of achievement (when we got through Bring On The Dancing Horses without murdering each other) we'd find any conceivable space that would allow us to make our noise.

The equipment we used was at best rudimentary and mostly awful. The buzz we had was both literal and metaphorical. I swear the earth hum coming through our two, slaved together Sound City 100W PA's was louder than our singer's actual vocal... but it didn't matter. Entire weekends would disappear as we strived to make the noise in that space match the noise in our heads and our hearts.

At that point, in those very early years when we'd have been 15 or 16 years old, we had no plan, really. We were just trying to get through our favourite songs, ape the sounds our heroes made, and share a crafty bottle of cider and a stolen pack of Benson & Hedges between us. It was all about the thrill of the moment, and although we dreamed of being rock stars, that wasn't really what fired our enthusiasm, or made those entire afternoons dwindle as quickly as match flames. We simply adored making a noise together.

If you've been in a band as a kid, you'll recognise that. You'll know that the 'getting better' bit is a lot more about enjoying yourself than adhering to a plan or a regime. However you approach 'practising' or 'playing' or – round about the same time you start dreaming of demo tapes and record labels – 'rehearsing', the longer you can keep fun at the forefront the quicker you will become better.

Even Radiohead have fun when they're playing together. Probably.

You can have fun in the crappiest of surroundings with the most rudimentary equipment, if the spirit is right.

You learn a lot about the dedication of fellow band members from band practise. The kids who make excuses, or who don't – happily – let all the hours wash by without moaning or pointing out that they have a date they need to go on, aren't worth it. Unless their parents own a van and the best sounding P.A in Christendom, they're not worth bothering with.

Sometimes your decision making has to be that pragmatic and ruthless.

Finding somewhere to practise is a challenge. Other people don't like your noise, take that as a given. Neighbours could have The Carpenters rehearsing through the connecting wall, in their melodic pomp, and they'd still complain. If you sound like Bolt Thrower, you're going to be very unpopular with anyone who lives within a mile of the epicentre of your rehearsals. Which is fine... as long as you aren't breaching noise regulations. They probably get up first thing on a Sunday morning and fire up the lawn mower. Anti-social noise is all subjective, isn't it?

Just don't move close to my house, OK?

206

Band Practise

If you can afford it, and there is one within easy driving distance, a good, professional rehearsal room is the ideal. Cardiff's Music Box grew out of a frustration felt by its founders, all musicians, that there was nowhere local to cater diligently for the particular needs of music-making folk:

We went to too many rehearsal rooms as kids where things were broken, there weren't enough leads, you couldn't buy a battery or a pair of sticks and worst of all there was no one around to even ask if there was a problem or request. Too much time was spent wandering around looking for assistance.

Ultimately we try to make sure that everything works, that it's in good condition and that there's always someone around to help with any problems or questions.

The rooms themselves are designed to make sure that they're accessible and ultimately mean the band can use as much of their booking as possible actually rehearsing. It's a customer service thing I guess.

We learnt this the hard way having been both the the people in a band and the people running the place. What really matter is that our customers achieve what they want to achieve.

Mark Foley, Music Box, Cardiff

Sadly not everyone has access to such facilities or the money to pay for them. Fairly priced as they are, in my experience, 15 year old kids have enough trouble affording strings and plectrums... there's only so much a paper round will pay for.

If that is the case, you will be relying on garages / function rooms / village or town halls / the back rooms of pubs. Spread the word that you need somewhere to practise. There are magnanimous souls out there, altruistic old gits who want to live vicariously through your music. Somewhere relatively self-contained, secure (if you're going to have to store equipment) and warm is vital. I killed the friendship I had with band-members by forcing them to sit for hours on end in a *freezing* industrial unit while I found my 'muse'. Making your music needn't be as tortuous or uncomfortable.

Use Earth Leakage Circuit Breakers (R.C.D's / Earth Leakage Trips). A lot of band practises are in places with less than ideal electrics. There's nothing romantically bohemian about the singer getting a buzz every time their lips touch the microphone. An R.C.D.. will protect you from electrocution. If it trips out when you plug it in, there's something wrong and *potentially fatal* with the electricity supply.

Check the fuses and the wiring in *all* of your plugs. The majority of musical equipment is secondhand. I bought two Pioneer record decks at Christmas and didn't think twice about the way that they were wired. I used them for a live, all vinyl radio show which meant that they had to be P.A.T. Tested by the BBC, an unnecessary formality as far as I was concerned... until the engineer testing the gear discovered a loose live wire, a loose earth and two incorrect fuses. Any of these rudimentary faults could have caused a fire or electrocution. All for the sake of 2 minutes with a screwdriver and a packet of fuses from the local supermarket.

If there's one piece of wisdom that you act upon in this entire book, make it that one. It could save your life.

What benefits will rehearsing bring and why is it important?

The answers to this are multifold and are mostly obvious. You can know your music, so that you're familiar with its details and where your fingers, your feet or your larynx should 'go' next, but you can also *know* your music, so that the ebb and flow of it is almost as natural to you as breathing in and out. When a band get to that point, when they're so at one with each other and what they're playing, it raises them to another level, it gives them a musical aura that sets them apart.

This isn't about 'tightness'… it really isn't about 'tightness'. 'Tight' is the faintest of compliments, generally only ever given by other musicians who are being polite because they haven't been awed by your songs or the dynamic of your performance.

What you're actually aiming for is a telepathic looseness. All of the best bands I have ever seen know how to play off each other, to trust that every element of the sound is buoying the others aloft. To bring an element of the unknown or the unexpected to every performance of every song, even the ones that are most familiar and well-worn.

I hope this doesn't sound like bullshit. It isn't. When an ensemble of music-makers truly know each other, musically – and that's a knowledge that can only come from playing together – they have the confidence to be able to play around the music. It's the difference between something nailed or riveted together and something that has an organic and natural flow to it. I'm not talking about improvised jazz here. This applies to a three-piece banging out a traditional 1-4-5 chord sequence to a Bo Diddley beat as much as it does to an improvised jazz orchestra.

If anything, it applies more.

Give your music flow and intrigue and space – and all of those elements come from playing together again, and again, and again – and you make it much more alluring to the listener.

It's common sense. Doing something frequently makes you better at it. A large part of the most exciting rock 'n' roll is instinct but practising gives you the freedom to trust your instincts, to let them flow. Don't fool yourself that hard work is the antithesis of the rock 'n' roll spirit. It makes it more easily summonable. And invoking spirit is what it's all about.

How frequently should you rehearse?

This very much depends on how good you are and how long you've been playing music. Seasoned veterans can shake any rust out of their system astonishingly quickly. It surprises me how much even I can remember of pieces of music that I learnt, or wrote, twenty years ago and have rarely – if ever – played in the interim. And my memory, generally, isn't great. I would forget your name five minutes after meeting you, and frequently forget my own PIN number.

The musical memories are stowed deeply and accurately because I was practising all the time – initially for the joy of it, then, in the final months, out of some soul-sapping desperation and sense of duty.

In those early years, it didn't feel like practising. It felt like fun – probably the best fun I've ever had. If you love what you do, and that's key to you deriving satisfaction out of music, you won't even need to ask a question like: *how frequently should you rehearse?*

So at some point we lost the fun. I think we worked too hard and spent too much time in a freezing room trying to chase down an inspiration that had long since bolted. Beware of doing that. *Commandment no. 4 is 'thou shalt have fun'.*

What should you rehearse?

Music Box is used by everyone from bands taking their first tentative steps to international, touring artists like Manic Street Preachers.

Band Practise

If you're writing new material as a band where it's an open forum then there will certain things you would hope to achieve in whatever timeframe has been set.

If you're a solo artist rehearsing with a backing band then getting your message across as clearly as possible will be the focus.

If you're rehearsing for a tour or a gig then focusing on the performance side and making sure it becomes second nature would be a focus, if it were me.

Mark Foley, Music Box, Cardiff

So, if you have a big gig or a series of gigs coming up, it's common sense to use rehearsal time to refine your set. Work on the shape of it. Great, memorable gigs have a beginning, a middle and an end. If you know your songs well, you'll know where they fit in the set. There's generally something a little disappointing when you watch a band busk their setlist, stopping after every song and interrupting the flow while they deliberate, or argue over, what to play next.

You can add spontaneity to a structured set in the moment itself – for example, if someone requests a song that isn't in the setlist but that you're happy to play. I'd advise against making the structure entirely spontaneous but, there isn't, of course, any hard fast rule. I imagine Jonathan Richman busked every one of his gigs, very much in the moment, and that has made him one of rock 'n' roll's most idiosyncratic performers. At the other end of the spectrum, Muse – who I saw in Madison Square Garden in 2013 – gave the impression, with their spectacular, programmed lightshow, that they're about as spontaneous as a tax deadline. With a few more fireworks involved. OK, a *lot* more fireworks involved.

One of the advantages to practising a set from start to finish is that things like switching sounds on guitars and keyboards become second nature. If the drummer sings backing vocals on the third song in the set, that means they know to swing the boom mic around after the second song has finished. Drummers need all of the cues they can get.

Can I take this opportunity to implore you to always think twice, if not twenty-twice, about including that new song you just wrote 5 minutes ago in the set?

We all get carried away by the excitement of having something new to show people. It's important to be realistic, though. For bands starting out, and particularly for their audience, everything is new, anyway. Introducing a song as "a new one" at your second gig when no one in the room knows your music is pointless. In fact seasoned gig goers will know that this is the time to go for a piss or get a drink. The new ones tend to be the least well-realised. My advice is to only include new songs when you know them inside out and you can bring them to the set as rounded and well-rehearsed as the other songs around them.

I fully expect you to get so carried away that you ignore that last piece of advice. I will be slightly disappointed with you if you don't. Please do bear it in mind, though.

If you're rehearsing for some gigs, try and make the rehearsal area as gig-like as possible. Set up as you would on stage. Face an imaginary audience. Position monitors where you'd expect them to be (if you have them) and adjust the volume of the backline (amplifiers) to match your intended environment.

Volume is a key consideration. There are few things in life that come close to the thrill you get from playing music at an obscene volume. No amount of arguments about health and safety and db limits will persuade you otherwise. It's important to state that there are serious issues regarding permanent hearing damage and loud volume. I've had persistent tinnitus for twenty years because I loved volume in the rehearsal room. Make your own decision. I'm not your dad. But make yourself aware of the risks.

Also realise that – in the vast majority of bands and the overwhelming majority of circumstances – a really loud backline will give a sound engineer enough of a headache that they may just give up on you and switch front of house off. It may feel better on stage, to play with the equivalent power of a jet engine roaring through the speaker behind you, but it will almost definitely lose itself in translation for anyone in the room.

Practise at as low a volume as you can so that the thrill is still there. Being able to hear everything in the rehearsal room pays huge dividends for your writing and performance. And when you turn up to your local venue, and have your amps at a sensible volume on stage, the engineer will love you. They may even marry you. They will definitely turn you up front of house so that the audience get the full blast of your eviscerating power.

I know valve amps will only overdrive or produce desirable harmonics and feedback at certain volumes. Try and buy your amps accordingly, if you can. A Marshall 4 x 12 stack in the local pub is overkill. In fact, it could kill and prison time isn't going to do anything for your band's chances.

Some sound engineers will recommend that you angle speaker cabs away from front of house if you insist on having them loud on stage – but this reduces the amount of control they have over your sound. Working well and graciously with the sound engineer improves your chances of a good gig exponentially. And preparing for that starts in the rehearsal room.

Remember, if you can sound good playing at a moderate volume you can sound good anywhere.

Discount any of the preceding advice if volume absolutely is your mien. I appreciate that not everybody wants to be Bon Iver. Some of you will want to be very noisy bastards. Turn it up to 11 for me, will you?

Frequently a rehearsal room is the only place where you'll have the opportunity to practice vocals and harmonies (backing vocals) at the requisite volume over the full band's sonic assault. So defer to the vocalists so that they can hear what they're doing.

It's much easier for a singer to hear what they're doing if they have a decent microphone and / or monitor. Drummers spend at least a grand on their kit. A poncey guitarist may spend double that on a name guitar, amp and effects pedals. Singers shouldn't baulk at paying a lot less for a good dynamic microphone (an SM58 or equivalent), a decent, sturdy mic stand and a monitor. Mics at the cheaper end of the market will feedback like broken-hearted banshees. Pay the extra for something decent if you can at all afford to. It will make a difference. Read reviews online, but check out what your music making acquaintances are using, too.

And when you have bought the mic, try to keep it in a dry place when you're not using it. They rust and the foam inside can rot quickly due to spittle and other expectorated substances (yummy!) which effect the mic's performance and make it smell like Satan's arse.

Rehearsal is an opportunity for you to find where you can truly express yourselves within a piece of music. Push the envelope. That doesn't mean "make your songs longer and proggy" (but it might). It means, "focus in on what makes a song special and learn how to highlight it."

It's easier to do this if you record your rehearsals. If you've set your amplifiers at a volume conducive to a decent sound in the room, getting a representative recording of what you're playing and what you sound like shouldn't be too difficult. A phone will do the trick... you don't need expensive technology.

We should also talk about getting wrecked. I've known a few bands: some of the most spectacularly unsuccessful (however you might want to measure that success) were the ones who tried to live a rock 'n' roll fantasy in every aspect of their existence. Drinking a bottle of Thunderbird Blue Label in a shithole in Saltney, stoned out your gourd on Uncle Tony's homegrown skunk, may make you think you're operating at a similar level to Brian Jones-era Rolling Stones, but it doesn't. Most of the great bands worked hard and sober in rehearsal. The hard work enabled the twattish excesses on the road. It's no chicken and egg scenario. You may think it opens up new dimensions to your sound but those 'new dimensions' won't be much use to you if you can't remember them.

As mentioned earlier, as much as is humanely possible in this world of creativity, ego and over-enthusiasm, try to listen to the whole and not just your part.

Bring spares and any tools you may need with you. A fishing box with Gaffer tape, insulation or drum tape, spare guitar & bass strings, plectrums, fuses, a drum key, spare kettle leads, a spare snare skin / snare, WD40, a power adaptor, a torch, painkillers, earplugs, pliers, a wire-snip, a screwdriver, plasters (as much for blisters as any cuts), a pen and a pad for set-lists and batteries for effects pedals.

There's little as frustrating as a rehearsal having to be abandoned partway through because the guitarist breaks a string and has no spares.

Finally remember that it takes a lot of rehearsing to get anywhere close to being really good. Don't rush yourselves. And don't forget, most important of all: have fun!

The only constant throughout is the enjoyment factor. I learnt that there's no point in being in a band that makes you miserable, for whatever reason.

Sometimes the politics or the business side can take over so much that you start to resent it and that's when I tend to get out. Bands and musicians should concentrate on the task at hand and the atmosphere they are trying to create and not each others personal flaws. Easier said than done...

Mark Foley, Music Box, Cardiff

PLAYLIST:

Echo & the Bunnymen - Bring On The Dancing Horses
Jonathan Richman & the Modern Lovers - Ice Cream Man
Iggy Pop - I'm Bored
The Velvet Underground & Nico - Femme Fatale
Bruce Springsteen & the E Street Band - Born To Run
The Cult - Love Removal Machine
The Carpenters - Solitaire
Bolt Thrower - For Victory

20: <u>Arrangement</u>

I don't think that it's always necessary to have an instrument play through a whole song, sometimes it sounds best just in the one part. It can go away and leave more space for other things to take the spotlight.

Arrangement is about keeping the parts that matter and taking away the parts that, maybe sound OK, but are just sitting on top of the song and play along without really mattering.

Elliott Smith

If all that rehearsing has gone well, you'll have music that you'll want the world to hear. We'll talk about getting gigs in due course. Many original music-making folk deliberate over what should come first, recording a demo or trying to get gigs.

What should come first, of course, is getting good and writing as many great songs as you can.

Songs are your currency – if you don't have any good ones, no one beyond friends and family is going to want to see you, and if no one wants to come and see you, then no one will be willing to put you on.

That's an echo from a previous chapter, but it bears repeating.

Once you have your embryonic song, perhaps something you've strummed through on an acoustic guitar, sung acapella into your phone or a bunch of loops and ideas patched together in Garageband, you'll bring it to the rest of the band and you'll start to hone it. Perhaps you'll have a drummer to give it a rhythmic foundation; a synth player who'll bring some colour and texture; a bassist who'll provide bottom end and (maybe) counterpoint or groove; backing vocalists who'll highlight certain phrases and motifs from the vocal melody and the lyric.

Maybe there will be a guitarist who'll weld a riff you hadn't anticipated to the song, giving it an excitement and urgency.

If you're a solo artist, you're free to fulfil all of these roles, and more besides. Do try to surprise, or push yourself, though. Solo recordings can suffer from torpor caused by an easy consensus. Understandably, people tend to agree with themselves.

That can make things staid.

If you lay down a chord sequence on a guitar, say, and then play a bass-line that mirrors what you already know about the song – not just the chords, but the rhythms and inflections of the guitar line – you're in danger of flattening some of the potential musical charisma out of your arrangement.

Yes, things should – to an extent – match one another, but another player will bring a them-ness, a not-you-ness, to their part which adds another dimension.

Fight against autopilot at every point in the arrangement, whether you're in a band or flying solo. The opportunities are limited only by your imagination and ability. Mostly the former, though. Imagination counts double. Don't let a perceived lack of technique get in the way of a great idea.

If you hear a riff in your head, or you can hum something that works well with the song, you'll usually be able to teach yourself how to play it. In fact making instrumental lines up in your head, or by singing along rather than by playing your instrument, is a good way to find more instinctive, complimentary and melodic parts.

Fingers have a tendency to seek familiar places on your instrument of choice. The great classical composers did much of their best work in their heads, or on a piece of paper.

As each of you (or just you individually, if you're a solo artist) defines your part for the song, the whole arrangement will come together.

Arranging for live work is a little different to arranging for the studio in that you're limited by what you can reproduce convincingly, on stage. First and foremost arrange for the song. Every member of the band is working together to make the song shine. It's all too clear, and frustrating, when I hear demos that have been railroaded or ruined by a particularly egotistical band member showing off their 'talent' at every available opportunity, to the detriment of the song.

It's generally the guitarist.

Force them to listen to Hendrix's version of All Along The Watchtower. That's a masterclass of the understated flowing like liquid into the virtuoso and back again without ever detracting from the whole.

Don't use a lot of pre-programmed junk or obsess over guitars. Play it from the ghetto of your soul. Keep it cool. Keep it natural. Don't contrive it and keep it close.

Jeremy Gluck, The Barracudas

I feel fairly confident in making quick decisions while I'm recording and not to over think them too much. Does this sound good? Is it making the song sound better? Then keep it. If it's like "Oh, I don't know...", then let's get rid of it.

Repetition is a big part of music, but I like it if you

can change things as much as possible, too.

Elliott Smith

Less is almost always more. I hear thousands of bands who strum and thunder their way through a song like it's a race to fill every moment with as much noise as possible, rushing to the end as if that is the main aim of the composition. Fierce energy, power and volume are all important weapons in your arsenal — but they're so much more effective if they're used sparingly.

By definition a great arrangement of a song highlights the song itself. Usually this means the vocals but it can also mean the lead melody, if it's an instrumental piece.

Make sure that you give the lead vocal enough room to breathe. There are exceptions, where a buried or obscured vocal is more suited to the sound of the band, but they are exceptions. Shine an empathetic light on that vocal. That's the rôle of the rest of the arrangement.

Little melodic phrases that compliment the main melody elevate a piece and maintain interest for the listener. It doesn't have to be florid, by any means, just memorable.

Listen to Cat Stevens' Matthew and Son to hear how the main, vocal melody is complimented and driven along by equally memorable melodies on the harpsichord, the strings and the horns. It's a brilliant example of an arrangement that lifts and colours each section of the song.

Most of you won't have access to an orchestra, of course – but you may have synths that could mimic the parts of an orchestra, or you could just play the melodies on a lead guitar or keyboard. It's the quality of the hooks that makes them memorable, not the instrumentation.

A fine example of how this can be achieved in a more

raucous and primal setting is The Ramones' California Sun. Listen to how effective the lead guitar is in echoing the vocal line.

Listening to orchestral 'classical' music can inspire you to a dizzying array of possibilities in harmony, voicings, counterpoint (melodies that are a mirror image of the main tune). You can apply those inspirations to the most basic line-up. A lead and rhythm guitar, a bass, a lead vocal and some backing vocals open up a huge amount of scope for arranging.

When people talk about the most remarkable arrangements in The Beatles' back catalogue, they mostly laud the orchestration on Sgt. Pepper's Lonely Hearts Club Band, or explain how the trumpets on Penny Lane were inspired by McCartney hearing the Brandenburg Concerto, but instead listen to the minimal arrangement of I Saw Her Standing There on their debut L.P. It sounds so simple. Everything has its own space and purpose. Every part contributes to the melody or the drive of the piece. The guitars, in particular, are the epitome of understated rock 'n' roll: deceptively simple and punctuating and highlighting the vocal and the spaces in between the vocal. It's no wonder this recording caused such a riot on radios throughout the world. Those handclaps... so simple, so brilliantly effective.

It's also demonstrable proof that an irresistible explosion of energy is rarely conveyed by a wall of (just) noise. Other than a little overdrive on the guitars, it's an incredibly clear and defined arrangement.

The Buzzcocks' Boredom manages a similar feat. It's claustrophobic, riddled with frustration and seethes... yet, despite the frantic nature of the song, nothing is competing sonically for the same space. The fact that you can hear, clearly, the drums powering the track along and how the guitar compliments the voice, gives the whole mix a thrilling, sharp-edged definition.

And that (mostly) two-note, police siren of a guitar solo...

One of my favourite, most unhinged arrangements is mclusky's Lightsabre Cocksucking Blues. The energy of the song is, initially, bound up in the hi-hats and the vocal. By the time the guitars crash in, it's akin to someone attacking your skull with a nitroglycerine-filled wrecking ball. Which is a great sensation, obviously – although unlikely to earn itself a play on daytime radio anywhere in the world (except on Triple J in Australia... god bless Australia!).

Another of my favourite arrangements – because it's clever, musical and incredibly accessible – is ABBA's 1975 single 'S.O.S.' All you could ever need to know about the arrangement and composition of pop songs glitters as divinely as the spires of heaven in its 3 minutes and 21 seconds.

Don't back away! You can listen to it in private and appreciate its genius without anyone pouring scorn over your punk rock credibility. As acclaimed journalist and broadcaster Pete Paphides said on BBC Four's 'The Joy Of Abba': "you can drop the needle anywhere on this single and you'll hear a hook."

John Lydon loved S.O.S. The Sex Pistols co-opted the opening riff for Pretty Vacant. With, admittedly, more distorted guitar. A blitzkrieg-more of distorted guitar.

It's a recording that exemplifies so much of what can be achieved when you're working out how best to present a song. They're lessons that ring as true for Swedish pop masterminds as they do for E.D.M. evangelists, black metallers or hip indie kids.

It begins with an intro that leads us down into the melancholic heart of the song, a series of descending chords over a recurring pedal note on the piano, lifted by the arrival of the guitar. It's not overtly dramatic. It persuades us into the song, rather than trying to drag us along with it. By the time Agnetha starts singing, we're adrift in a stark wilderness with only her presence to cling on to: a perfectly sad voice singing a perfectly sad melody with heartbreaking clarity over piano arpeggios and similarly minimal and effective broken chords on the guitar.

And then that Bach-like fugue of notes on the Mini Moog rises out of nowhere and lifts us breathlessly into the chorus. That little motif deserves a paragraph of its own. It's complete musical genius and a perfect example of how even a great song can be sustained and improved by its arrangement. Play this song to yourself on acoustic guitar, or piano, and it's still a thing of melancholic wonder… but add in the simple, memorable lines from the electric guitar and the synth and you have one of pop music's finest productions, to my mind.

It has more hooks than Muhammed Ali in a Hall of Mirrors… or everything else in the pop music canon, smelted down and cast into hook after hook after hook…

Sorry, I do get carried away… especially when a piece of music is as perfectly realised as this is.

Listen to how every aspect of the arrangement compliments and highlights the song. The sun-from-behind-a-cloud chorus sparkles with acoustic guitar; the distorted guitar that gives the "when you're gone…" section a real rock 'n' roll drive; the double tracked vocals and harmonies that highlight the chorus; the phase on the piano as it slows right at the end.

The arrangement is as restless and unresolved as the song's subject matter. Nothing is exactly the same twice. It keeps our interest, even if it's mostly on a subconscious level.

It shows how the arrangement of a song should build, or have its own narrative. Even if you're a solo artist recording and performing very simply you can bring dynamics to your performance. It's not (just) simply a case of being loud or quiet: it's picking a volume and a tone to emphasise where you are in the song.

I refer you back to Elliott Smith's quote that opens this chapter.

How you decide to interpret or exercise that is, of course, entirely up to you.

Arrange your songs, and recordings, so that they have a shape: a beginning, a middle and an end. It doesn't have to be overtly done, or signposted. Even a 90 second thrash can have a shape to it. Shapes make things more interesting for the artist and for the listener.

A flatline arrangement will kill your audience's interest.

Great soul, disco and dance music will teach you about minimalism, bottom-end and groove. Jackie WIlson's ubiquitous '(Your Love Keeps Lifting Me) Higher' shows that the vocal can take centre stage even on a dance record. The backing is built upwards from that insidious and irresistible bass-line and the so-simple-anyone-could-play-it guitar riff. The horns brilliantly fill the gaps between the vocal lines. The strings do exactly what it says on the tin, lifting us higher and higher towards the end of the song. Bongos, tambourine, vibraphone all play in and around the beat to bring syncopation. And it's that syncopation that gets our feet tapping.

Chic's Good Times, such a full-sounding record and yet one that has a tremendous amount of space and clarity in it, also shows how powerful a weapon syncopation can be. Nile Rodger's guitar plays continuously, driving the song along more so than the drums. His trademark, damped, rhythmic style, flirting with the off-beat is both simple, complex and signature. If you have something unique in your sound, make sure your arrangements show it off, but only if it compliments the song.

I could list hundreds more songs and records, here. This chapter would stretch until the end of time itself. Soundtrack'd be good, though.

I picked songs that are, other than the mclusky one, pretty well-known and easy to hear. They illustrate some of the different aspects of what makes for an interesting arrangement. The key thing for you to do now is to listen to your own favourite songs and try to fathom what it is about the way they've been arranged that highlights the song's strengths.

As with many of the more subjective topics in this book, this advice isn't something I'd want you to have at the forefront of your mind when you're performing, practising or recording a song. Absorb the fundamentals and allow them to become second nature.

Yes, there's an awful lot to be said for just plugging in and bashing away. We shouldn't forget the importance of gut instinct and the thrill of noise-for-noise's sake.

The thing is, you don't have to adopt the same philosophy for every arrangement, in fact I'd recommend that you don't. Whatever the song calls for, invest yourselves as deeply and as convincingly in it as you can.

If you want the song to be unhinged, unscrew your hinges, cast them aside, and go to whatever sonic extremities are required to fully realise your vision.

If you want the song to be crafted and considered, filled with musical delights and surprises, map it out. Paint it in your mind, seek out the places where it gets a little grey and illuminate them with more interesting detail.

There is no point in half-measures. Too frequently, subtlety becomes a by-word for bland.

If you serve the mood and atmosphere of the song well, you will make better recordings.

Arrangement

Ah, recording…

PLAYLIST:
Elliott Smith - Happiness
Cat Stevens - Matthew and Son
The Ramones - California Sun
The Beatles - I Saw Her Standing There
Mclusky - Lightsabre Cocksucking Blues
The Buzzcocks - Boredom
ABBA - S.O.S
The Sex Pistols - Pretty Vacant
Jackie Wilson - (Your Love Keeps Lifting Me) Higher
Chic - Good Times

21: <u>Trwbador On Electronic Sounds</u>

Very, very late in On Making Music's genesis (significantly longer than 7 days, no day off, no gods involved in the creation… apart from Elliott Smith), I realised that I hadn't, explicitly, spoken to anyone about technology and the challenges innate in finding the right sounds to work with when – in theory – you have a near infinite palette at your digitally-enhanced fingertips. Or analog-enhanced, if ancient synthesisers that don't speak in 1's and 0's are your thing.

See? So many choices…

Trwbador are Angharad, Owain and a fascinating grab bag of software, synthesisers, acoustic guitars, loops, glockenspiel and harp. They're young enough to get asked for ID every time they buy a drink and sound so unique and wonderful that I go into a meltdown of palpitations and hyperbole every time I play them on the radio. Which is a lot.

Playing them ruins my image of hard-to-impress, cool detachment, I can tell you.

Their imaginative use of electronics brings a terrific and revitalising energy to some more traditional, folkish and acoustic influences. Although those influences are an echo rather than a dominating force. This isn't folktronica, or whatever that heinous, compound phrase is. This is experimental pop music, and it's generally as hummable as it is ground-breaking.

Their eponymous debut album was nominated for the 2013 Welsh Music Prize. A promo of their second album,

Several Wolves, has been on a constant loop through my speakers since it arrived a month ago. They've evolved so much since I started playing Angharad's early, electronic demos on my show. Even then, her art was intriguing, unselfconscious and sounded quite unlike anything else I'd heard.

They agreed, kindly, to answer some of my questions about using technology to make their intriguing music.

Angharad, you've been making electronic music since you were very young... what inspired you to do that? How did you make your earliest electronic forays?

As a kid my favourite video games were MTV Music Maker and Pop Star Maker on the original Playstation and I was always interested in production, so I saved up and bought Logic pro 8 and an Apple Mac when I was 17. I didn't go out much and didn't watch TV, so I used to stay in my room, chain smoke fags and drink cider on Logic and then show the tunes to my friends.

Owain, you're a wonderful guitarist, did you come to synths and technology well after you'd learnt the guitar. How do you think that may have influenced your approach?

Thanks Adam. I've been playing guitar on and off since I was in primary school. I came to use synths after the boom in software instruments around the mid to late 00's, when my tutor at college handed me a load on a CD-R. They've definitely given me something else to work from and have opened up more sonic territory. I still usually have parts written on guitar first, though, and then later they become synth riffs instead.

With reference, particularly, to your V.S.T's, synths and plug-ins, how do you find the sounds that you use?

We often hear sounds we like on other records and try to see if we can get close to those sounds through a mixture of hardware and software plug-ins, and some trial and error. When we get a new tool we also play around with it for a while and see what it makes possible, then try and run with any ideas that come from that.

Are you careful to try to pick sounds that haven't been worn thin by overuse, or is it handy to use recognisable sounds, sometimes, to 'place' a piece of music?

Because it's pop music we think It's handy for us to make clear references to styles and genres that influence us, so we know what we're making and how to place it / carry it forward. We're also very keen on experimenting with new ways of making sounds that excite us and figuring out how to incorporate them. It's very hit or miss but the two approaches combined usually means we end up with music that we understand but that also interests us in some way.

How frequently do your songs come directly out from sounds you stumble across and then get inspired by (as opposed to pieces you've composed in a more traditional way on the guitar)?

Owain: *This virtually never happens at the moment because Angharad has lost Logic on her studio set-up and I've only been using guitars and synths for the last year. While making our first record there were a lot of tracks being built around samples and sequencer flow. This is something that will creep back into our work, though, because Angharad is going to get set up again with a studio system and I've started messing around with hardware* *samplers.*

Is it important to experiment or allow yourselves to make mistakes when you make sounds?

We enjoy experimenting. It's something built in to the idea behind what we do. It sometimes makes things harder, though, and requires a lot of time and patience because 80% of what comes out has to be discarded. Happy mistakes are great things. They usually happen late at night when we're far too tired to know what were doing and can never be recreated, so it's very important to go with it.

What is your favourite piece of kit, currently, to get your creative juices flowing?

Angharad: *Looping for me really seems to work. I make loops and vocal hooks on my phone and then bring them to the table and we build them into songs. Playing harp is something I also use to come up with hooks or melody lines.*

Owain: *My mobile phone has been great because now when I'm walking or driving somewhere, I can quickly record a voice memo of an idea. My main piece of kit, though, is a synth called the Analog 4. It's done every synth part on the new record and we've consequently sold every other synth we owned. It's just a synth monster in so many ways.*

Is technology something that you have a particular fascination with? Or is it just a tool to get you closer to the sounds you want?

Angharad: *My fascination with technology is up and down and bounces back and forth between acoustic interests. I* *think you need a balance of the two.*

Owain: *There's definitely a power in using technology for sounds. It opens up a whole new world of noises and possible reactions, but you lose a certain 'real world' human relatability. Technology is everywhere and all around us, therefore it feels right to use it for creating music because it's part of everyone's lives.*

What are your main considerations when you're choosing the sounds for one of your recordings?

Do they sound good? If not, do they fit the narrative and theme of the song? We try and get contrasting textures, if possible, and we also try not to over do it. Most recordings we make would have had about 8 tracks or so of takes and sounds taken out before mixing down. For instance on 'Breakthrough' there was a whole percussion section, but to include that we'd have to sacrifice some of the harp sound and we felt that the harp provides a strong driving rhythm anyway. Sometimes sounds are so powerful it's good to let them be and give them space – we had this problem with our synth, it's such a powerful sound that we couldn't really fit any other instruments in with it unless we cut away at it and let it lose its power.

The writing on your new album is more sure-footed than on the (still excellent) debut. How much of that is down to being more confident with the technology that you use?

Angharad: *I don't think we were more confident with the technology this album, quite the opposite, actually, because all the instruments were new and we were very lucky to be able to update our whole set up. While making the record, we were just learning how to use these new toys. I do have a better idea of what I like and what I want* *now, though.*

Owain: *A fair amount of it really. A lot of the sound of the album was focused around the synth we used. We also bought a drum machine before starting recording and these things all help the sound become a little sharper. We may have gone a little too far and based songs around the instruments perhaps more than our own initial ideas and plans, but it's all good.*

Are there limitations that frustrate you? We (laypeople) almost assume that music makers have access to any sound they can dream up... is that the case?

Angharad: *For my taste in sounds I can pretty much get whatever sound I want. We don't have access to string quartets or an orchestra but you can always recreate these things with samples and synths. I guess finding the sounds I want has never been an issue for me.*

Owain: *I'm definitely limited to what I sounds I can achieve. I think with all the software tools available now there's sounds out there that people can easily get that no one could have dreamed up. I'd like to be able to use reverb more effectively – I've always struggled to get nice sounding, heavy reverb. Songs I make rarely match up to what I have planned in my head before making them. I usually like limitations in musical instruments because I find it easier to make something when you know what you've got to use.*

Who are your technological inspirations, musically-speaking?

Angharad: *We're both really into Broadcast and their stuff with The Focus Group (and most things on Ghost Box). The way they make ghostly and otherworldly retro music that sounds current and contemporary is amazing. We've* both been into Diplo these past two years, as well. We love his sense of fun and awareness. The tracks are just designed for dancing to in every way.

Owain: I thinks it's the people building instruments and pieces of software. Using them to make songs with is the easy bit I guess. Companies like 'Bastl' from Czech Republic and 'Teenage Engineering' from Sweden all make such fun and interesting instruments that it would be hard not to be inspired.

Have you experimented with any of the multitude of intuitive music apps that are available, that don't necessarily work like traditional instruments?

Angharad: I have experimented with music apps, I use them mainly for rehearsing with or getting ideas flowing. They're great for planting seeds of ideas. I use some drum apps and a drone one. They're all mainly for jamming out ideas.

Owain: Yeah I've used a load on Ableton and they usually come piled in with Digital Audio Workstations now. There's some great ones out there, especially ones people are just making themselves and giving away free. Native Instruments have just released 'Molekular' and they've been pushing it all over YouTube. It looks ace though! Really easy ways to push and bend sound for fun through a series of apps. I think you might need to own a copy of Reaktor to run it, though.

It always sounds like you're having a lot of fun. How important is a sense of fun when you're making music with technology?

Owain: I don't think it's important to sound like you're having fun but you definitely have to mean what you're doing and be trying to communicate something. Fun's as *good a message as any! As is nostalgia or euphoria, and I guess love or revenge or whatever, if you're that way inclined. We always have to feel like a song is taking us somewhere and we're riding along with it or it goes in the bin.*

Diolch yn fawr iawn Angharad ac Owain. Both of Trwbador's albums are a rainbow of sonic possibilities, exquisite songs and, certainly on the second album, propulsive, bass-drenched rhythms. They're original and beautiful records filled with unexpected wonders.

I could try to recommend their music highly enough, using all of my favourite, clunky adjectives, but it wouldn't get anywhere close to doing it justice. Check it out for yourselves. Your efforts will be rewarded many times over.

Trwbador's excellent second album, Several Wolves, is out now on Owlet Records (8/10 - Mixmag, **** - 'Q' Magazine).

http://trwbador.co.uk

@Trwbador

PLAYLIST:
Trwbador - Trwbador (2012), Several Wolves (2014)
Cornelius - Drop
Broadcast   - Come On Let's Go
Diplo & GTA - Boy Oh Boy

22: <u>Recording</u>

For a band, being in a studio is the most cherished time that you can have because it's enjoyable and creative and miles away from all the industry bullshit.

Tjinder Singh, Cornershop

Dave Datblygu once criticised one track minds working in forty-eight track studios, so we thought that we would be respectful of that.

Gruff Rhys, Super Furry Animals / solo artist

Datblygu are an influential, underground Welsh band. Their singer, David R. Edwards, is one of the finest songwriters of his generation. His words seethe with insight, poetry and dark humour. The anecdote relayed by Gruff Rhys, above, is typical of Edwards' ability to stick a pin through the heart of a subject.

No matter how well you record your music, the most important parts of any recording – the creativity, imagination and decision making – happen in your head. If we get lost in technical details later, or mired in contradictory recording philosophies, do not lose sight of Edwards' baseline wisdom.

At school we had a Tascam Porta One Mini Studio 4-track cassette recorder. One weekend, Mrs Parr – head of music, soon-to-be nurturer of Coldplay's Jonny Buckland – gave me permission to take it home to record my tinpot band. Unfortunately the instruction booklet had been swiped. It bemuses me that someone stole that and not the 4-track itself. At about the same time, 15 glockenspiels were stolen, too. I still imagine I may stumble across them all, boxed together, at a car-boot sale in Chirk being flogged by a sheepish, former schoolmate.

The lack of an instruction booklet meant we didn't know what the hell we were doing. The Tascam wasn't at all intuitive. We spent 5 or 6 hours buggering about with it, trying every imaginable combination of button presses, but didn't record anything more than a guitar line, all afternoon.

This was my introduction to the world of recording music. That pattern of high expectations and excitement followed by frustration and disappointment was fated to repeat itself throughout the rest of my musical life.

These next two chapters are designed to help you avoid that potentially expensive disappointment.

The Boy Scout motto, 'be prepared', is key to successful recording. It's also important to have access to the right technology to record your music adequately, with someone who's savvy enough to know how to use it. That could be you, a bandmate, or a paid professional.

The 'paid professionals' wear two, but relatively similar-looking, hats.

A producer oversees the recording and helps draw out and capture the artist's vision, in all of the different ways that that is best enabled. The next chapter is an in-depth interview with respected music producer Charlie Francis, where he explains the role in detail.

An engineer is responsible for the technical aspects of a recording: microphone choice and placement, levels on the desk, equalisation etc.

Neither role is strictly-defined. They overlap and intertwine like a particularly incestuous Venn Diagram.

Whole books are dedicated to music production,

recording and mixing. I only have room to make the faintest scratch on the surface of the subject, here. Like playing an instrument there are technical aspects (understanding the technology and how to apply it) and creative aspects (making intuitive decisions to best capture a piece of music).

And like musicians, there are producers and engineers with very different philosophies and technical approaches. Steve Albini is renowned for his uncluttered approach to recording. He refuses to be credited on album sleeves as anything 'more' than an engineer and has made his signature sound the band's signature sound. Artists are encouraged to play live. He sees his job as, first and foremost, capturing them: their spirit and their songs. His landmark albums include Nirvana's 'In Utero', The Pixies' 'Surfer Rosa', mclusky's 'mclusky Do Dallas' and The Breeders' 'Pod'.

At the other end of the spectrum, Phil Spector's lavish and melodramatic Wall of Sound – massive, echoing, orchestrated arrangements – is as much a feature of his recordings as the songs themselves. Spector's key albums include Ike and Tina Turner's 'River Deep Mountain High', The Beatles 'Let It Be', George Harrison's 'All Things Must Pass' and the festive classic 'A Christmas Gift For You From Phil Spector'.

Albini and Spector aren't entirely different beasts; they both favour the sound of a band playing together, live, in a room, and both ends of this (somewhat contrived) scale have produced great recordings of remarkable longevity. Neither is right or wrong. Artists lucky enough to have the budget to work with a producer, pick someone with an aesthetic that matches the music they want to record.

Finding a good producer or engineer is a case of keeping an ear out for recordings you like, listening to recommendations (or otherwise) from fellow music-making people, and then talking to those engineers and producers to see if you have a similar approach and perspective. A good working relationship is fundamental to a successful recording session.

If you can't afford to pay for a producer, it's still worth considering your recording session as a producer might: bringing a consistent vision and quality to proceedings.

Some new bands think it's important to show off as many different dimensions to their sound as possible with their initial recordings, as if variety and flexibility are valuable musical attributes. Your demos aren't a C.V – they're an artistic statement of intent. Showcasing multiple genres or approaches will demonstrate that you have no focus or vision. Ask yourself how often you've had a good meal from a restaurant that professes to do Chinese, Indian and Italian food? You haven't. The 'jack of all trades, master of none' adage is applicable especially to music.

Where should you record? Home computers, some 'free' software (for example, Garageband and Audacity) and a rudimentary set of microphones can achieve decent results if you have good ears and the perseverance to teach yourself the technology. If you're recording solo electronic music, with little or no live instrumentation, you may never want to leave the confines of a well set-up home studio.

If you're a solo acoustic artist, and you invest in a decent condenser microphone, a mixer with a good microphone pre-amp and you can find a quiet room to record in, you won't need to leave the home studio, either. Initially, anyway.

A good, professional recording studio brings with it a level of engineering expertise that will help you achieve results to best represent your music. The rooms will have been acoustically-designed to suit different approaches and line-ups. There will be a 'live' room, with just enough ambience and sparkle, to give performances a natural, 'live' sound. And acoustically-treated 'dead' rooms, with little or no reverberation, so that sounds can be recorded as drily as possible. After all, not everyone wants their acoustic guitar or a lead vocal to sound like it's being beamed in from the other side of Wookey Hole.

A good, professional recording studio will also have a choice of decent microphones to compliment and capture your arrangements. This can make a lot of difference to a finished recording. Although a £1000 valve condenser mic can't, in itself, make someone sing better, it can bring a warmth and intimacy to a recording that makes it more attractive to the listener and a singer will generally sing better if the voice they hear in their headphones sounds good.

Different types of microphone can have a major influence over how a vocalist approaches the recording: if the vocal is quiet, breathy and atmospheric, that valve condenser mic will make a big difference to the sound and will pick up every nuance of the singer's performance. If the vocal is louder and more aggressive, a dynamic mic would usually be a better option.

In a good recording studio you will have the choice to find rooms and microphones that work for you and your music.

What should you record? That's simple. Record whatever it is that you're most excited by. If you can transmit your own enthusiasm through a recording, it will excite an audience too.

I'd advise against recording new for new's sake. Trust your instincts, though. If you know that previous songs you have written improved over time, or changed shape, give new compositions breathing time before you record them. If you're just starting out and have no idea what benefits hindsight may bring, don't worry about it. Enjoy the recording experience and learn as you go along.

Be realistic about what you can finish in the allotted time. This is most applicable when you're paying for studio time. Sometimes, because you're paying, it's tempting to squeeze as many different songs into the session as you can while you have access to the facilities. With respect, that's a foolish approach.

Recording one or two songs really well will give you a more enduring result than recording five or six songs shoddily. If recording 'roughly', or lo-fi, is part of your philosophy, it's still worth setting aside more time than you think for the recordings themselves. Great 'lo fi' recordings are about capturing a performance, generally live, with minimal overdubs. So allow enough time to nail that performance. There's an allure to first takes that rarely extends beyond your own pride.

Get it right, no matter how many takes you need, within a disciplined and realistic time-frame. Multiple takes of a guide track, or the live spine of a track, are a real option in modern recording, not just the preserve of disgustingly well-financed, major label bands.

Remember to label the takes and mark them out of ten so you can find the best ones later.

Once you have a satisfactory take, go for one more pass. It's surprising how much better the results can be when you're relaxed in the knowledge that you already have something you can use in the can.

How long you spend recording is much less of a financial issue if you're not paying for studio time, but I'd advise that you still work to a deadline. Otherwise you will be tempted to tweak endlessly, adding chaff to the recording. Each subsequent addition risks diminishing the initial spirit of the music.

The trick is to get a good, working, monitor mix that you can take home at the end of the session, and to sit on it for a few days, so that you come back to it with alert ears and hear afresh any inherent weaknesses in the recording and the mix. We'll return to this advice at the end of the chapter.

Prior to starting your recording session, make sure you know your songs well. Knowing the song is different from just knowing your part. Frequently in the studio you'll have to adapt what you play – maybe what you do live just doesn't sound great on tape. Live music is generating thunder; recording music captures lightning.

Knowing the song, as a whole, will make it easier for you to adapt and keep track of where you are if the landscape of the composition changes. Rehearse the songs until you stop having to think about what you're playing, so that you'd know where you were if you were playing it on a waltzer with someone else's music blasting out of the sound system.

Practise, in particular, the beginnings and endings of songs. Both can trip up inexperienced bands in the studio when they don't have the visual cues they're used to, to conduct them along. If you're used to watching the drummer, or rely on a head nod before thundering into the climax of a song, be aware that those signals won't be visible if you're recording your tracks separately from each other.

Set-up your instruments and amplifiers before you start a session. Check fretboards for buzzes and amplifiers for dying valves or dirty pots. Set the action and intonation on stringed instruments. Tune the drums. Replace skins where necessary and tape / pad them to prevent too much ring or resonance. Unless you want ring or resonance!

Oil the bassdrum pedal.

You wouldn't believe how loud a squeaky bassdrum pedal can be.

Teching your instruments during a session is a waste of time and money. Do it beforehand.

Build your recording upwards from a solid foundation.

Recording

Mistakes made early on in a session will have to be compensated for subsequently, potentially weakening the whole recording. You can ignore errors at the time, out of embarrassment (if you're the one responsible for the bum note) or in the name of progressing the session, but they will bother and annoy you increasingly as time passes.

It's much better to try and get everything as right as can be at each stage of the recording process.

At the start of the session this, generally, means getting a great guide track down (if you're planning to overdub individual parts later). Wet-nosed bands, over-keen to hear the fully-fledged result of their musical vision, can rush through the recording of the rhythm section. Don't. If you get a great drum take down, your recording will already be better than most.

Do pay attention to tempo. If you have live drums it is a shame to play to a click track because rigidity, whilst desirable in some scenarios (metronomic electronic music) can sap the natural ebb and flow from from your recording. If you're, first and foremost, a live band looking to replicate that 'liveness', then ditch the click track and try to get a drum take that encompasses the song's natural pacing. This is generally done by everyone playing together as 'live' as possible.

"Trying to capture the live sound" is one of recording's biggest cliches. However sayings become cliches because they're oft-repeated and have some truth to them. Many artists want a 'live' sound because layering each successive part, using a studio's multitrack capabilities, can result in something clinical, stilted and uninvolving.

That's a generalisation but it applies in many circumstances.

If the final mix is your masterpiece painting, then the sounds you choose are your paints and colours. Be imaginative and fearless. A lot of music sounds the same because people choose the same sounds. If you want to distinguish yourselves, try to find sounds of your own.

Of course, many music-makers choose the same sounds as their peers to fit in to a particular movement, or genre, so that their music is recognisable to the audience they want to attract. Pizzas are made with dough, mozzarella, tomato sauce and basil, just as pop punk is made with shiny, overdriven guitars, clicky bass drums and Blink 182 vocal harmonies.

People look for consistency with food; they revere originality in music.

Decide whether you're making pizza or music and choose sounds accordingly.

Original sounds don't have to come from inordinately expensive equipment, quite the opposite. Working with enforced limitations can make you necessarily more creative, sonically. And can improve your chances of stumbling across something truly original.

Synth pre-sets may help you sound like the flavour of the month but screwing with a synth pre-set, then feeding it through a broken valve amp and recording it on a dictaphone in a bucket of sand may help (*may help!*) you to become the flavour of next month.

You will already have decided whether you want to lead or whether you want to follow. The studio is where that choice manifests itself most clearly.

Blending familiar, run of the mill sounds is one option for fresh noises.

My favourite kinds of sounds are the sounds that you can't identify. I like to mix different sounds together to make their own sound. I find I really enjoy a record if I'm not sure what the sound of it is, because then you're not consciously thinking 'Oh, that's a guitar', you're getting the message of the music. You're brain's not interfering so much.

E, Eels

Whichever sounds you choose, if you're on a schedule, know how to call them up prior to the session. If you have a day to record a couple of songs, it's best to ignore the temptation to morph into Brian Wilson and order in a sandpit. Studios give you huge scope to make thrilling, new sounds – but have a baseline, working, sonic palette if time is tight.

You can add an awful lot, in the way of effects and eq, when you're mixing.

Lots of 'Mwng' is out of tune completely! It's not that proficient at times, but that wasn't the point.

Gruff Rhys, Super Furry Animals

There are few records I have listened to as frequently as Mwng, Super Furry Animals' wonderful, stripped-back 4th album. I can't think of a moment where it's "out of tune completely". That's not to contradict Gruff, just to say that – as a listener – it's not really evident.

Instruments slip in and out of tune according to circumstance. If a band are recording live in a hot room, with sweat on fretboards, yanking guitar necks and thumping strings due to the spirit and energy evoked by the song, it's likely that tunings will shift. In those particular circumstances, bent, dis-hamornic notes, vibrating on anti-nodes, can help to better communicate the spirit of the recording.

Can help.

But it's not something to aim for consciously, or to use as an excuse when the music doesn't warrant such leeway.

So, tune your instruments. Being in tune isn't a compromise to 'the Man'. It's not a fey thing to do. It's not un-punk-rock. Being out of tune doesn't make you sound like The Velvet Underground. It makes you sound shit. There is the width of a gnat's memory between charmingly slapdash and gratingly out of tune. If you want to aim for that tiny patch, when you're paying god knows how many pounds an hour, be my guest.

Out of tune instruments are my no.1 reason for rejecting a demo. It's the first thing I hear. The rest of the song becomes redundant, especially as it's so bloody easy to keep your instruments in tune, these days.

There *are* exceptions. But they are rare exceptions.

Submitting a demo with an out of tune instrument prominent in the mix is like turning up for a date with egg all over your shirt.

Having said all of that, don't let an inability to tune your instrument stop you from making music. Too frequently whether you can tune an instrument is used as an elitist test to see if you pass muster to join the muso ranks. I quite like musos, but I don't think I'd aspire to joining their pedantic ranks.

Tuning is only an issue when people record music that they know should be in tune, but can't be arsed going to the effort of tuning themselves. If you're making a primal, sonic howl, and your music is borne out of frustration at petty rules and bureaucracies (like my stipulating you *must* be in tune), then ignore me, ignore me loud!

In most other circumstances, though, if your music has 'musical' aspirations, tune your fucking instruments. Or die. Figuratively speaking.

When you do get round to making a recording, make it extreme. Initially you have to grab someone's attention. My ears will always prick up when I hear something leaping out of the radio that makes me think: "what's going on there?" It's not always a good thing but it will attract attention -- and once you've got someone's attention with that you can go, "well, that was that, here's something that's even better, you know... we've got these good songs in reserve." I think it's probably a mistake to waste your good material too soon anyway. Do something extreme.

David Gedge, The Wedding Present

One of the other recurring weaknesses in new artists' recordings is tameness and over reverence for the process itself, strangling the life and the spirit out of the recording. If you're tip-toeing through a song, worried about making mistakes, that tentativeness will result in a tame and insipid recording.

So, go for it!

You're capturing a moment – of spirit and vision – as much as you're capturing notes played in a particular order.

Put every ounce of soul you can into the session. That doesn't mean over-emoting, or ignoring subtlety, it just means bringing as much of you – whether collectively or as a solo artist – to the song as possible.

Make loud bits loud. Make unhinged bits unhinged. Be fearless. Be you. Be *fearlessly you*!

Spirit and atmosphere are the things that elevate a recording and set it apart.

Don't hesitate to sound weird or real. The other day a pal of mine sent me a demo his band had done of an obscure Stooges song. It sounded like it was recorded in an oil barrel half-filled with sludge. Lately I've been looking for crystal clear reproduction of my voice and words but his humble noise made me remember all over again how important to rock 'n' roll music it is that you can have the fidelity of a tin can telephone.

But I don't mean go and be lo-fi. We've been there. I mean go with what's right for the sound that you make.

Jeremy Gluck, The Barracudas

It's difficult to 'go for it', to be extreme or weird, if the process is new to you. Recording can be an intimidating experience, and not just for new artists. One of the most experienced songwriters that I know, a man who has recorded over twenty critically-lauded and influential albums, can't sleep the night before he goes into the studio; a combination of excitement, anxiety that the new songs won't prove to be as good as he hopes they are (they invariably are), and a concern that he won't be able to get his parts down quickly.

Mitigate against most of these nerves by being well-rehearsed. And remember, you can't expect to be an expert when you start out. That comes as you learn from each recording experience.

Remember to listen, attentively, to everything that's going on, as it's going on. It's easy to get drawn along in a session's slipstream, losing objectivity, only to discover that the session's almost over and you don't like the snare sound or the bass is out of tune. Be picky and demanding (but be civil, too). You're paying, whether it's paying money or investing your time into your band's own session. If you hear something that isn't right, now is the time to speak up. Good engineers and producers have pride in their work, whoever they're working with, but matters of quality

248

control are fundamentally your responsibility.

If you're paying for studio time, make sure that you leave enough time for a decent mix. A decent mix will bring focus to all of the good work you've laid down so far, weaving it together to best demonstrate the qualities of the song and you as an artist.

If you're in a band, it's important to approach the mix collectively, listening to the whole and *not just your part.*

Ideally mixing is done in, at least, two stages. A quick, working 'monitor mix' that you take home with you when the recording session has finished and then, after you've had time (days, weeks, preferably not months, because – by then – you may have forgotten your way around what you've recorded) to assimilate and consider the strengths and weaknesses of the recording, a final mix.

The final mix is the most magical part of the recording process, in that you get to fully realise, or as close as dammit, the vision you have for your music.

This is the point when you can start to play with your composition, working out what you want to highlight, what you want to sparkle and what you want to smash into the listener's eardrums.

You will, probably, have access to a bewildering array of effects, equalisation and panning options. Approach them fearlessly. One of the recurring mantras in this book is "less is more" but do feel free, time-allowing, to have fun in the studio and fun with your own music, even if that music is dark as Hades in a power-cut.

Don't feel the need to be too civilised or to stand on perceived formalities. You shouldn't be too frightened to reach for extremes or to try things that mightn't work.

Experiment. Again, if you have the time. This is another reason why setting aside more time than you think for fewer tracks, at the start of the session, can reap real dividends.

If you have a day to mix two tracks, you're going to have lots of scope to refine your final vision for the recordings. If you try to mix four or five songs in a day, your options are limited. Maybe that, in itself, will suit your music but even very minimal and simple arrangements can benefit from a patient and thoughtful, rather than a rushed, mix.

Try to do things in the mix that make your recording stand out, but things that still compliment and enhance the song, as that is frequently the main consideration when you're mixing.

Do not hesitate. A lot of the music I hear is competent, but bland and uniform. The recordings don't have the courage to distinguish themselves from their chosen genre, they lurk against the walls, tentative and awkward.

If your music is introspective, it doesn't need to sound tentative, too. Nick Drake's recordings are rich, sonically, and ring with truth. Way To Blue is one of the saddest and most beautiful recordings I have ever heard but it's fearlessly sad. It doesn't try to hide its melancholy. It's not embarrassed to emote. Neither should you be.

Have the courage to make your songs sound full of life in the speakers: whether the music is melancholy, joyful, vicious, shy... highlight the emotional atmosphere with your choices in the mix.

Check the 'eq' of the overall track as you go along, through different monitors, if you can. Boosting the bottom-end because it sounds amazing on the studio's gargantuan main speakers, will probably mean that the track will distort smaller speakers and cheap headphones.

Remember that the majority of people listen to music on small speakers and cheap headphones – deferring to them may compromise, somewhat, your audiophile vision, but it's wise to meet the majority of listeners at least partway. Don't limit the potential audience for your music by making it sound crap on the majority of devices.

Good studios have a choice of speakers through which you can monitor the mix. Take an .mp3 or a freshly burnt CD to a car to hear how things sound on much smaller speakers. Check the mix on a laptop or your smartphone. Alternatively invest in a device like the VRM Box that will simulate a range of differently-sized speakers and how they will respond to your mix.

A good mix is about balance, allowing each part of the arrangement to exist without it being drowned out or obscured, especially where instruments or vocals occupy the same tonal range. It can help to visualise the mix – where each instrument should be, from the bottom end (kick drum, bass) to the higher frequencies (hi hats, presence on vocals, guitars and strings) – but the most important sense to tune in is, of course, your ears.

Ears get tired easily. Don't be afraid to rest them when you can no longer hear the wood for the trees, or the fuzz guitar for the bass harmonica.

It's remarkable how a walk, or a cup of tea, can sluice your ears out and bring a fresh and final perspective on what you need to do to finalise the mix.

As a final consideration, during the mixing process it is important to have in mind what you are mixing your recording for. If your intention is to have the final mix pressed on vinyl or duplicated on CD (but especially the former), avoid 'mastering' your mix at this stage. Applying compression across the master track, for example, will give the mastering engineer who eventually works on your tracks less scope to optimise the recordings for your desired format. Please see **Chapter 24:** *'Mastering Your Recordings'*.

PLAYLIST:
Datblygu - Y Teimlad
Nirvana - Scentless Apprentice
Pixies - Bone Machine
mclusky - Whoyouknow
The Breeders - Only In 3's
Ike & Tina Turner - River Deep Mountain High
George Harrison - Wah Wah
Super Furry Animals - Ymaelodi A'r Ymylon
Nick Drake - Way To Blue

252

23: <u>Charlie Francis On Production</u>

To my mind, Charlie Francis is one of the UK's finest record producers. There's a great sonic precision to his recordings but never at the expense of the spirit of the songs. His reputation was forged working with internationally-renowned artists like R.E.M., The High Llamas, Will Oldham and Robyn Hitchcock. His expertise has, more recently, helped capture many of my favourite Welsh records: Future of the Left's 'How To Stop Your Brain In An Accident'; Sweet Baboo's 'Motorhome E.P.' and Shhh…apes' eponymous debut E.P.

If these are names that are new to you, I implore you to check them out. One of Charlie's great strengths is his ability to produce artists with wildly differing sounds and approaches. These three releases epitomise that rare skill.

No doubt his empathy with the people he records stems from his experiences as a fine musician in his own right, having played with a number of notable artists (Jon McLoughlin, Toyah, Bert Jansch) over the years. He understands an artist's needs as well as anyone in his field.

Charlie has been kind enough to answer my questions about the role of a producer. He did this out of the goodness of his own considerable heart. And for the vague promise of a pint the next time I see him.

What is the role of a producer?

The role of a producer varies according to genre, budget and era.

I could write a book about this but I think it will be more helpful to lay out my approach.

My personal take on it is that I am there to help the artist create the best version of their vision, maximising its appeal without detracting from its core values.

There are so many facets to what I may do on a given recording. They include any or all of the following:

* *Getting to know the artist/band in a way that creates trust (more on this to come) and clear communication. Helping to dispel any fears about the process which may hinder the artist and foster a spirit of optimism and a desire to aim high. Getting to know the music beforehand and establishing the desired outcome in principle. Just 'being there' for the person/people you are working with is incredibly important if you are going to collectively do your best work.*

* *Keeping in mind the motto 'whatever it takes'.*

* *Helping with song choice if required, then examining song arrangements, structure, key and tempo.*

* *Suggesting and finding any additional musicians required and establishing their rates and hours.*

* *Choosing and liaising with a studio or studios.*

* *Engineering the session.*

* *Working to get the best performance possible from everyone involved.*

* *Encouraging and supporting the artist where needed, reigning in where needed.*

* *Keeping to the budget and timescale agreed.*

* *Editing quickly and judiciously.*

• *Knowing when to stop.*

• *Mixing the record.*

• *Sometimes I may also play a part, typically keyboards or bass but also sometimes guitar, percussion, backing vocals.*

• *Having an opinion about the running order of an album. Very often a band has suggested a sequence which I think is mistaken, at which point it helps if I have one in mind which may work better.*

• *Overseeing the mastering process.*

When a band work with a producer, how important is it for them to relinquish a little of their control over the songs?

This question seems to presuppose that there is a conflict of interest between the band and the producer which would be a recipe for disaster.

The key ingredient in the relationship is trust – if there is mutual respect then control is not an issue as you will be working together to reach a common goal.

Most artists are only too happy to take intelligent suggestions from someone they trust.

It is the producer's duty to be sensitive to the artist and provide clear arguments for anything contentious they may have to suggest.

If everyone takes the process seriously, the final result becomes the only thing everyone cares about.

What – for you – makes a great recording?

A great recording for me is one I want to play many times for any number of reasons. It can be an amazing band performance, a heart-wrenching vocal, or a seductive electronic soundscape. The defining factor is a sense of something unique which also has integrity, and speaks to me in some way.

A great recording I have worked on is one which makes everyone involved in it feel like they have surpassed all their expectations and created something unique and lasting. If it is well-received and popular all the better! I like my recordings to sound as good (vivid, 3-dimensional, spectrally balanced, 'alive') as possible but it's clearly not such a big deal for some people.

How best to imbue a recording with spirit?

The spirit has to come from the artist and be fiercely protected by the producer. Things that kill the spirit are working to a formula, having rigid working methods, or working with a set of preconceptions which are at odds with the artist's natural direction.

Making it seem like hard work or over-labouring things can really kill the spirit. It's possible to work very hard but remain passionate and engaged, and have fun doing it. One of the most important and hardest things to do is to keep in touch with the instinct that tells you immediately if something is 'right' or not. Learning to recognise and protect that instinct is vitally important.

Should bands consider their live and studio arrangements differently?

I think it's sensible to do so. Sometimes people get hung up on being able to reproduce their recordings live but they are two totally different arenas and listening experiences.

An immersive record and a captivating live performance work in very different ways, not least being the simple physical presence of the performer at a gig. A recording can be listened to very closely and repeatedly – a performance is much more impressionistic.

If the record is seen as strictly documentary then that is a different story but even in jazz and classical music, editing and post-production are commonplace these days.

How well-rehearsed should a band be before they consider recording? Should they know their individual parts inside out?

The more experience, the less rehearsal necessary in my experience. A new band would be advised to be very well-rehearsed. Not knowing your own songs isn't too clever. Having a great part is very useful but what is also a useful skill to develop is being able to modify a part on the spot when necessary without losing the sense of performance.

Paradoxically very experienced and capable musicians very often come up with their best stuff in the white heat of the moment, and start to over-think and over-elaborate if you let them get bored. It's incredibly important to capture the first thing they do.

How does a band best communicate their sonic needs to a producer / engineer? Should they bring in example sounds?

There's nothing wrong with being able to hold up examples of things you like and it can really help define the parameters of what you're doing. The downside is the 'make me sound like John Bonham' factor which neglects the fact that unless you actually are John Bonham no drum kit, gothic mansion or microphone array will make you 'sound like him'.

I very often like to sit around with the people I'm working with and listen to a variety of things which might inspire discussion at the very least, and can really help to illustrate a specific idea. It's also usually a lot of fun, and brings out everyone's passion.

How important is it to record in a way that keeps all options open for the mix? i.e. flat eq / minimal effects

Not important at all. If you like it a certain way, go for it.

A better argument for not eq'ing is that there is probably something else you should do first – try a different instrument, play it softer/harder, move the microphone. A brighter microphone will be a much better option than eq'ing a dull one, if it needs to be brighter.

Trying to get the record to sound the way you want to from the start is a better strategy than leaving all those decisions to the end. That doesn't mean that there won't be a ton of eq used in the mix, however!

Sometimes an effect recorded with a part becomes a defining factor in the recording which influences all the decisions taken subsequently.

Having said all that, if you aren't experienced and someone else more experienced is going to be mixing the record, you will probably do less harm if you avoid eq and compression unless you're sure.

How important is 'breathing time' between a recording session, a rough mix and the final mix?

It can really help. Not hearing something for a week gives you the chance to listen to it far more objectively when you go back to it. I'm a fan of that.

What are the main mistakes that inexperienced bands make in the studio?

Trying to record too many songs at once. Thinking that the gear is more important than the performance. Not being in the studio with the right person to start with. Thinking that the flaws in your musical approach won't become magnified horribly by the microscope that is the recording process. Oh, and only listening to yourself and not the whole - a tricky discipline.

Given the fact that the digital revolution has enabled so much, in the way of home recording, what are the advantages of a recording studio?

Acoustic spaces for performance and monitoring. Good monitoring. A choice of microphones. Properly installed cabling, good headphone mixes and communication, isolation where required, a clean earth (less noise). A sense of 'the moment'.

What are the most important pieces of kit a home recordist can invest in that will give them more chance of 'pro' / studio results?

The equipment is secondary by a galactic difference to the ability to use it properly. The 'pro result' is more about the working method than anything else. Having said that - the right microphone for your voice (not necessarily 'the best' microphone) and good monitors which you understand and have listened critically to a wide range of music on will certainly both help. Having a room to listen in that isn't a small square box will also be very useful if possible.

The only criteria a good 'pro' would have for a piece of equipment would be whether it enabled him to do the job to the best of his ability. If it didn't, it's not good enough.

Find out more about Charlie Francis' work at:

http://charliefrancismusic.co.uk

PLAYLIST:
The High Llamas - Checking In, Checking Out
R.E.M - Suspicion
Sweet Baboo - Motorhome
Shhh... Apes! - Painkiller
Led Zeppelin - When The Levee Breaks

24: <u>Mastering</u>

If you've written a great song, arranged it well and managed to capture its spirit in the studio, do please consider making the effort – or paying a few extra pounds – to have it mastered. From a non-technical point of view, mastering makes things sound better. It applies a quality control and consistency to your recordings that can be the difference between them sounding good enough to be played on the radio (for example), or being rejected because they sound poor, especially alongside the pro releases elsewhere on a playlist.

From a slightly more technical point of view, mastering compresses and equalises your recording to an optimum level for the different environments that the music will be played in, on your desired formats.

I asked a respected mastering engineer how the process, and his expertise, benefits your recordings:

1. Giving the song a final once-over with a fresh pair of ears for perspective. In a professional context that means the mix engineer handing it over to a pro, mastering engineer. In a home mastering context that means: put the recording to one side and don't listen to it for a few days, then come back to it fresh to make the final decisions.

2. Achieve a consistency across the tracks on an album or EP.

3. Get a balanced sound that translates across all listening environments.

4. Preparing the final music in the correct technical way for each intended format – for CD that means burned to a disc or as a DDP (CD Master File for online delivery to the factory) with all the correct metadata encoded, for download it means a WAV at 44.1kHz 16bit, for vinyl either get a mastering engineer with a lathe to do it, or for home mastering pan all low frequencies (100Hz down) dead centre, go easy on the top end and kill any sibilance, get test pressings and listen to them carefully before giving the go-ahead to the manufacturers.

For iTunes, accredited mastering studios can now deliver high resolution files to iTunes which will sound better through their converters and you can get the "Mastered for iTunes" logo when your music comes up on iTunes. You definitely can't do that at home.

5. Setting tasteful gaps between the songs so the pace of an album feels good.

Donal Whelan, Hafod Mastering

For digital releases, mastering at home is entirely feasible:

As much of the book encourages the DIY approach, I don't think you should be discouraging of home mastering – vinyl certainly is a specialist job, although I've done it myself a couple of times, but there's enough decent software around these days that it's quite possible to do it yourself for a CD or download release if you have a decent pair of ears.

Alan Holmes, DIY label / producer / engineer / music-maker

If it's just a digital release, DIY mastering is achievable with the right software and monitoring. I've been doing quite a lot for local bands and the results have been hugely satisfying. Monitoring has to be a cut above though – you have to know the sound of your room.

Matthew Evans, Keys / engineer

Alan and Matt stress the need for good ears and good monitoring (speakers). Both have excellent ears and significant experience of making records. They have learnt how to master a recording so that it will sound good on an iPod and a car speaker and a radio (in mono or stereo) and a top-end hi fi system.

In my opinion, the most important job for a mastering engineer is about the bigger picture – making sure the volume of each song is matched correctly so listening to the work as a whole is a pleasurable experience. And it's about translating on different systems... every musician will tell you "Well, it sounded amazing in the studio!! Why does it sound pants on my stereo???" ...thats where mastering can really help out; getting the balanced mix to sound gorgeous and exciting on most systems, from laptops to boomboxes.

Matthew Evans, Keys / engineer

Each of these environments represents the tonal range and dynamics of your recording differently. An iPod's headphones or car speaker will have a different tonal response to a top-end hi fi. If your recording is destined for radioplay[1], it is wise for it to match the sonic qualities of the pro recordings around it (especially with regards its volume levels).

Assuming that you won't master separate versions for each of these environments (some do), mastering your recordings will apply a best-fit-for-all-scenarios approach. If you have good ears and you're prepared to test your

264

mastered recordings in different environments (or by using a device like the VRM Box, that simulates a multitude of different listening environments), it is eminently possible for you to master your recordings yourself.

If you are going to do it yourself, the greatest danger to be aware of is over-doing it. Things tend to instantly sound exciting with loads of compression / limiting on them but soon become flat and tiring to listen to.

But remember there is no 'right' way to do things. The fantastic Japanese group High Rise use extreme compression and limiting as part of their sound – just be aware of what you're doing, and why!

Alan Holmes, DIY label / producer / engineer / music-maker

The most (in)famous mastering plugin is probably Ozone 5. It's a beast and you have to know what you're doing, but it is a very powerful bit of software. The danger is overdoing it...a little dab'll do ya! 'Louder' doesn't necessarily mean 'better', a tip I like to practice is level matching so you're comparing the processing fairly; that way you can judge whether you've improved things and then turn up to finished volume (-3db for CD).

Matthew Evans, Keys / engineer

Matthew also pointed out that during the mastering process, it's possible to encode a recording's ISRC code into the music. (ISRC codes will be talked about again in **Chapter 40:** *'Paper Work(s) - Making Money From Your Music'.)* In the UK, ISRC codes are allocated when you register your recordings (*not* the composition) with PPL.

Encoding that identifier into your final product, as a digital (and inaudible) watermark, helps agencies to track where your music is being played (on the radio, for example), thus making it easier and more efficient for you to get paid any royalty that is due.

Generally speaking, recordings that will be reproduced on vinyl should be mastered differently to recordings that are going to be reproduced digitally. Vinyl's eq response isn't the same as a CD or a download's eq response (which is, theoretically 'perfect'). Vinyl also handles stereo 'differently' to a CD. It's recommended that, for a vinyl release, you get your tracks professionally mastered to take these differences into account.

For example, certain bass frequencies on vinyl, especially those that aren't in the middle of the stereo field, can cause the needle to pop out of the groove on playback, making the finished record skip.

And it's not just the bass frequencies you should be mindful of...

People are largely aware of how bass sounds can cause problems in vinyl, but high sounds can be just as bad – they don't make the needle jump, but cause the most unpleasant type of distortion.

Alan Holmes, DIY label / producer / engineer / music-maker

If there are problems with the finished records that mean they sound unsatisfactory to your customers, or don't play all the way through without skipping, it will result in returned records, potential refunds, and damage to your label's reputation.

Please note that mastering engineers prefer your

recordings to be submitted minus any previously applied 'mastering' – i.e. compression / limiting or equalisation processing the final mixdown. Mastering something that has already had the dynamics smoothed out of it gives the engineers less scope to optimise your recordings. Their knowledge and equipment will produce results that should be exponentially better than Garageband, say.

Be especially mindful to send tracks with no limiting. Also get a proper mastering engineer to cut your vinyl, don't just leave it to the plant. There are some very dark goings on in the world of vinyl pressing these days which explain the recent quality drop in a lot of pressings.

David Wrench, producer / engineer Caribou, Georgia Ruth, Zun Zun Egui, Gruff Rhys et al

Don't present your mix for mastering already limited (made loud), whether you're mastering it yourself or getting a pro on the case. For a pro it seriously restricts what we're able to do to it because there's no room left in the mix to make any changes, and most things that you try just introduce distortion.

If you're mastering it yourself then give yourself the best chance of getting a good mix in the first place by mixing with some decent headroom. Between 1 and 6dB is what I advise my clients, but we still get a lot of mixes in already slammed. It's very frustrating.

Donal Whelan, Hafod Mastering

So, submit your mix for mastering as clean as possible and peaking at a maximum of -6dB (this is 'headroom'). Even if you're careful to avoid clipping and max out your levels at 0dB in the final mix, the likelihood is that some of the frequencies will be distorted, or on the threshold of distortion. Keeping the volume level you mixdown to low (-6dB) gives you enough headroom to be confident that no element in your final mix will distort. And it gives a mastering engineer plenty of scope to dynamically process your mix, to give it the desired power or punch.

Considerations about headroom and keeping the recording as dry as possible (with regards compression and limiting) are worth keeping in mind right from the start of the recording process.

If you are mastering for vinyl, it is imperative that you request test pressings and listen to them carefully.

Play the test pressings on the best turntable, in the best listening environment, available to you. Make sure that the turntable has been set up properly, that the stylus you use isn't worn or damaged, and that it is seated correctly and plays music that you're familiar with accurately, with no degradation in sound quality, and a consistent volume level across the stereo pair (if it's a stereo recording). Damaged, bent styluses tend to reproduce one channel of the recording more loudly than the other. Listen out for this before you assess your test pressing.

When you're satisfied that your set-up will reproduce the test pressing accurately, play it and listen carefully to make sure that every part of the recording is present and correct. Phase issues can cancel out and seemingly 'delete' important parts of the arrangement. Listen out for distortion that may be apparent at low volume at the extremes of the frequency range.

If the test pressing is a faithful reproduction of your master, all is well and the pressing can go ahead. If you have any problems, or misgivings whatsoever, contact the pressing plant and / or the mastering engineer and explain what they are. These are best presented with as much specificity as possible: i.e. *hi-hat sounds splashy and distorted from 0'48 onwards. Main vocal isn't a present as it sounded on our final mix.*

You don't need to be able to talk in terms of specific frequencies. Competent engineers will know where to listen out for splashiness, distortion, (lack of) presence etc.

With vinyl, always get a test pressing and listen to it on a good system. Listen out for buildup of hiss which shouldn't be there (this has happened twice for me in the last week and is down to something called a separation issue when they are growing the negative), and for squashed or overly sibilant 's' sounds. If you want to be really sure the pressing is ok, get your mastering engineer to cut an acetate for you to hear first.

David Wrench, producer / engineer Caribou, Georgia Ruth, Zun Zun Egui, Gruff Rhys et al

This advice is especially pertinent if you are planning to self release your records (see **Chapter 41:** *'DIY Releases'* for more information on that subject) but having your recordings mastered well also improves CD and other digital releases.

I'll leave the penultimate words to Alan Holmes. They're pertinent and wise...

No amount of professional mastering can make a shit song sound good.

Alan Holmes, DIY label / producer / engineer / music-maker

So now, having mastered your recordings and preserved your sonic vision for eternity, you'll want to know what to do with it next, won't you?

[1]*If your recording is destined for radioplay* - since the growth in use of the BBC's iPlayer radio-on-demand service, mastering – even on a rudimentary level – has become more important for (BBC) radio. When people listened to my show exclusively via the FM or AM signal, everything we broadcast (unmastered demos included) went through the eye-wateringly expensive Optimod compressors we use to process and 'master' the signal for radio transmission (smooth out any peaks, lift any quiet sections so that people don't think their radio has broken or lost signal). The iPlayer broadcast doesn't go through those same compressors. An unmastered demo can, therefore, sound awful in comparison to a pro recording.

USEFUL LINKS:

http://www.masteringworld.com

http://www.hafodmastering.co.uk

http://www.brynderwen.co.uk

https://www.facebook.com/BrissettMusic

PLAYLIST:
Ectogram - Dancing At Sparrows
Keys - Bad Girls
HIGH RISE - Whirl
Caribou - Can't Do Without You
Mowbird - HAHO

25: <u>What Next?</u>

We've never really seen the point in just appealing to an esoteric, cult-type audience. I think – without wishing to sound like a muso or anything – music should be about communication, so if you say something then you want as many people as possible to hear it.

Jarvis Cocker, Pulp

The music business has absolutely nothing to do with music. In my opinion, on the rare occasions that the recording industry has engaged in the marketing of something of quality, it's been by accident. In other words, the quality of the music itself was of secondary importance. So – conversely – if you would like to succeed in the music business: whine, flirt, dress like a bimbo, be a bimbo, be frighteningly ambitious and don't play an instrument and don't care about your product at all.

Caring really bugs them.

Otherwise celebrate your ugly, beautiful, hard life in sound and leave it somebody else to care about whether or not anyone else ever hears it.

Kristin Hersh, Throwing Muses / 50ft Wave

The autobiographical interludes in this book aren't here because I'm a rampant egotist, a radio presenter desperate to nail threadbare musical credentials to the mast in an attempt to elevate myself to the level of the artists I've subsisted off for the last two decades. Ah, OK — maybe there's a tiny bit of that going on...

What Next?

These tattered, sobering recollections are here because they're illustrative, mostly self-deprecating and, I hope, a mildly humorous yang to the remainder of the book's sanctimonious ying.

Nowhere will that be more apparent than in these next few paragraphs.

I started recording music 'properly' in 1990. In the 7 years that I was in a dedicated, 'pro' band we didn't send a demo tape out to *anyone*. There were numerous studio sessions in that time. We self-recorded an album and more or less lived in a studio in Blaenau Ffestiniog for three years. Yet none of that painfully-crafted music ever went into a jiffy bag to Creation, or Ankst, or Blanco Y Negro, or One Little Indian, or any of the other amazing labels we worshipped at the time.

None of it.

The gigs we got were due to word of mouth. I think our manager for the last year, or so, of our existence did send some tapes out to publishers and contacts he had in the industry, but nothing came of his enterprise.

The motivation, the desire, the belief has to come from within the band.

We had bucketfuls of motivation – you need that to spend a sunless summer in a leaky, chemical bunker in Blaenau Ffestiniog, concocting fifteen minute magnum opuses that no one is ever feted to hear.

We had a fair amount of desire, although not enough to stop us from deciding to get a tow-truck back to our local curry house rather than to our last, ever gig, after our deathtrap van fatefully broke down in Hereford.

I think we had belief, too – but it was a very provincial, localised kind of belief. For example, we believed, to a man, that we were better than Baby Milk Plant, another local Mold band, but most of that was based on their heinously awful name. We spent the majority of our existence working hard but doing nothing with that hard work. Perhaps deep down we knew that we'd be found out if we went to play with the big boys and girls.

I think it was enough for us to be making music, to fill our otherwise dole-drum days with rehearsal room dreams. Those dreams didn't have the audacity to look far beyond the local gig circuit. We suffocated ourselves to death in that rehearsal room. It's the only palpable regret that I have. And it does make me sad, make me want to shake 24 year old me by the shoulders and ask me what the hell I think I'm up to.

The primary motivation for this book it is to stop you from making that same mistake.

We were signed to Virgin Records in 1979 for a year: that was a real disaster. The accountants came along and threw us off the label.

We kept going and we always wanted to keep playing music, but those were the low-points for me, being on a major label. Maybe that's not a problem any more with major labels crumbling to dust before our very eyes. Which I think is a good thing for musicians.

When the music industry is in crisis, it's a time of great opportunity, for artists. We always treated what we did as art, it was never really an attempt to have a career, or get money.

It's more interesting to do what you want to do and not do what you're told to do.

When we were on major labels we went from brilliant, revolutionary punk rockers to corporate employees with the slash of a pen. Don't sign that contract! Please, please don't sign that contract!

Jon Langford, The Mekons / The Three Johns etc.

What Next?

It's fine, of course, to make music simply for making music's sake, and to have no over-riding ambition for it. However I imagine that anyone reading a book like this will have bigger ambitions. Identify those ambitions – maybe you wrote down your aims for your music as advised in **Chapter 1:** *'No Rules'*? – and do not shirk from trying to fulfil them. Particularly, do not delude yourself as to what you should be doing to achieve them.

I wanted to be in a big, touring band, living off music, being feted by journalists and revered for the music we recorded. I didn't have a lack of ambition. But I ignored, for the majority of my music-making life, the fact that I would need to send my music out into the wild beyond to get anywhere near achieving those dreams.

I was waiting for someone to come and discover me. Even in 2014, with the multitude of tools available to music-makers that weren't around in the 90's (BBC Introducing, the internet, bandcamp, Soundcloud, Arts Council grants etc. etc.) that would be a laughably naive strategy.

In 1994, it was dream suicide.

The chances of someone – a sizeable audience or a record label – coming to find you are slimmer than a spider web ballerina.

Remember, if there are 100 steps to being No. 1 in the world, and if the first 97 are correct and the last 3 are incorrect, the first 97 steps don't count.

Kim Fowley, producer / impresario

If you want to be discovered, you have to put yourself on a map.

You choose which map. Is it the map of Worldwide Musical Domination? Or the map of Underground Acclaim and Artistic Integrity? Does the map feature the vast, slow moving continents of the major record labels that remain? Or is it dotted with an archipelago of smaller, independent islands?

Will you be aiming for the summit of a quick record deal or an album release? Or do you want to spend time in the lowlands, building up a reputation playing to as many people as possible first?

This doesn't mean that by aiming for a major label deal you'll get one, of course, but you have little chance of getting one if you don't aim high and follow your dream through.

Actually, that's something of a misnomer.

If you're young, good looking, and the music that you've written, rehearsed and recorded has something ineffable, thrilling and commercial about it, the rest of this book is destined to be an untraversed territory for you. Stick a remarkable song on Soundcloud, alongside a picture that makes loins yearn, and the music world, and an audience, will fall over themselves to adore you.

I'm sorry if that sounds reductive or unfair. It's the truth.

Hundreds of radio shows, thousands of bloggers, tens of (decent) labels and live agents all have their senses finely attuned to discovering you. You will not slip through the cracks. You will not go unnoticed. There is no such thing as a great lost band in 2014. Well, unless the band lose themselves, which is an entirely different matter.

So that's the .1% of bands who have it all accounted for. The rest of you, the 10% of music-makers who make fascinating music that does much to improve and soundtrack many of our lives, should formulate a plan, of sorts, to get your music heard by the audience you desire.

What Next?

This is where chickens and eggs and which should come first can start to overwhelm artistic sensibilities. How do you write a band biography to get yourself a gig when you haven't got anything of any substance to put in the band biography? Wouldn't you be better off releasing some music to get an audience interested in seeing you live before approaching promoters or agents for live gigs? How can you afford to record that music if you don't have any money coming in from gigs or merchandise?

'What should we do first? WHAT SHOULD WE DO FIRST?'

Well, if you've followed the advice so far in the book, you've done the most important bit first, already. You have a set of songs… great songs… the best you can make them. They must be the best you can make them because you have also been your own worst critics.

Having great songs and good recordings doesn't just open up doors, they're the things that carve out the doorways into an otherwise obdurate, unforgiving and unclimbable cliff wall.

My advice is that you do a low-key, digital release first… a free download on bandcamp or Soundcloud, or whatever comes to replace these services in the future, and coincide that with a local gig, or two, maybe three if the area is rich with altruistic venues. It will help you to have a biography, a decent photo and some social networking set-up, even at this early stage.

I acknowledge that there are great bands who have 'come out of nowhere', bands like Islet whose initial selling point, beyond the originality of their music, was that they had no social networking presence and no one knew anything about them. That trick can only be performed a number of times, though.

If you want to try it yourself, be my guest, and good luck.

So this is what I would do next, in chronological order:

1.   Write a biography.

2.   Get a decent photograph.

3.   Set up your social networking sites. Register with PRS and PPL.

4.   Identify your best song. Make it available as a free download.

5.   Use any interest generated by the above to get yourself a local gig.

6.   Contact local press / radio / blogs to promote gig and demo.

7.   Add substance generated by steps 4-6 to biography. Rinse and repeat.

So, this is the plan of action that I would advise. It's most applicable to new artists starting out, of course, but the order of having a platform in place to share your music and communicate with a potential audience; making some good, well-recorded music available to generate interest in your band; getting a gig to take advantage of that interest; and then promoting both, is sound and logical.

You can embellish that strategy however you please, it's just a basic template, a set of stepping stones to get you moving forwards.

Don't strand yourself or your music, like I did. Have no regrets.

We'll deal with each of these steps in turn over the coming chapters. It'll be much more exciting than it sounds! A little bit of pragmatism now creates more opportunity for your fireworks to go off with a real fizz and bang later on.

26: <u>Writing A Biography</u>

You need to concentrate on being a great group. I meet bands from London and they come up to me and say "we've got management and we've got a press officer and we've got a label interested and we've got an agent interested... they're all coming to this showcase gig that we're doing."

And I think: it's all too soon for that. You're not actually a very good group yet and I think ultimately the first objective should be to be a good band and have great songs and good concerts and then the rest of it falls in place. I think a lot of people do waste a lot of time trying to publicise themselves when they haven't got that much to publicise, yet.

David Gedge, The Wedding Present

This chapter's key piece of wisdom is here: *a good biography won't open any doors for you but a bad biography can shut them in your face.*

The quality of your music is much more important than the quality of your biog (biography) but a bad biog – and presenting your music in the wrong way – can mean that your music won't even get listened to.

First impressions count. And when it comes to rock 'n' roll and pop music, first impressions count double.

For the remainder of this chapter, we'll concentrate on what makes a good biog and introductory letter / email. I'm not talking about a press release, here. There is a difference and it's an important difference.

Your **biog** introduces you to a label, an agent, a journalist, a booker or a blogger. It's factual. It's not trying to sell anything. Its intention is to provide key information about you as an artist: where you're from, what your experience is, the kind of music you make and what your intentions are for it.

A **press release** will incorporate elements of the biog, but it is much more likely (and valid, if you feel the need) to use hype and exaggeration to sell a release or a tour. The mistake that many new bands make is to write their biography as if it's a press release.

One is factual and should avoid the unnecessary and overblown, the other is necessarily overblown.

Unnecessarily and improperly bigging up your music is an obvious trap that you should avoid. It's not easy, though. Hype has been inextricably linked with rock 'n' roll since the very beginning when the singles charts debuted in the US and UK music papers (1940 and 1952 respectively). As the popularity of the charts increased, so did their influence, with record labels and artists realising that higher placings generated more interest and more money.

That was the beginning of pop music as we know it.

Music as a marketed item for mass consumption hadn't really existed before that. As it left the primeval sludge of sheet music sales, and rolled onto the land in its black, vinyl glory, teams of hawkers, salespeople, marketeers, DeeJays and general bullshit merchants were quick to follow.

Whoever could shout loudly enough, and with enough snake oil charm and persuasion, got the most attention and the biggest chance of placing highly on the chart.

And this is how the marketing side of the music industry has played it ever since. It's no wonder, then, that bands who've grown up in this ecosystem, reading hyperbolic articles in music magazines and on music blogs; who've heard radio people talk in exaggerated tones about the music they're playing, and who've grown up in the commercial (not) free-for-all of capitalist society, have been socialised into talking about their music in the same way.

We learnt a very valuable experience in The Alarm in the very early days, we thought we were the great band from north Wales and if someone from the industry came to see us, then that would be enough.

We went to the offices of the NME and tried to kidnap one of their journalists – Adrian Thrills – who now writes for the Daily Mail. We actually got as far as bundling him into the lift and it all got a bit out of hand and ugly. We got separated from him and Adrian Thrills ran away. We've never spoken to him since. I'm sure he hates The Alarm with a vengeance, and quite rightly so.

We were separated from him by a guy called Roy Carr who was one of the editors at the time. Roy took us to one side and said: "Look lads, I know what you're trying to do but you can't force people to come and see your band, or listen to your music, but if you put enough energy into it and if it becomes really good, and you let the music speak for itself, then that will bring people around the world to see you and that's what you should be aiming for. And that really struck a chord with us. It was probably one of the most powerful sets of words we'd heard spoken to us as a band. It really resonated with us. It was a big turning point into us becoming The Alarm.

Mike Peters, The Alarm

Ninety percent of the demos that arrive in my inbox are accompanied by sales patter, a biography that is like the worst kind of spiel you'd hear coming out of a double glazing salesperson on their first day at work. If, due to illness, they hadn't received the necessary training.

If you think that I'm exaggerating, try to remember the last time the double glazing salesperson told you that their unique thermo-tuned, aluminium and PVC light-directing, revelation installation would be the biggest unique thermo-tuned, aluminium and PVC, light-directing, revelation installation in The World come next month, and you'd better get that unique thermo-tuned, aluminium and PVC, light-directing, revelation installation NOW so that you wouldn't look stupid for turning it down, like the guy who rejected THE BEATLES.

Neither is the double glazing salesperson likely to threaten you with an exclusive: "if you don't take our unique thermo-tuned, aluminium and PVC, light-directing, revelation installation RIGHT NOW, I'll give it to your competitor down the road and they will become the coolest kid on the road and everyone will laugh at you for being a past-it loser."

It's also rare for double glazing salespeople to claim that they have the finest and most unique thermo-tuned, aluminium and PVC, light-directing, revelation installation when, in reality, all they have to offer you is a hole for your wall.

"It's a bit of a rough hole because the singer had a sore throat that day and we had to record it in a biscuit tin but if you can hear beyond the pneumatic drill and the out of tune universe in the background, it's definitely a worldwide hit. We're free next week, if you want to give Pharrell a call."

Generally when a band writes its own biography, the outcome is as successful as when toddlers are allowed to build their own bonfires.

This is because bands don't really like writing their own biographies. Those that do – the ones who pen reams and reams of self-satisfied, clever-dick bilge – are always... that's *always*... rubbish. I can't think of a single occasion when this rule of thumb has been disproven. The length of an unknown band's biog is in inverse proportion to the quality of the music.

Music-makers who haven't done much of note feel an understandable need to flesh out their biographies with trivialities but here's the irony: people on the look out for interesting new music tend to *prefer* a band with little or no backstory.

There's an allure for a record label in bringing a great, hitherto unheralded band into the world; one that arrives fully-formed, blemish-free and godlike. Bulking out a biography with mundane details about your debut gigs in the Dog & Duck, playing Stereophonics cover versions, will make you sound moribund, not like the essential and mysterious future of rock 'n' roll.

You may think that providing lots of details about your band's history, and – as a soul-sappingly recurring example – the wacky musical tastes of individual members, will make a journalist more likely to write about you because you'll have made their job easier for them, but it doesn't work like that. That's not how good writers work.

Keep the biog tight. Leave scope for labels to imagine what they can do with you (they're creative and imaginative people, too). Reveal just enough of your story for a blogger or journalist to want to ask more questions. Feature details that a DJ can wrap around the broadcast of one of your songs so that they sound authoritative. DJ's love to sound authoritative. Although my knowing that may surprise those of you who have heard my radio show.

As your biography represents your art, it's important for it to have a similar attention to detail as the music itself. If the biog is long-winded and error-strewn, it's a safe bet that the music will be too. When a venue owner or a label manager has a couple of hundred demos to listen to, that impression can dictate whether your music get listened to or not.

Writing A Biography

It's worth imagining who you're sending your music to and their situation when they receive it.

Your biog is your 'Welcome' mat to all manner of influential music people, including promoters. One of the promoters I spoke to while researching On Making Music thought it would be more useful for you if they were entirely honest, warts and all. All hail the Anonymous Promoter…

Having a good biography is majorly important. It is your musical CV and should be well-written, informative and interesting.

One major factor I would suggest to bands when compiling this is to make the first paragraph usable as a short biog in itself. Again we promoters don't have time to write things: Copy & Paste is a good friend of ours!

The Anonymous Promoter

The people who run record labels, even the smallest record labels, will have a large surfeit of unsolicited demos to listen to. They're typically pressed for time and pressed for money. They may dip into the slush pile while they're making their morning coffee or dealing with housekeeping tasks. Listening to you is their good deed of the day, squashed in amongst a hundred other onerous tasks.

People who work in the media – radio / TV / bloggers – will also have a large surfeit of unsolicited demos to listen to. They're typically less pressed for time than label owners, but their time is still precious. They have deadlines to work to and an urgent need to find artists they can write about, or broadcast, who will earn them kudos. A large proportion of them are unpaid hobbyists and enthusiasts. They'll also dip into the slush pile in a spare 20 or 30 minutes. Or they'll set aside a morning to listen through the seemingly infinite backlog. They do it quickly not because they don't care about music but because experience has taught them that the best music rarely arrives from unknown sources.

Promoters and venue owners are in the exact same position as the above – with the added complication that they tend to be on a tighter financial reign and they're probably bleary-eyed after a late night, perhaps an unproductive one where they've lost money.

Into all of these peoples' challenging and time-arid lives comes your demo. A judgement about your potential interestingness and value (artistic as well as commercial) will be made quickly and on factors unrelated to the music. If any of the following challenge the patience or the aesthetic sense of the recipient: the packaging, your greeting, the biog, the format in which you've submitted your music, the validity of accompanying materials (photos, bribes, machetes)… you'll be discarded, ignored, *unlistened to*.

It'll be a reflex action for these people, not done with any malice but just because their instincts have taught them how to recognise unsuitable submissions quickly.

You'd be unwise to try and challenge those preconceptions.

Be brief and be factual.

Here is an example of a concise biog for a (completely) fabricated band. Rather than deriding the innumerable bad biogs I receive, I thought it'd be more constructive to start by focusing on what to do, not what not to do.

The Silent Atoms are a four-piece band from Cardiff. We formed in 2011. We play psychedelic pop music inspired by The 13th Floor Elevators, Love, XTC and more contemporary bands like Temples.

We've played sold out shows in our home city (including supporting The Wytches) and received radio support for our first demo on Huw Stephens' Introducing Show on BBC Radio 1.

The demo is available as a free download from http:// thesilentatoms.bandcamp.com There is also a video for the lead song, 'Crimpolene Factotum Hole', on YouTube. It has received over 10,000 views.

And that's it.

If The Silent Atoms hadn't received (hypothetical) airplay on Huw Stephens' Radio 1 show, and hadn't played any sold-out gigs, the first and last paragraphs would still suffice. You don't need to write any more than that.

I can sense your disbelief from here!

"Where do we show people what charismatic and cool rock 'n' roll mavericks we are?"

"That's no way to grab someone's attention!"

"But our bass player has a *really funny* nickname…"

Your charisma and your coolness should come through in the music. You'll grab more peoples' attention (and keep it) by being succinct and bullshit-free. Humour in a biography is as attractive as mouth sores at a kissing contest. Here is a concise list of other do's and don'ts.

Avoid writing about yourself in the third person, especially if you're going to ladle it all over with steaming hype sauce.

The Silent Atoms are the greatest band to have come out of South Wales since The Stereophonics and are destined to be acclaimed as songwriting geniuses.

The line above came from a bona fide biography accompanying a demo submission to my show. Any proclamation of greatness is naff, and that naffness rises to almost toxic levels when the line is written by the band themselves.

Writing in the first person (I / We) makes the biog sound more personal and believable. Whoever is reading it is more likely to warm to it than the supposed professionalism of a biog written in the third person.

Do include germane and impressive factual information about your achievements:

We have been played on Huw Stephens' Radio 1 show and supported Chvrches at their recent show in Cardiff.

Do double check that the information you include *is* both germane and impressive.

Our bass player, Simon, used to play speed dominos for St Cuthbert's Elementary School.

Or:

Daisychain played their debut gig at the Kings Arms in Wrexham and were so amazing that their fans tore the venue down so that they could each take a brick home as a memento.

What kind of a luminous dong writes a line like that in their first, self-written, band biography, eh? < COUGH! >

The biog is usually accompanied by, or incorporated into, an email or letter of introduction.

It's vital that you research who you submit your music to. Far too many artists make the profound mistake of compiling a mailing list of every music industry contact they can find, online or in over-priced, under-researched 'unsigned guides', and the like. Firing emails off anonymously, to all and sundry, without making even a token effort to discriminate between who you're sending your music to, will irritate the bcc'd recipient.

Don't irritate the recipient before they've even had a chance to listen to you.

If you're going to have the audacity to impose on a stranger's time, at least do it respectfully.

Research each and every person you submit your music to. It's of paramount importance to find out whether the label, station, blog or publication supports the type of music you make. There's no point in sending glossy R&B cover versions to a label that specialises in twee indie pop. If it's a label, a station or a publication that you're unfamiliar with, ask yourself why you think it's a good idea to send them music? The law of really diminishing returns applies to music industry entities the more removed they are from where you are and what you do.

Don't waste their time and, more particularly, don't waste your own.

Focusing your energies and maintaining positivity are important. The ratio of open doors to closed ones is dispiritingly low. There's no need to reinforce that fact on a daily basis by targeting doors you know will be closed or that you aren't suited to fitting through.

Most labels / stations and publications have addresses to which you can send new releases / demos and an online submissions policy.

Endeavour to find out what you should send beforehand – preferred music format (CD through the post / download link / attached .mp3 / via an online uploader system) / photo? (if so, what resolution?)

There are sites and guides that you can subscribe to that promise direct industry contact details for a monthly fee. Most of these contact details are available freely and publicly anyway. The problem with such guides is that they don't contain relevant information about the nature or tastes of the contacts they provide. They encourage a random, hit and hope strategy that *rarely, if ever,* works. Save your money! Do your own research, it will serve you better.

If you can demonstrate that you have some knowledge and love for the label / station / publication that you're sending your music to, the chances of you finding an empathetic and enthusiastic ear increase markedly.

Dear 6Music,

I'm an avid listener to your station (the Little Dragon session on Lauren Laverne's show last Wednesday was magnificent!) and I'd be honoured to have my latest single considered for airplay.

I think it'd complement the broad range of fascinating music that you play.

A download link for the promo and a short biography are attached.

Thank you for your time.

I look forward to hearing back from you.

Yours,

Adam (The Silent Atoms)

email@emailaddress.co.uk

01234 567890

Or a label:

Dear Shape Records,

We're sending you a copy of our current single because we're big fans of mowbird and Sweet Baboo. We don't sound like either but think we share a freshness and sense of adventure with them and the other artists you have on your excellent label.

We understand that labels rarely work with artists they don't know. We hope you like what you hear (download link and biog attached) enough to buck that trend.

Thank you for your time.

I look forward to hearing back from you.

Yours,

Adam (The Silent Atoms)

email@emailaddress.co.uk

01234 567890

The correspondence is short, clear and to the point. They demonstrate knowledge of, and enthusiasm for, the people they're contacting.

Other things to avoid in your introductory email / letter are:

Over familiarity – good manners won't put anyone off your music. I get irked by over familiarity, people who I've never met calling me 'mate' or 'fella'. People starting their emails with a cheery 'Hey!' as if they're shouting at me from across a hipster-filled room.

OK, I sound like I have a battery farm of chicken bones up my arse. A simple 'Hello' or a 'Dear', followed by a concise and factual biog; some words that make it clear the sender isn't throwing music out at random and has some knowledge of my show, and I'm *desperate* for their music to be good.

Making excuses for your music – if you feel the need to excuse something about your recordings *they're not ready to send to anyone*. Don't let your name become synonymous with half-arsed music. People will stop listening and are likely to mentally blacklist submissions from you in the future.

Desperation – giving the impression that you'll do anything to get yourself a deal / airplay / an interview won't get you any of these things. At least not for any worthwhile label / station or publication. It's a fact of human nature that the harder you're perceived to be trying to get someone to like you, the less likely that is to happen.

Arrogance – my favourite introductory email, ever, promised me a prominent mention in the band's future biography (book, that is) when I made history and became the first person to play them on the radio. The demo sounded like a malfunctioning 80's robot trying to play an unloved Oasis album track on a one-stringed ukulele in a discarded, rusty barrel half-filled with liquid shit.

Hubris in a biography is a sure sign of mundane music. Keep the swagger for the sounds. Artists who are justifiably confident and proud of their music say very little about it. They certainly don't have to tell the reader how great it is. Its greatness is evident in the listening. That's how great music works.

Misleading / tokenistic influences – try to be specific and honest about your musical influences. If you've been inspired by and sound like Coldplay, mention it. Don't –

out of a misguided attempt to make yourselves appear cooler – namecheck King Tubby, Husker Du or Stereolab – if those artists have no discernible influence on your music.

Also, avoid mentioning genres in your list of influences, but not artists or actual records... when I see a band do that, my tokenisticy senses start tingling.

It's better to be specific when you list influences. Anyone searching for a reggae band (as one example) is going to be more impressed by someone citing Toots & The Maytals, say, than just broadly 'reggae'. That reads as though it's undiscerning and ticking boxes.

I just had a band submit a piece of music and list these as their influences: "Electronic Music, Classical, Hip Hop, Rock, European, Jazz, Cuban, Funk, Soul, Blues, Tribal, Brazilian, House, African, Ska, Reggae, Blue Grass, World Folk, Drum and Bass, Country, Punk, Polkas and Waltzes."

Reads like they're more influenced by the rhythm buttons on a Casio keyboard than by the depths, shades and subtleties of all the music they list. Bionically tokenistic.

Mentioning previous bands that no one has heard of – this is surprisingly common. I think some unknown bands feel it gives them gravitas and heritage if they mention other unknown bands that the members were in before their current unknown band. Hopefully repetition of the word 'unknown' will have hammered home the cluelessness of this approach. If only your mum or your best mates know who you're referring to, don't refer to them at all. Past failures rarely expedite a shot at future glories.

Sign off by politely making it clear that you'd appreciate a reply. That's a given and doesn't need to be expressed explicitly. It's another fact of music-receiving life that no one has time to reply to all of the people who send them music, not even anywhere close if my experience is anything to go by.

Why else would I spend 100's of hours writing a hulking, great (free) book and still feel as though it would save me time in the long-run?

If one of the people you've sent music to is remotely excited by it, they will get in touch with you, of that you can be assured. If they feel you show some potential and would like to hear more in the future, they will probably reply, time-allowing. They may even offer some observations or constructive criticisms.

If you hear nothing, it's possible that you've been inadvertently overlooked. Give it a *couple of weeks* before either re-sending, or sending a very polite reminder asking whether your submission was received.

'Couple of weeks' is in italics to underline its value as good advice. Pushy artists who demand a full critique hours after submission will be ignored – or have their email address added to the 'Junk' list.

No doubt that curdles your sense of fairness – it does mine, to an extent – but this is the unburnished reality of the music industry in 2014. Yes, the power is in the hands of a sanctified, self-important cabal whose indifference to your music may drive you mad with frustration, but that's the way it is. Hopefully this chapter will have helped you to improve the odds in your favour.

That's the music, the biog and the introductory email sorted... is there anything else you should include in your submission? A photo, perhaps?

27: **<u>Pictures Of You</u>**

When we finally did make a record, it got favourably reviewed in the NME by Tony Parsons. He said it "made the Sex Pistols sound like Paper Lace". They needed a photograph to go with it so we constructed something out of an old coat and a bucket with a face drawn on it and they didn't really want to put that in the paper. So then we went off and stood in some trees and you could barely see us.

Jon Langford, The Mekons

There's a hot air balloon filled with irony in my trying to talk, with any authority, about band photos. I don't enjoy having my picture taken. I resented it particularly when I was in a band. I wanted our music to be accepted on its own terms. Most ugly buggers do feel that way about videos and photographs.

My appreciation of the band photograph hasn't improved much in the twenty years I've been making radio shows, either. I've spent that time receiving photos from artists seeking radio play, wondering what the hell I'm supposed to do with them? Show them to the microphone? Or do they think my loins will overrule my ears when it comes to decisions about airplay?

Maybe that's how it works elsewhere? It's the only possible explanation for Cheryl Cole, after all. And if that sounds sexist, I'd say exactly the same thing about Harry Styles and co., too. Their limited musical abilities are very much secondary to the way they look. That's indisputable unless you're a hormone-ravaged Directioner who hasn't, yet, progressed beyond Syco's siphon of saccharine ear slurry.

People who are good-looking get breaks in the music industry – in any industry – that pass the rest of us by.

I'm not beautiful-ist or sexy-ist. I am just evangelically music-ist. I'd rather believe that the interesting-ness of the music is always the most important factor, but – all too frequently for my liking – it isn't.

I do understand that my requirements, as a graveyard-shift radio presenter who likes to play odd shit to freak out unsuspecting pensioners on the Llŷn Peninsula, are singular. The rest of the industry is much keener to see, and to be able to show, those responsible for the sounds they froth over.

In that neck of the woods, looking good – being young, insouciant, sexy and having demonstrable proof in hi res .jpeg format – can be important.

Thankfully, in the contrary world of rock 'n' roll and pop music, strange-looking misfits with vampiric skin tones and heads as oddly disproportionate and compelling as the rock outcrops in Monument Valley can be deemed cool and attractive. If you're average-looking (and I'm unashamedly average-looking!), you're not a lost cause, not by any stretch of the imagination.

Just make sure you don't present yourself averagely, is all.

Rather like a bad biog, a bad photo can also get your demo chucked into the bin, with prejudice.

A bad photo has very little to do with the attractiveness of the subjects. Beautiful people are sinners, too, with regard terrible photos. Having eyes like sparkling, chestnut cabachons or hair as lustrous as a sunset on the Nile, doesn't disqualify you from soft focus naffness, or dressing up like you've been dragged through Top Shop (or Man) by a girlfriend (or boyfriend) who's just stumbled across that damning text message from her (or his) best friend on your phone, and whose revenge is going to be slow-baked, subtle and ever-so-embarrassing for you.

"Don't be silly! You look great in those faux leather trousers, with the Mickey Mouse slippers, and that luminous green, string vest on. Very you! Perfect for your photo-shoot with Acoustic Roots magazine. Of course it won't balls your career up! You need to make a splash! Yes, even one that looks like neon vomit on a Persian rug."

Having some sense of how you're presented, through your biography / photographs / artwork / videos, is important in the digital age, because all of these facets of you as an original music-maker will be readily accessible to anyone, existing at the same web-democratic level as 'proper', established artists.

Your Facebook page is a click away from Grimes' Facebook page. Or Beirut's. Or whoever it is that's flavour of the month while I'm writing this.

Although you can't compete with their stylists, graphic designers and pro-photographers, you can ensure that however much of yourselves you decide to present alongside the music is presented tastefully and with care.

A badly-lit shambles of a photo, where you're all wearing new clothes bought for the occasion that make you look like mongrels in tuxedoes, posed un-serendipitously as the camera goes off by accident in an Asda car-park, will give the impression that your music is equally as clueless.

Aim for a consistent vision across all different media, something that best represents you and your music.

Whatever mood is evoked by the music should be evoked by the biog, the photo and any videos you shoot, too.

A band who look like accountants, but who also make precise music and convey themselves in a business-like

298

manner have a 'thing'.

If you make moody and atmospheric music, and your photos and videos are similarly impressionistic, you also have a 'thing'.

If you're a straight down-the-line, classic rock band, and the things that are satellite to your music are also redolent of denim and Jack Daniels, you have a 'thing', too.

If you're that classic rock band and you look like a boy band – all permatan and painstaking, mirror-struck hair styles – you won't have a 'thing' and you'll have a much more difficult time persuading people into your world.

You don't have to adhere to stereotypes, but whatever you do to present your music, be convincing. A straight down-the-line classic rock band who dress like accountants might jar, but if it's done with conviction, it could be a heck of a 'thing'. Well, it worked for Dr Feelgood.

Sorry. Got distracted. Just spent the last hour listening to Dr Feelgood. What a band! And, as a friend pointed out on Twitter, they looked like secondhand car salesmen, not accountants. The point remains, though.

Be yourselves. If you're being yourself you'll feel comfortable. If you feel comfortable you'll look 'cool', or whatever the correct rock 'n' roll word for 'unawkward' is.

You don't have to contrive an image or sell-out. Be you. Be you. BE (really) YOU!

Who should take the picture or film the video? Well, everyone feels as if they're capable of taking a great band portrait. That's one of the by-products of the Instagram generation. So you may not feel the need to find a pro photographer, or a photographer aspiring to be professional.

You've got to have a good dialogue between the band and photographer – the photographer can't read minds. Meeting up beforehand to bounce ideas off each other is really helpful. Make sketches, bring photos for inspiration etc. Tell the photographer what trends you like as well as what you don't like.

Polly Thomas, professional photographer / pollythomas.co.uk

If you employ someone who knows what they're doing, your chances of getting pictures, or a video, that embellish your music are significantly higher. Good photographers understand format, composition, lighting, depth of field, tone, post-processing and how best to deliver usable images. A mate may get a lucky shot of you on their phone, and then apply a filter that everyone else is using to make it look suitably treated and 'pro', but there is little chance of that shot being scalable (for use, say, on an A3 poster or as the splash image on a webpage).

Trawl local photographers' Facebook, Instagram, Flickr and web pages. Find someone who has a similar sensibility to you... who's taking shots that make your heart beat faster. Check out photography exhibitions at local colleges. Keep an eye on the audience at your gigs, does someone come to see you with a decent camera, who seems to know what they're doing?

Of course, pro photographers will want to be paid, that's a given. You get what you pay for, that's a given, too.

Beware of offering photographers (and graphic designers, for that matter) 'exposure' for their work in lieu of payment. People in the creative industries hear that argument all the time. It drives the good ones insensate with rage, mainly because they know their work has been cheapened by the tens of thousands of enthusiastic amateurs who think they're photographers because they have an SLR or graphic designers because they have a copy of Adobe Illustrator (a cracked version, naturally).

Negotiate whatever suits both parties best, but don't be surprised if professionals expect payment.

If you don't have any money, it's an idea to get in touch with photography courses at a local college. Frequently the students need interesting subjects so that they can refine their technique and build up a portfolio. A free exchange in those circumstances suits everyone.

It's understandable for a young, upcoming band to try to forge partnerships with other upcoming artists, but if you're 30-something, semi-professionals with day jobs, seeking to exploit the cheapest option is pretty much indefensible.

Things to consider about band photographs: have them shot in landscape format, most blogs / music sites won't consider an image in (ironically) portrait format. If they function as a square crop, that's useful for avatars, too.

Prominent / readable logos, shop signs etc. could prove problematic. As one example, The Beatles' estate do not like Beatles imagery (album sleeves, pictures of the band or The Beatles logo) to feature in other people's (unlicensed and uncleared) photos, even if it's accidental and in the background. I have a promo photo taken in a local 2nd hand record shop and we had to blank out the Beatles' album cover in the background, to avert any potential lawsuit.

Any images with sexist, racist, homophobic or potentially blasphemous content (even for satirical purposes or to raise awareness about these issues) are unlikely to be usable in other people's publications. Rock 'n' roll has a history of challenging society's mores, but rock 'n' roll isn't an excuse to offend people for the sake of cheap controversy, certainly not over truly sensitive issues like race and gender.

Ask the photographer to compose and shoot images that will work at a number of different sizes and in colour and black and white. The moody, Anton Corbijn-like image of you all standing in a wilderness may look great on a full-size album sleeve, but its effectiveness will diminish at smaller sizes.

If you use a professional photographer, ask them what the terms of use are for the images they shoot. You may think you can use them however you wish, for perpetuity, having paid for them, but sometimes that is not the case.

There's nothing wrong with a smile. The majority of music photos I see are of miserable-looking bastards who look like they've just had all their equipment nicked out of the back of a van. Appearing pissed off isn't always cool. A natural smile, or the hint of a natural smile, may warm someone's heart enough to listen to your music in a positive frame of mind, or to stick you on the front page of their blog.

The littlest things can sometimes make the biggest difference.

Be creative. A striking and original image, that resonates with your music, will linger in the mind much longer than something formulaic and humdrum.

Of course, all of the above applies to videos (and graphic design and artwork), too.

However you decide to represent your music, have fun with it and revel in the creative collaborations you can forge with photographers, film-makers and graphic designers.

With a brilliant demo, a succinct blog and a decent photo, you're ready to take on the world. Who knows where this may take you?

28: <u>Social Networking</u>

Once upon a time, in a land very, very close by, troubadours and minstrels travelled from village to village on foot, carrying music in nothing more complicated than a lice-ridden head. Their renown was based on musicianship and an ability to learn the latest ballads. Like you, their mums and dads probably banged on at them about getting "ye propere job", but there's nothing like the allure of the road. Even one riddled with outlaws and lepers.

These travelling music folk didn't have to do anything to announce their imminent arrival in a town. Mediaeval York wasn't papered over with gaudy billboards proclaiming Blondel's appearance at the O2 Amphitheatre.

No one shared the event on Faceslate, so they didn't have the ignominy of 100 people chalking 'attend' but then only 2 turning up. If it was tweeted about, it was only the local witch who understood, on account of her ability to talk to the birds.

No one took a 10% booking fee for an automated transaction on YeTickets... in fact, tickets weren't sold at all; concerts were performed for food, splinters from the cross, a tankard of mead, magic beans and in the hope of a romp behind the haywain.

In many respects, then, medieval music-makers were better off than their modern equivalents. Although, what with the threat of plague or a pike through the throat from a Norman lord who wasn't so keen on lute 'n' bass, it wasn't all perfect.

Like Chelsea's growing global reach, Jeremy Kyle or dental bills, whoring yourself on social networks has become an unavoidable truth of modern life.

The internet has done much to irrevocably change the landscape and expectations for musical artists. Only 20 years ago, the cycle of an unsigned band's existence was: gig to make enough money to -> record demo -> send demo to record labels hoping for A&R interest -> send demo to local papers / radio in hope of growing audience to generate 'buzz' should A&R man find way out of London -> despair when A&R man (and it was generally a man) didn't arrive because he couldn't find his way out of London -> repeat until quick fade.

It would be misleading to suggest that bands in the 80's and 90's weren't autonomous and didn't self release or put their own gigs on, of course they did. Autonomy back then involved fly-posting, fanzines and fliers, three f's that have (some might say) been replaced by the capital 'F' in Facebook. Promoting your music – or letting people know about your gigs and releases, if you prefer that terminology – has been revolutionised by the internet. Of course, the internet has also eroded the power of record labels. Things are much more democratic now or – more accurately, given the ready access so many have to a means of production and distribution for their music – more Marxist, now.

But this levelling of the playing field has meant that, to be noticed, you have to make yourself heard amongst a chaotic and deafening babble.

Artists who rely on Facebook, as a most obvious example, to promote their gigs soon learn that it's an increasingly inefficient way to spread the word about what they're doing.

Everyone on Facebook is bombarded by messages and invites. Most of us reflexively hit 'Attend' or 'Maybe' as an automated courtesy, without taking in any of the specific details of the event we're responding to.

So 67 people out of 3,000 invited click 'Attend' but only 24 actually turn up.

It's worth remembering this example for the remainder of our discussion of social media. They are incredible new tools. They enable you, the contemporary music-maker, to do things that I, a seasoned old fart, could only have dreamed of in 1994. Our mailing list, as a case in point, took hours of maintenance every week. If we'd misplaced that one A4 pad with all of the names detailed in it, we'd have lost the entire mailing list, for good.

Every time we contacted the thousand, or so, people on that list, it cost us a veritable fortune. We had to consider, deeply, every mail-out we posted. Spam was an expensive luxury in the olden days that only the behemoth major labels could afford. And we know what happened to them and their budgets.

Communicating with your audience and promoting yourself, then, is easier now – but easier doesn't necessarily mean better or more effective. We'll get to that in more detail in due course.

If you use social networking in a creative and effective way, there's no doubt that it can have a positive effect for your music. There are even cases where phenomenally successful YouTube channels, or MySpace pages (back in the day – a key factor in Kate Nash's record deal), or huge amounts of followers on Twitter, have been instrumental in artists signing record deals.

My instincts tell me that any label, station or publication that is mostly interested in you because of numbers (of followers) are to be avoided. Their chief focus should, of course, be your music but it may be unwise to discount other factors that can get influential people to listen to your music, however vulgar those factors may be.

Pursuing strategies to generate huge numbers of followers (using one of the many services to buy YouTube

views and Twitter followers), regardless of their actual interest in your music, in the belief that those numbers alone will be deal-breakers for you, is unwise. Truly influential labels, stations and publications see through that ruse as if it were made of cellophane. And it has just as much substance and longevity.

However while I was writing this chapter, The Guardian newspaper published an article about how influential an artist's social networking statistics are in securing a playlist on BBC Radio 1[1]. The whole notion of airplay being determined by anything other than an artist's music (or demographic... I can see why station's targeting a young audience would want to feature young artists, too) is a depressing anathema to me. Nevertheless it's important that you're aware that decisions are made on this basis, if you aspire to receiving support on these networks.

For those of you who want to exist autonomously, and who aren't interested in chasing labels or the industry, social networking provides an accessible and cheap[2] conduit to your audience.

Social networking is also an accessible and cheap conduit to record labels, promoters, venues and the media.

It is no good having a Facebook page with no tracks, very few photos, no event details (past or present), no interaction and – most frustratingly – no biography.

We only need to hear 30 seconds of a song to know if it's what we are looking for and, in fact, decent. If it is then the next step would be to look at what tools you have provided for us to promote the show.

If your tunes have captivated us enough to click on your 'About' section and there is no information on your band, do you really think we have the time to scribble a paragraph describing your music?

Have a profile on every available platform. Some are more popular than others. Potential fans might be 'too cool' for Facebook but a whore for Instagram. You cannot pass on these free advertising platforms.

The Anonymous Promoter

Some degree of a presence on these platforms, then, is a pre-requisite for music-makers in the digital age. At the most basic level, that would be just a contact e-mail address. Many artists exist on a number of different sites, in a range of different media: Facebook, their own official website, Twitter, Soundcloud, bandcamp, YouTube, SnapChat, MixCloud, Vimeo, Spotify, iTunes, Amazon…

These are all part of your (potential) digital arsenal. No doubt the names of these services will change as the years pass and, no doubt, new services, sites and platforms that we can't predict will grow and be adopted by music-makers in the coming months and years. For example, SnapChat is only beginning to be exploited by bands as I write this and if I'd have been writing this book 6 or 7 years ago, MySpace would have dominated the conversation.

Regardless of the brands or the platforms, the challenge for you is to identify which of the available services will be most useful to help you raise the profile of your music.

A streamlined presence is more effective. Double-posting your content – hosting videos on YouTube and Vimeo, running a blogging site as well as a news page on an official site that mirrors the same content, that's also, probably, posted to Facebook too – is likely to reduce the number of visitors to any one of those services and to confuse anyone who's looking for definitive news updates about what you're doing.

Decide what you will post to which service and try to make each service distinctive from the others, according to their specialism. Breaking gig & releases news is perfect for a service like Twitter / press releases and more in depth developments can be posted on Facebook, or equivalent / videos to either YouTube or Vimeo / demos or new releases to bandcamp or Soundcloud, and – perhaps – you can amalgamate all of this output on a central, official website.

Given the very low signal to noise ratio on social networking (i.e. more chaff than a threshing convention, less wheat than a smallholding in Oklahoma during the American dustbowl of the 1930's), it's important to keep your updates relevant.

Provide enough content to maintain interest without bombarding people – like the band-who-cried-wolf – so that they notice when you have important announcements to make about gigs and releases. That's not to say that you shouldn't have a dialogue with your followers, of course you should, but perhaps more informal content should come from a separate source: an individual Twitter account, say, rather than your official feed.

It's a case, with all of these platforms, of getting the balance right. Of giving just enough away, whether information, music, photographs or videos, to keep people interested, but not too much to drive them away, or to stop the services from being effective.

Don't feel the need – in fact, be particularly careful to not – reveal too much. One of my favourite bands of recent years, who will remain nameless, had a garrulous and eccentric bass player whose favourite trick was to post pictures of himself on the toilet to Twitter and Facebook. He didn't realise that interested parties at record labels and radio were somewhat aghast at his behaviour, and subsequently didn't pursue their interest in the band.

As has been mentioned many times already in this book, and it's applicable here, too: *less is more*.

One of the truly revolutionary aspects of social networking, with regards music-makers, has been the level of access that it enables for fans and supporters. In the good old days, you'd post something to a PO Box fanclub address and get, if you were lucky, a 'signed' photo and a badge back, three months later, by which time you'd gone off the bloody Bay City Rollers, anyway.

I had to cool that paragraph up a bit. For me it was Brotherhood of Man. Save Your Kisses For Me still makes me go gooey.

Be as accessible to those who show an interest in your music as is natural for you. Some music-makers don't feel comfortable talking about the minutiae of their existence or their sounds. Don't feel you have to feign anything. Behaviour that's consistent with your music and philosophies is key.

A band like The Joy Formidable keep their 100,000 plus Facebook fans interested by regularly updating them on what they're up to, which has proven to be of particular value when they're between albums. They run competitions, link to relevant interviews and articles about the band, and – very occasionally – give a glimpse into their lives and interests away from the band. They don't post anything that's superfluous to the music but help foster in their followers a real sense of community, access and insight, without spoiling the mystery or the magic of the band.

Because, rest assured, if you post too much flannel and nonsense, you'll give the impression that your music is flannel and nonsense – which is to be avoided.

Don't underestimate the value of mystery. Give enough of yourselves to keep people intrigued, not satiated. We're music fans. The loyalty we feel to our favourite bands can be more enduring than the bond we have with our partners or friends. But we can also get bored quickly and be more fickle than a bankrupt spy at a general meeting of the United Nations.

Nurture that loyalty, don't give excuses for people to move on: like a picture of you grinning on the loo, or bad mouthing other artists, or moaning about how hard it all is, or riling public figures for cheap controversy, or begging hoards of music industry people for support, or trying to encourage members of your favourite sexual flavour into the dressing room.

I've seen music-makers do all of these things, to their detriment.

I should acknowledge that social networking isn't for everyone. A minority of artists I play on my show eschew a web presence. For some of them, that's presumably to foster an air of mystery, but that stance feels like something of a cliched affectation in 2014.

Others distrust the digital world and feel strongly that music is cheapened by it being streamable, and easily accessible. For them, only having their music available as a physical item, a piece of vinyl or a CD, or when they're playing live, is a strongly-held principle.

If you feel only want to exist in the material world, be aware that you won't benefit from the easy methods of communication or getting the word out about your music enabled by social networking, but don't feel pressured into compromising your values.

Social networking shouldn't be done at the expense of everything else. Cate Le Bon, a brilliant and idiosyncratic Welsh songwriter, still maintains a postal mailing list, sending occasional postcards to those who've expressed an interest in her music. Receiving something tangible from one of your favourite music-makers is a real buzz. The fact that so few do that nowadays, makes it distinctive and laudable.

The good promoters that I know well, will tell you – each and every one of them – that the most effective promotion for a gig is still done in the 'real world': posters,

310

press coverage, flyers, word of mouth, radio support. Social networking is complimentary to these old school methods, it's not a replacement for them and it's risky to put all of your Facebook-event-shaped eggs in that particular basket.

It's also important to note the revival in vinyl, cassette and – no doubt soon, as these things are entirely cyclical – CD's. Downloads from social networking sites are convenient and will help sow your music far and wide, but having the option of a physical release is wise, too, if you can afford it. We'll talk about this later in the book (**Chapter 41:** *'DIY Releases'*).

At the outset, set up an e-mailing list that people can subscribe to. This should be in addition to a Facebook page, or equivalent. As we've discussed already, most people ignore Facebook messages, unless they're from close friends. A (free, for lower volumes of messages) mailing list service like MailChimp is a cheap and effective way to keep in touch with your fanbase. Someone who has gone to the trouble of subscribing to your mailing list is much more likely to respond positively to mail-outs about gigs and releases. E-mailing 20 people who care about what you're doing is far more effective than messaging a couple of thousand people who've 'Liked' your Facebook page, but who've liked hundreds of others and won't even notice your message amongst the multitude they receive every week.

As we've mentioned Facebook frequently in this chapter, it's worth pointing out that access to their 'free' service has changed markedly over recent years. The reach of its pages is being purposefully limited to encourage users to pay for greater reach and / or advertising.

If you're thinking of promoting your gigs through Facebook, you may find that you're only promoting it to you and your closest friends, if you're not prepared to pay for the privilege. That's Facebook's prerogative. It's a business and it needs to make money for its investors and to maintain its service.

The lesson here is to not rely on any one 'free' service. Terms and conditions can change quickly. Where your music is involved, it's important to read the small-print.

Finally, don't lose sight of your priorities or get trapped in this infinite web of potential prevarication. A song, a riff, a genius sound are all considerably more important to you than a witty Tweet.

You're a music-maker not an I.T. support worker. Don't forget it.

[1]The Guardian newspaper published an article about how influential an artist's social networking statistics can be for securing a playlist on BBC Radio 1 - *http://www.theguardian.com/media/2014/may/25/radio-1-playlist-secrets-uncovered-battle-of-brands Sunday, May 25th. 2014.*

[2]cheap - *I'm not sure that an internet presence is cheap. We take it as a given that everyone has ready access to the internet but I'm sure that there are exceptions. Probably in the areas and socio economic groups that have traditionally been the catalyst for music's most thrilling evolutions: rock 'n' roll, mod, two tone, hip hop, punk, house, garage, grime... all genres that grew out of the underclass / working class. Libraries and educational institutions offer free access to the internet, as I'm sure you know. If you have great ideas, make the effort to share them. Trite and patronising as it may sound: the more disenfranchised you are, the more likely you are to have something interesting to say.*

29: <u>The Perfect Demo</u>

We're developed, know what I mean? We're ready to rock 'n' roll at the end of the day. We've got the songs. We've got it. We've got songs, songs, songs!

Liam Gallagher, Oasis

The *less is more* philosophy I'm foghorn-ing throughout this book is shouted at twice the volume when it comes to submitting your songs to labels, stations and publications.

Be as prolific as you like with your writing and your recording, but don't overwhelm your audience with substandard or half-finished ideas just because, with the freedoms afforded by the internet and social networking, you can.

Each new release should be an event for all concerned. Be especially careful of what, and how much, you submit to labels and media outlets.

When I started out in radio, I received official singles and album releases from radio pluggers and unsigned artists submitted *demos*. The separation between the two was pretty clearly delineated.

Nowadays all bands – regardless of whether they're signed or not – submit singles or albums, the 'demo' has been usurped. No one has to wait for a label to find them, A&R them, produce and record them, or distribute them before they can 'officially' release their music. This was the new, gold dawn that many music-makers, jaded at having been ignored by record labels, had desired.

Well, perhaps we should have been more careful what we wished for.

The Perfect Demo

That A&R process, derided as it has become, was a filter for quality and quantity of music. Yes, it was a process that became drunk on self-importance, too prescriptive and overblown for its own good, but it was the most reliable system we've had for finding, preparing and presenting original music-makers.

Twenty years ago, if someone sent you a single, you expected a certain quality of writing and recording. These days, a 'single' or an 'album' ranges from something A&R'd in the traditional way and recorded with high production values to a new band's very first, stuttering and rather awkward steps in a home studio.

It's like kids dressing as adults. It's unlikely to fool anyone. Trying to haul yourself up on an equal platform as official releases from established artists and labels, by using the same terminology as they do, is a mistake. It has a tendency to highlight any weaknesses.

Industry people who hear a *demo* are already empathetic to a new artist's intentions, but industry people who are presented with an 'album' or a 'single' judge it as such, against a pantheon of greatness. Only put yourself in that position if you're sure. *Really* sure. Having-been-your-own-worst-critics-sure…

The message is clear: music-makers, love your demo!

I can remember, even now, addled and arthritic of brain as I have become, the best demos that have landed in my lap. In particular, I recall a cassette tape arriving in the post in 1994 that was the singular most exciting musical thing I ever heard, before or since.

It had three songs on it. It sounded like a nicotine-ravaged Otis Redding fronting The Who Clash, if both Otis and The Who Clash had met in a queue at the Job Centre in Newport, Gwent. It was the rawest, most soulful explosion of white, working class noise I've ever heard. And I listened to that cassette so often in my car, at work on the Amstrad Hi Fi and in my Walkman, that it eventually went translucent and snapped, breaking my musical heart.

It was 60ft Dolls. They're the best band you've never heard of, unless you have... in which case, you'll know exactly what I mean.

Sadly if you go and explore their commercially available recorded output, you won't hear anything that quite matches the description above. Their first demo was their finest sonic statement.

The most perfect demo.

I wish, more than many things, that I still had a copy.

It had great songs. It was recorded well enough for you to hear the fizzing, unpredictable chemistry of the band. It had great vocals. All of the songs sounded like they'd been written and recorded by the same group. It was brazen and defiant, and not at all eager to please.

Subsequently it pleased me a lot. I'm getting lightning goosebumps just thinking about it.

That and Georgia Ruth's demo as eulogised at the beginning of **Chapter 17** were monumental and unforgettable moments. OK, I'm prone to a bit of melodrama, but I'm doing my best to circumvent that particular gene and be objective here.

The perfect demo features an artist's one or two best songs – no more. You don't need to demonstrate flexibility – you're not a gymnast – and variety is only desirable in redcoats and cruise ship bands.

You'll have gone partway through this process when you decided what to record. Picking two best tracks is a matter of being honest with yourself. You'll know which ones best represents your music. Be decisive. If you've made great music it will, of course, be difficult to make the choice.

"But our whole album's brilliant! They're all classic songs!"

This is rarely, if ever, true in my experience.

You'll probably be aware of a consensus in your audience, amongst the people who you've played your music to. It mightn't be a clear-cut consensus, but whichever song it is that is most loved by your audience – the one that gets the biggest cheer at gigs, for example – is your best bet and it would be foolish to deny that weight of opinion.

At this point, it's worth remembering that 'hit' songs are elevated to that status by an audience, not by the artist.

The perfect demo understands who it is being sent to and what their requirements are. It has context.

For example, radio will very rarely entertain the idea of playing a piece of music from an unknown artist that's much more than 3 minutes long. A leftfield record label, however, will be more prepared to embrace your 15 minute black psych metal overture, especially if that's the kind of thing the label has a track record of releasing (you've already done your research into that, haven't you?).

Music-makers adopt an unintuitive one-size-fits-all approach to music submissions, when taking the time to consider what you're submitting, and to whom, can improve your chances of success.

Just because you send the shorter and more accessible track to radio doesn't mean you have to send the shorter and more accessible track to labels or promoters.

Choose whichever is the best song for the person to whom you're submitting your music. Do not shirk from the small amount of research into your intended recipients recommended in **Chapter 26:** *'Writing A Biography'.*

On Making Music

The perfect demo is well-recorded and represents the artist's music to the best of its ability. It is not a live recording from an iPhone held aloft in the middle of the floor at the Dog and Duck.

Nor does it arrive with a litany of excuses: "these aren't really our best songs…" "we couldn't afford to record it properly…" "we don't really sound like Mumford & Sons anymore…" "I've got rid of the band who recorded these because they weren't very good…"

The perfect demo instils in the listener a desire to hear more, not less.

The perfect demo is sent in a format that the artist is 100% confident is listenable by the recipient (your hipster, cassette-only release is likely to rattle into a bin rather than a cassette player).

The perfect demo, whether on cassette or CD or .mp3 or wax cylinder, is clearly marked with the artist's name and a contact email address and telephone number. If it's submitted digitally, then that means correctly 'tagging' the track or naming the file so that it's clearly and unambiguously you.

I have 2,682 unidentifiable 'Track 1's' by 'Unknown Artist' on my music drive. That's no exaggeration. It astounds me how many artists submit music that isn't clearly identifiable. When you mail your blank CD-R with a covering letter / biog, understand that it will arrive in an office with hundreds of other blank CD-R's and covering letters / biogs. The covering letters / biogs get separated from the CD the moment the jiffy bag is opened. Pixar could make a tear-jerking animated feature about the fraught journey one abandoned CD-R has to undertake to be reunited with its attendant biography. There would be little chance of a happy ending, either.

And although the notion of sending a piece of music through the post may strike you as archaic, this piece of wisdom extends to digital submissions, too. Untagged and untitled .mp3's are like grains of sand. There is no need to take the risk that they will be lost and unidentifiable.

Make sure the filename is: artist name - track name.

And, similarly, make sure that the ID3 tags for the .mp3 are correctly filled in.

If you don't know what an ID3 tag is, look it up, it'll take you whole seconds.

For these reasons, I recommend you don't submit .wav files, or files that aren't easily tagged. High fidelity is much less important than getting your music heard and recognised.

The perfect demo is not an 'album'.

I can't stress to you how time-poor we 'industry folk' are as a species. Don't assume that hard-pressed label owners, the few A&R who remain and overwhelmed radio people will have the time to listen to an entire album of your work – especially if you're an unknown artist.

Your magnum opus, this wonderful musical tapestry that you have spent months writing, arranging and recording, is likely to get judged on the first couple of tracks alone, if you're lucky.

Label people and media folk **do** listen to entire albums, but very rarely in the white, unscrupulous heat of listening through the slush pile.

We faceless drones want nothing more than to bask in the reflected glory of working with an artist who releases an album widely-regarded as a classic. However we have learnt that there is a well-worn path to those albums. One that doesn't have them appear, fully-formed and out of nowhere, from an artist that we've never heard of before.

So I'm not, by any means, album-ist. I still believe that

the album is the ultimate musical format, the medium through which some of humankind's finest artistic statements have been made. However reaching for the next submission in the teetering 'unlistened to' pile, when I have an hour to go before my show starts, and discovering that it's an album from an unknown band, is like having a garrulous, drunk neighbour knock on your door at 11:55pm, when you have to be up for a theoretical physics exam at 6 the following morning.

It's distinctly unsatisfactory to have to skim through an album of someone else's hard-work. It feels like a dereliction of duty, even if I have spent the previous eight hours straight listening to music submissions. Everyone works to a deadline. If you're working in radio, your deadline is the start of your show. The BBC aren't going to shift my start-time back by an hour so I can listen to another album.

So it goes back on the shelf, or into a folder in my inbox, to be considered for the following week's programme, by which time another couple of hundred submissions have arrived, some of which are albums from unknown artists, too.

Eventually the album may get a perfunctory listen. Then, inevitably, it ends up in the bin or in a charity shop.

Again, this may read as if I'm being unnecessarily harsh, a prima donna demanding that your music arrives just-so otherwise I will refuse to listen to it. I'm just letting you know, in the clearest possible terms, the situation that your music arrives in: cheek-by-jowl with hundreds of other submissions, with barely enough time to listen to half of them 'properly' (i.e. in full).

By all means record an album, if that is what fulfils your vision and your creative urge, but I'd recommend that you don't make it your first submission to a label, a radio station or a music publication. If your name is unknown and doesn't come from a trusted source (i.e. it isn't a release on a recognised label or you haven't been recommended) it is likely to get a skim listen, at best.

I try to listen to every album that I'm sent, but I am one of the exceptions. You don't want to predicate your entire strategy for getting your music supported by the industry on exceptions.

The perfect demo, then, is 10% research, shape, format and context. 90% of what constitutes a perfect demo is still the music contained therein. The advice above will just improve the effectiveness of that music's delivery and the likelihood of it being heard and responded to.

PLAYLIST:
Oasis - Columbia
60ft Dolls - Happy Shopper (original Townhill recording)

30: <u>Moshi Moshi On A Label's Perspective</u>

As has been mentioned more than once in this book, and at least twice more than was probably necessary, I've been making new music-orientated radio shows for over twenty years. The only frustrating aspect of the role, above and beyond the out of tune guitars, is hearing people who've fallen out of love with new music, bemoaning the state of new music.

Comments sections on the major newspapers' music pages reek of holier than thou proclamations from the bumptious, unaware that by echoing variations on the fuddy duddy mantra – "music just isn't as good as it was back in my day" – they demonstrate they're far staler than any of the music they criticise.

The dry rustle of their cultural death throes isn't anywhere near as exciting as the sounds I'm hearing. And music *is* so much more exciting now than at any point that I can remember. For a start, it doesn't need media-fabricated scenes to propel it into the mass consciousness, four or five bands who've half-inched the same influences and patronise the same second-hand clothes stall at Camden Market, following a prescribed media vector.

What's remotely fucking exciting about that?

And the constant cycle of that, that we've had since 1957?

Perhaps I take things too literally but from where I'm listening, music's more exciting, now, because the music, itself, is – you know – more exciting.

It mightn't incite movements – a 'new' punk to give

'individuals' an identikit persona... – but movements were always about herds, and there's nothing less original than being in a herd.

So contemporary music-makers can be more themselves and follow their own muse without having to bend towards an obvious zeitgeist. I've bemoaned the diminishing importance, generally, of A&R elsewhere in this book, but music has benefited from being less determined by unimaginative A&R departments contriving, and clogging media channels with, desperate facsimiles of whatever it is that is the flavour of the month.

The labels that survive and prosper in the modern age do so by reflecting quality, originality and a strong aesthetic.

Moshi Moshi Records are an ideal example. Their knack, to have discovered and released a who's who of the UK's most imaginative (leftfield) pop artists of the last 16 years (Bloc Party, Hot Chip, Florence and the Machine, Slow Club, The Wave Pictures, Hercules and Love Affair, Teleman, Sweet Baboo – amongst many others) demonstrates that it isn't, actually, a 'knack' at all. Running a label with great releases is about having excellent ears, the instinct to know where to find intriguing new music-makers, and the imagination and wherewithal to know what to do with them. A bit of money helps, too.

Stephen Bass co-founded Moshi Moshi Records in 1998 and kindly, and very quickly, agreed to answering a few of my questions from a label's perspective.

Given the longevity, success (both commercial and artistic) and prolificness of Moshi Moshi, please pay particular attention to the answer to the first question...

Have Moshi Moshi ever first heard about an artist they went on to sign via an unsolicited demo?

No.

Do you listen to demos from unsolicited artists?

Occasionally, if someone sends a particularly nice email, I will weaken.

What constitutes the 'perfect demo' for you?

Interesting artwork, no flannel, something with some character.

Unsigned artists are told, frequently, that word of mouth is a more persuasive factor in getting yourselves heard by a label. How can an unsigned artist generate that word of mouth?

A&R people are the same as anyone else and will pay more attention to something that has been written about or talked about or played by someone else, preferably not the band in question, or their mates, or their mum.

It's pretty easy just to think about how you yourself find music and try and do the same really.

There are a few things that people pay attention to – the BBC introducing system seems to be fairly powerful, certain radio shows, certain websites that will go the extra mile in unearthing new stuff. Get yourself on their radar!

There is still, even in 2014, a belief that being in London can help a band. Your roster come from all over the UK... was London (your artists coming to play the city) at all

influential or helpful for you?

You don't have to be in London and you certainly shouldn't need to be in London to be discovered. In fact, in the discovery phase you might be better off not being in London.

Once you are signed and working it might be practical to move here. I think the important thing is to start <u>somewhere</u> – you need some sort of scene and following. It might be that it is easier or more logical to be elsewhere than in London to do that.

You need some sort of initial, real, active fan base, though, something genuine and often those sort of scenes develop outside of London in smaller, cheaper cities that are a little less forgiving to wallets and critique.

It's also good to learn your craft before you come and do that big London show with perhaps a load (or perhaps just one or two) industry insiders there to watch you.

Are numbers, of Twitter followers / YouTube views etc., at all persuasive or impressive to a very music-focused label like Moshi Moshi?

What we need is people who are smart enough to know what matters and hard-working enough to actually do something about it and start building these things up.

Generally we are in fairly early so don't expect the number of people following those artists on social networks to be massive. but we need to know that there is an awareness of how to start doing these things. or an idea that might make us confident that people will care and will want to follow you or watch your videos... it's all about communication, after all.

How have you tended to find the artists that you have released on the record label?

Mostly personal recommendation whether that is through industry contacts or perhaps, more often, from other musicians.

What are the qualities you look for in an artist?

Creativity, character, charisma, originality. A strong work ethic. A lack of bullshit.

Does there have to be scope for you to imagine being able to work with and help an artist develop? (i.e. not being presented with something too 'finished'.)

I don't think so. I think just something we feel that we can relate to. It's more fun if we need to work on the development side of things but that is probably best worked on via our management arm.

Moshi Moshi are renowned for featuring artists who are slightly leftfield, but who it would be easy to imagine in the Top 10, in an ideal world. Is that philosophy of interesting *pop* music key to the label and key to the artists that you seek to work with?

Yes… we have always liked music that comes from the leftfield to become pop rather than going for the mainstream. It's just a matter of personal taste, really.

In fact it is actually the only way we could survive. To launch a new mainstream pop artist is a much more expensive affair.

We have a different definition of success and that is sometimes the distinction. I actually think that all our bands are pop acts and obviously we have worked with a lot of acts who have gone on to be big pop acts, but they weren't necessarily seen as that from the outset.

How important is it that artists who approach you are familiar with Moshi Moshi's philosophy (and artists)? Is research key?

Well, we don't have a particular style of artist so there aren't any restrictions there. But I think it's obvious that we are going to be looking for something that isn't derivative.

Perhaps we make ourselves a lot of work with this approach and sometimes it does feel like we are constantly trying to push square pegs into round holes or banging our heads against the wall, but, historically, the acts that go from being something new and unique, to connecting with people, have been the ones that make life interesting and end up having long-lasting careers that bring a little more satisfaction to both parties – creator and fan.

Thank you Stephen.

Keep up to date with Moshi Moshi's new releases, and investigate their excellent back catalogue, by visiting: http://moshimoshimusic.com

Follow them on Twitter @moshimoshimusic

PLAYLIST:
Bloc Party - Banquet
Slow Club - It Doesn't Have To Be Beautiful
Florence + the Machine - Rabbit Heart (Raise It Up)
the Wave Pictures - Little Surprise
Hot Chip - Hittin' Skittles
Hercules & Love Affair - My House
Teleman - Steam Train Girl

31: <u>Huw Stephens On Getting Radio Play</u>

Huw Stephens is one of that rare breed of broadcasters who has musical authority, but also manages to be accessible (and entertaining) to eye-wateringly massive audiences.

His BBC Introducing show on Radio 1 (Thursday mornings midnight - 2am) is a renowned breaking ground for new artists. The XX, Frankie and the Heartstrings, Jake Bugg and Lorde (amongst many others) all received early support on Huw's show before filtering elsewhere on the Radio 1 schedule.

His new music show on Monday nights on Wales' national Welsh language station, C2 is, again, an invaluable platform for new noise-makers.

Some of the artists Huw enthuses about also manage to find their way onto the playlists for his weekend afternoon shows on BBC Radio 1, getting heard by a whole other audience of potential fans. One play on Huw's weekend show is equivalent to a year's worth of exposure on my show. Network radio is a massive, potential shop window for music-makers. Huw wields the responsibility with enthusiasm, knowledge and fairness.

He co-founded Sŵn Festival in 2007, now one of the most enjoyable (and important – but most importantly, enjoyable) festivals of new music on the UK calendar. In 2011, Huw and John Rostron conceived the Welsh Music Prize – an annual celebration of Wales' finest albums.

On a personal level, having watched and listened to Huw in action over the last decade and a half, I can say with some authority, I think, that he is one of the most genuine, hard-working and musically astute broadcasters it has been my privilege to listen to, or, on happy occasion, work with.

Don't think I'm exaggerating. I mean every last word.

It struck me that by this stage in the book, you'd probably be sick of my radio-shaped demands, so I asked Huw some questions about getting airplay on his excellent transmissions.

What excites you about a piece of music enough to make you want to play it on your shows?

Something that grabs me, shakes me, soothes me, leaves me wanting to hear it again or more from the artist, and something I think will sound good on the show and that I think will fit in with the other tracks.

Are there aspects of a recording that can set a band apart (in a good way)?

Although a little roughness in a recording is fine, I am looking for something that is broadcast quality, as the show is listened to all over the world, and I think a certain quality of recording and producing is fair enough.

I freely (but sadly) admit that I rarely get more than 30 seconds into some demos before I move on to the next track, because the music is just wrong for me, or is littered with mistakes, or is recorded badly. What are the factors that make a recording unsuitable for you?

It has to sound good on the show. Simple as that really!

Do music makers sometimes submit their music in the wrong way… i.e. the incorrect format / to the wrong e-mail address (or as a message via Twitter that you don't see until weeks later)?

I don't often find new music via Twitter to be honest. Links get sent to me during radio shows, which is the worst time to send a DJ music I think – I'm busy doing a show![1] I get sent CD's through the post, but I don't think that'll happen for much longer. I'm emailed music by pluggers / promoters / agents / friends and I listen to the SoundCloud links. They're a lot easier to handle than CD's, to be honest.

What is the best way for music-makers to submit their recordings to you?

A CD, or a link to the BBC email.

How important is it that people do their research first? (i.e. check out your show to hear what it is you support.)

Vital I think. Although I play a bit of everything really, it's mostly bands. All I ask is that the music I'm sent is good and ready to played on the radio. A lot of it isn't suitable for my show, and it's a waste of everyone's time then!

How much unsigned, unsolicited music can you play on your Radio 1 show? I assume that quite a high proportion comes via radio pluggers?

I do get a bit from radio pluggers. We play a few tracks from the BBC Introducing Uploader. I listen to everything I'm sent, and as long as it's interesting, it's in. I try and create some familiarity with forthcoming session artists. And because it's all new music, it doesn't mean it has to be scary or unfamiliar – I try and create mini-hits, not the late night show, which means repeating great tracks quite a bit. Although I do move on when the artist gets played in a more prominent slot, otherwise my show sounds like other DJ's shows!

Unsigned means something very different to what it used to. A lot of music comes in on small labels, labels the bands themselves have set up. I don't care about the label really, it's about the tune.

Can a radio plugger, then, be a useful (if expensive) tool for a band?

Yes, if there's some sort of plan in place. Radio play, I think, falls into a big jigsaw that includes playing live, being ready to record songs and generally getting out there. Pluggers do have relationships with radio stations and DJ's, and particularly I think if you are after getting on a playlist, or more than one play on a certain group of shows, then a plugger can help take you to the next level. Because it's very competitive to get on playlists, and pluggers can push for your music to be heard and considered.

How influential can a biog / a good photo / a huge amount of Twitter followers be?

Again, on a playlist level, web statistics can be important. Social media followers, and Shazam tags, Youtube plays, that kind of thing. But the music needs to be up there too, of course! I'll be honest, I don't read a lot of biogs, unless I like the music. And sometimes a photo does more harm than good. I genuinely don't think they matter. Listen to the music, see if it's good / suitable / quality and then go from there.

Don't worry about photos, and biogs - keep them short and simple if you have to do them. Concentrate on the music.

How important is word of mouth to you? Recommendations from friends? Seeing bands at festivals etc.

Very important. In fact, that's something you just can't buy, a friend telling you about something. I pick up the free music mags, get NME, read some blogs like The Line of Best Fit, the Quietus, check other DJ's shows and track listings to see what people are really liking, and not being paid to like.

Do you have any other tips for artists seeking radio play?

Choose your best two songs, and concentrate on those, get them out there to shows and DJ's and promoters and venues that you think will like them.

Diolch yn fawr iawn, Huw Stephens. Hear Huw every Monday, Tuesday and Wednesday night 10pm-1am on BBC Radio 1 and every Monday night at 7pm on C2.
Follow Huw on Twitter: @huwstephens

[1] **I'm busy doing a show!** – *This! This! This x 1,000! I can get anything up to forty or fifty demo submissions or requests to listen to a recording, during any given three hour show. I can also get many 10's of other messages around these invitations to listen to music. The invitations get buried quickly. The demos go unlistened to. Everybody ends up going to bed with a sadface :(*

PLAYLIST:
The xx - Crystallised
Frankie & the Heartstrings - Possibilites
Jake Bugg - Lightning Bolt
Lorde - Royals

32: <u>Getting Gigs</u>

I think the main thing to do is to get out of your hometown where you live and go and play live, as much as you can, and commit to the lifestyle.

Black Francis, The Pixies

Live music is like going to war.

Owen Powell, Catatonia

I'm sat at my laptop, drizzly April day outside, head fuzzy with a flu hangover, and I can hardly type the words fast enough to capture the memories evoked by that word... 'gigs'!

This bewilderment of recollections comes despite the fact that I haven't throttled a guitar in anger for 15 or 16 years, certainly not at a gig where I played my own songs on a stage with best friends, righteous in a belief that the noise we were making improved the world somehow and imbued us with temporary, superhuman powers.

The biggest audience we ever played in front of would have numbered a couple of thousand. The venues we tended to frequent held a tenth of that, but the buzz, regardless of audience-size, was overwhelming and unparalleled... when things went well.

Some of the best nights of my life happened in some of the dingiest shitholes imaginable.

Music is a wonderful thing. It can keep you locally,

playing with your friends... it doesn't have to take you to rock 'n' roll stadia around the world. Just playing in the local venue can be enough, in the youth club or the pub.

Some of the greatest experiences in rock 'n' roll that I've ever had are seeing bands in small places.

The greatest gig I've ever seen was the Sex Pistols in 1976 in Quaintways in Chester and they were right in my face. I stood in a room with a few hundred people – if that – watching Johnny Rotten and the Sex Pistols confront the world and it was incredible.

Mike Peters, The Alarm

Great live music, whether witnessed or performed, tops out the scale of awe-inspiring, human experiences – one hydrogen atom's width below the birth of my daughter – for me, at least.

Ace gigs are fucking ace. There's no excitement like the excitement of pushing yourself into the white heat and noise of your own music, loud, in front of an enthusiastic audience.

Equally, bad gigs are fucking bad. Screw something up, fail to connect with – or, indeed, attract – that audience, observing any interest in your noise wilt as you fight to conjure it, and the disappointment will kick you in the guts for days.

However experiencing the latter is key to achieving the former. No one did a great gig without learning their way through their fair share of bad ones.

It's not just about the spectacle and the thrill. Live music is part of a great social tradition that stretches back to mankind's earliest days. Music – and the communal sharing of music – underpins all of our most important rituals: birthdays, weddings, funerals, sporting events, worship, rites of passage, making friends, finding a mate

(yep, even if you're in a Tool t-shirt.)

When wise-arse commentators declare that live music has lost its allure, its cool and its place in our hearts to Xboxes and PlayStations, they are ignoring the indubitable fact that music – and the communal experience of music – is woven into our cultural souls.

Of course, this doesn't mean that you're guaranteed an audience at The Dog and Duck on a damp Thursday night in January.

There is *so much* live music on offer that you need to be better than good to draw an audience.

It's not, explicitly, a competition. You don't have to sully your art by having a survival-of-the-fittest philosophy at its core. Audiences will be drawn to something that thrills and awes them, so be thrilling and awe-inspiring – and if you can be the most thrilling and awe-inspiring live musical experience in your neighbourhood, or your town, or your city, or your country – and beyond – then you'll draw an audience accordingly.

Gigs are important to you because they're an opportunity to communicate with your audience, to sear your music into their lives, to give them an experience that is unforgettable and unique, that exists beyond music as 1's and 0's on their smartphone.

Gigs give you the chance to hook in and bewitch a new audience, to expand your congregation. If you're only playing in front of 5 people, but those 5 people have never heard you before, that gig is at least as worthwhile as preaching to a couple of hundred of the already-converted.

Remember that. It may help when you have those inevitable experiences of playing to almost empty rooms.

Now I'm sure that, principled and pure artist as you are, commerce is the furthest thing from your mind, however it would be priggish to ignore the fact that gigs are a perfect shop-front for your music. Having merchandise for sale – vinyl, CD's, badges, t-shirts, mugs, branded Sumo suits – doesn't dilute the integrity of what you're doing; it gives you the opportunity to make enough money to keep your transit van, or equivalent, rolling from town-to-town.

Gigs also give you the chance to test audience reaction to your songs. You don't have to do this explicitly – *"Hey guys, which of our songs do you think is the best? We're wondering what we should record as our next single..."* – may come across as too eager to please.

If you're sensitive to your audience's reaction, though, you'll get a great, objective sense of where the peaks and troughs lie in your set. Recording the peaks is a wise strategy.

When you start out, you want to play anywhere, to show off the fact that you're in a band and you've written a few half-decent songs. In those early days, it's wise to play wherever and whenever you can. Feeling comfortable on a stage, in front of an audience, is an invaluable state of mind to attain.

One of the first radio interviews I did was with Benji – then singer with Dub War, currently fronting the internationally-renowned Skindred. He told me that the stage, to him, was more familiar, even, than his front-room at home in Newport. The amps and the drum kit were the furniture, the rest of his band were his family and friends, the audience were guests they'd invited in. It was a brilliant metaphor that underlined why he is such a great frontman.

You don't get that sense of belonging overnight. It's earned over hundreds of nights.

So where do you start? How do you get a gig? Where is the first rung on the ladder, and how can you ensure that the ladder climbs upwards, and not to the side, or downwards.

Well, first make sure that you're ready to gig. Being 'ready' means having a 15-30 minute set of great songs – certainly as great as you can make them for the level you're at – and that you can play them all the way through without stopping, and without the singer needing to bring the lyrics up on stage in a notebook.

I spoke to a few promoters across the country about what it is that makes a band worth a punt, and what it is that consigns them to the 'rejected' pile.

A band's songs do have to be great. The ones who are thrashing around, out of time, with simplistic drumming and out of tune shouting, don't make the grade. Yet they're convinced they're the best act you will ever book. They're also not afraid to voice their opinions of promoters on social media, stating their disgust at not being booked, suggesting it's only a popularity contest.

This is a big NO NO! Spend less time behind the computer being a nerd and get practicing! I cannot even begin to tell you some of the statuses I've read recently from bands I've had to turn down for gigs. It's doing them no favours. To the point they will not get a gig, ever.

Social media is a great platform to promote your music and make it accessible to bookers, fans and potential agents. It is not a medium to give your opinion on being rejected. The reason, more than likely, is that your music is shit.

The Anonymous Promoter

It's much easier to build a reputation for being a bad live band than it is a good one. Reputation is pretty important for bands starting out. Don't stain yours by not being ready for any opportunities you do manage to eke out.

Paradoxically, gigs can be easier to find when you're really green. If you're just starting out, and you're young enough to be in, or associated with, an educational institution, take advantage – shamelessly – of any facilities and opportunities they provide. School and college gigs are a great way to learn your chops away from the cynical go-on-then-impress-me gaze of seasoned old buggers like me.
1

Make yourself known to local youth organisations. Many have funding to support artists from their catchment area. This is especially true (in the U.K., at least) in more socially and economically deprived areas.

It's worth contacting your local council to make yourselves available for any forthcoming events they are planning, and if there aren't any forthcoming events, offer them one!

Opportunities like these tend to go to bands who are prepared to knock on doors, not – necessarily – to the best bands. There's nothing wrong with knocking on a few doors between songwriting sessions. Most of those doors are easily accessible through the internet. These days you don't even have to muster the energy to do any real knocking.

If you're too young to play in licensed venues, play friends' parties; busk (if it's legal in your town / city)... do whatever you can to give yourself confidence and experience, and do it while people give you a certain amount of patronising leeway for being young.

For other bands / artists who can't rely on a school or college gig, and who have outgrown their ration of 'patronising leeway', your challenge is to turn yourselves into a *draw*, to make yourselves commercially viable to venues and promoters in your town... then further afield... and then – if your renown continues to expand – an agent is likely to be receptive to taking all of this gig-getting responsibility off your shoulders.

Bands have an internal logic all their own because you've got a band, you got to find gigs for the band to play and you're rehearsing for the gigs. If you're spending all your time hustling for gigs, rehearsing for gigs, playing gigs, you're kind of missing the point. Because the thing that's going to take you to the next level is – really – a killer song and the only way you get to the killer songs is by writing rubbish ones. So you have to be able to write 10 songs a month, or something, of which 9 are going to be rubbish, to get to the 10th one. So, write a great deal more than you think you need to.

Tom Robinson, songwriter / 6Music presenter

You become a draw by having great songs and by being able to perform them well. So, write and rehearse. No amount of fancy paper will cover over the cracks of not having great songs. They have to be your priority.

Gigging before you have great songs is to be avoided. If you don't have great songs, you're on a hiding to nothing... maybe not nothing, but certainly nothing more than Pay-To-Play and half a crate of beyond its Best Before Date Tuborg.

Achieving the balance between writing and gigging has to be intuitive. There's no hard-written formula. You'll soon learn which gigs are worth your while and which gigs sap your soul.

You become a draw by working your gigs, by doing the utmost you can to promote them: flyers, posters, word of mouth, social media. Artists who leave the responsibility for promoting their gigs in the hands of the promoter have taken things far too literally. This may become true when you're touring globally, working with agents and big fish promoters, but until you reach that point you are, in essence, co-promoting every gig that you play.

It's important to find promoters who have a similar sensibility to you and who promote nights that will provide the right stage for your sound. Random, unsolicited emails to venues will not bear any fruit. Don't be under the illusion that anyone working at a venue has the time to listen to a random submission and then place it with a suitable promoter. That just will not happen.

Do your research.

Of course, there are some magnanimous promoters and venues out there who will give unproven artists a chance. This rare breed of people are most benevolent towards friendly and familiar faces. If there's a good local venue, support it. Be a recognised presence at a promoter's nights and they will feel much more supportive of your cause if you approach them to ask for a gig.

Be polite, ask who you need to speak to about music bookings, and when you find that person, enquire when might be a good time to talk to them about getting a gig. Keep your spiel brief and to the point.

Take any 'no's' you receive gracefully. There will probably be a lot of 'no's' and even more 'maybes'. Don't turn the 'maybes' into 'no's'. Even in big cities, bridges are few and far between; you can't afford to burn them every time you're turned down.

Being an integral, positive part of any local scene doesn't mean you have to become music's answer to Mother Theresa. You can be positive without fawning and without compromise. Neither do you need to turn yourself into an extroverted gobshite or an inveterate blagger.

Hanging out with other bands, supporting their endeavours, is inspirational and fun. Getting involved in, or creating, a local scene is especially important in your early years as an artist.

Being right there in the thick of it, talking to other music-makers, will forge useful contacts and create opportunities for you. Even mediocre musicians can prosper (relatively) because they put the legwork in and make themselves known.

Carping from the outside, sitting in a caff bitching about the opportunities other bands are creating for themselves, won't earn you any gigs or goodwill. A sense of entitlement builds a reputation, but not the kind of reputation that will benefit you.

If you can't afford to buy tickets to get yourself into the local gigs, offer to hand out flyers or put up posters in return for 'free' entry. Go for a job behind the bar. Offer to DJ. Obviously you can't do this for every venue you want to play in, but most artists find a venue that is their spiritual home – somewhere that resonates with their own philosophies. Make that place your temple.

If there are nightclubs, town squares, bandstands, independent record shops, boutique secondhand shops or art spaces locally, tap them up for potential gigs. Bona fide, sticky-floored music venues aren't the only places you can play your music. Bringing live music to people in unexpected places opens up a new realm of opportunities. Thinking creatively doesn't just apply to songwriting.

One opportunity, available in almost every town in the land, is the Open Mic night. Some deride them for being exploitative, a short step away from Pay-To-Play. I feel more charitably towards them. A well-run open mic night, with supportive hosts, in a good venue with an enthusiastic crowd and a decent P.A., is a great learning ground for new artists, if their style of music can be accommodated.

Not much point in a balls-to-the-wall, bulging-vein hardcore band turning up to an acoustic-only open mic night. Well, unless it's for the perverse enjoyment of the crowd. I once saw a death metal band try their schtick with acoustic guitars, it was unintentionally hilarious and didn't do anything to further their cause... apart from teaching them the very valuable lesson of keeping a 500m safe distance away from all other acoustic open mic nights in the future.

Good open mic nights foster a sense of community – they're not just a transparent ploy for the venue to put live music on without having to pay for it.[2] Don't underestimate community. The musical community isn't a scene, as such, because its members will be from disparate musical movements and a range of ages.

There's a lot to be learned from experienced music-makers. Buy 'em a pint and listen to their stories. Even the least famous – *especially* the least famous – have wisdom you can learn from.

If you're that balls-to-the-wall, bulging-vein hardcore band I mentioned above, the likelihood is that you'll be steeped in DIY culture. DIY is a route open to any artist regardless of genre. Find a suitable space, hire it; rent or blag a PA; print up a few posters, and you're away.

It's incumbent on me, as a stuffy, old git who works for the BBC, to implore you to check the legality of anything you organise. Check that any space you hire has public indemnity insurance. This means that if someone has an accident at your event (gets crushed by a falling speaker; trips over a PA lead and knocks their teeth out; has their shoulder dislocated by a stage-diver... the possibilities are frightening and endless), you are *more likely* to be covered against any potential litigation, if you haven't been negligent.

Always check the electricity supply where you're playing, especially if it's a guerrilla / ad hoc gig. Check that they have RCD's. Being fastidious about your safety isn't anti-rock 'n' roll. Your audience need never know that you've compromised rock 'n' roll's live fast, die young credo. Not much romance in frying your eyeballs during a soundcheck, anyway.

Be aware of noise levels at DIY gigs, especially at house parties / squat gigs. You don't want your equipment confiscated by an over zealous environmental health officer.

Environmental Health officers are zealous by their very nature.

How much to charge for a gig is an inexact science. You're unlikely to get paid, not even fuel costs, for your earliest forays into gigging. This may seem unfair but a new band has to work their way up a bill and prove their worth to a promoter or venue before they start discussing money.

Early on, it'll be clear to you that those promoters and venue owners are doing you the favour by letting you play. When the power balance in that relationship has reversed, and your audience are bringing revenue to the venue, then is the time to negotiate a fee.

Another thing that really gets on my tits is when I hear about artists complaining they're not getting paid enough. It's annoying when artists moan about venues treating them as if the venue is doing them a favour by giving them exposure... we *are* providing you exposure! Deal with it.

A band loads £5000 worth of equipment into a £500 car to play a £50 gig. If you are hustling for shows, that's what you get. That only changes when you prove your worth.

I have recently had a band out price themselves for a weekend show. I broke down the show costs including his fee, rider, PA hire, lighting, sound engineer, security, staffing and promotion. I can imagine he felt quite embarrassed when it turned out that if we were to work this show on a contractual basis, he would owe me more than he was initially asking for.

The venue pays for it. The reason we cannot pay artists a lot of the time is because there is no money to spend. None. Zilch.

Most shows will just cover costs. Lowly promoters like myself are in it for passionate reasons, as should the musicians be, and not to make the big bucks. I am putting on these gigs to make it accessible for the people of the city I live in. Not to out-price shows and have an empty dancefloor. We provide you with a huge potential fan base.

We are giving you the exposure, make the most of it, and stop complaining.

The Anonymous Promoter

Some venues still operate a 'pay to play' policy, generally 'name' venues in bigger cities trading on their reputation.

If a venue or promoter expects you to sell tickets, but offers you only a small percentage of that money back, it is a pay-to-play venue. You're likely to end up on a bill with a handful of other artists who've all fallen for the same scam.

You judge whether playing in front of the other bands' fans, for the fun of it but nothing more, is worthwhile to you. If you get a gig in a city that's far from your home, and the other artists on the bill are at a similar level to you (i.e. there's no recognised, name artist to pull the punters in), and the only financial recompense on offer is a measly percentage of the tickets you manage to sell, your alarm bells should be ringing. Loudly.

But as one commenter put it when I discussed pay-to-play online: "doing gigs is fun, no matter how much you get paid or how far you have to go."

The consensus of opinion is that no venue worth its salt, and no promoter worth their reputation, operates a pay-to-play policy in 2014. This scenario prospered in the bad old days of the music industry, when a London gig – *any* London gig – was regarded as a golden fleece, something mythical that would guarantee a band exposure. Don't fall for false promises; the music industry is a rickety tower of false promises.

Start a mailing list as early in your gigging existence as you can. Have a pad, or a clipboard, on the merch stand at the venue... or just on a table if there's no merch stand. People who volunteer their e-mail addresses to you are telling you that they like you and that they'd be prepared to interrupt their busy lives to come and see you, or part with their hard-earned money to buy your music. That's a great compliment to your music. Value it.

A diligently-maintained mailing list is a very valuable resource when it comes to promoting your gigs, far more efficient than the social networking equivalents. Getting people to your gigs – and people are much more likely to go to your gigs if they know about them – can be the key to all that follows. For example, a burgeoning following is much more likely to lead to a label offer, or a successful self-release.

Where I come from we have a saying. You can't be in two places at once when you're nowhere at all. So be patient, bide your time. I mean this, learn your craft and keep moving. The opportunities will come. If you have anything worth hearing someone will hear it. They might like it and — if you're lucky — they might love it.

Jeremy Gluck, The Barracudas

Once you're regularly pulling 50 - 100 people to a gig, you've become a draw and venue owners and promoters will start to take notice.

When you've reached this stage, you'll have become useful to promoters as a potential local support for touring artists. These aren't always the best gigs to play – soundchecks are rare as panda orgasms, fees are (still) low or non-existent, audiences are generally chatting at the bar waiting for the main act – but they do provide valuable, factual embellishment for your biog and they are a great opportunity to forge new connections with, and get inspired by, touring bands.

If you play a great set, pull some enthusiastic punters and you're a positive presence at the gig you're very likely to be asked back, and not just by the venue.

Touring artists don't see too many other human beings. A friendly support band, who are musically simpatico with their vision, will be remembered. And who knows where that may lead?

Unfortunately some support bands think it's their rôle to act like uppity wankers. The black mark that goes through a support band's name who won't share an amp, or who play past their curfew, or who slag off the main band from the stage, is an indelible black mark.

This is a little bugbear of mine, really. If you're a support group, you should be respectful that you've been offered a position like that. Nobody likes a bigheaded support group who think they own it all and it's their right to be there and think they're popstars, when – ultimately – you're supporting a band whose audience isn't there for you, it's there for them. Basically what I'm saying is that I think people should be more grateful sometimes.

David Gedge, The Wedding Present

I imagine that artists who behave like David's outlined above are over-compensating for a massive insecurity complex. You don't have to supplicate yourselves to the headline band, but good manners breed good favour. There isn't a creative entity in the world that needs favours more than a new band needs favours.

The difficult balance for any new band to achieve, is playing enough to build their audience but not so much that they become over familiar and boring. People's goodwill can wear out quickly. So make sure that you reward any loyalty that is shown your way with great shows. If you can make every gig feel like an event, you're bringing excitement to our otherwise moribund lives.

If you can do that in a black shoebox that stinks of piss and stale Newcastle Brown, your magic will surely earn you international acclaim.

When you have great songs and you're attracting a three figure audience, it's not only the venues and promoters who will begin to take notice.

People will start blogging about you, you'll get played on the radio, venues and promoters in other towns and cities will start to be interested in putting you on. Momentum can build quickly. Or not at all.

Average bands reach a glass ceiling at this point. If you're struggling to get anyone's attention – or you can pack a pub with your mates and some of their mates, but no one else – then you don't have great music.

There's no shame, here. Great music is, by implication, rare and fucking difficult to conjure.

This is the bitterest pill you may have to swallow.

Maybe inspiration is just around the corner? Maybe you just need to work a little harder on writing those 'great' songs. They're the key to everything. Some bands who start out average do, eventually, bloom into something special.

It's always about the writing. Write! Write! Write! Do not give up!

For those of you whose audience is growing, and who are simultaneously garnering interest and support from labels, blogs and radio shows, the next logical step is to find yourself an agent.

A good live agent is an artist's best friend. More important, I'd suggest, than a manager.

On rare occasions agents can be engaged by submitting releases and biogs, if you can demonstrate a real and growing interest in your performances, but it is much more usual for an agent to contact an artist, generally because of a recommendation from a label or because they've noticed that the artist concerned is generating a buzz and selling out shows.

Agents work on a percentage of the ticket sales for shows. 20% of nothing is, clearly, nothing. But 20% of a £300 take, and the likelihood of that take being replicated across a healthy number of venues in different towns and cities, and you just about start to be an interesting proposition.

Agents, like the majority of people in the industry, require proof of concept before they'll invest time and their hard-earned contacts in you. They need to know, with as much confidence as they can have in this chaotic industry, that you're a draw live, that you can perform well enough for an audience to pay to see you, and then pay more to see you the next time, in a bigger venue.

Having a healthy mailing list, and a significant (and uncontrived) following on social networks, can be a major attraction for agents. Positive live reviews from authoritative sources help too, as do good quality live photos and videos, especially if the venues are obviously busy and the crowds enthusiastic.

Agents are music fans too and aim to build a roster of artists they like and are proud to represent, so don't think that it's just a case of impressing them with numbers.

The baseline is always great music. The truth of your music's greatness is in the number of people who want to hear it and who are happy to pay for the privilege.

[1]*Seasoned old buggers like me* – *pubs and venues across all lands are rank with jaded failures who ballsed up their chance, if they ever created a chance in the first place. Their bitterness is vampiric. Ignore them. Gloriously.*

[2]*Without having to pay for it* – *it's worth noting that every time a venue opens its doors, puts the power on, hires a P.A. and engineer, and employs someone to work behind the bar, they're "paying for it".*

350

33: <u>Playing Gigs</u>

Another thing I look for is image. Some bands just don't look right on stage. Work on this. I hate to say it, but with live performances it matters. I remember a story a friend of mine told about a hardcore show he once attended where, obviously, all the bands were in black hoodies and covered in tattoos and piercings. He said the band that received most attention all wore Daz white shirts and had UV lights pointing at the stage. A sharp contrast!

Work on the way you look and your performance. It will help for repeat bookings.

The Anonymous Promoter

In the interests of not wasting any more words than is absolutely necessary, I have reduced this chapter to a checklist of heavy-handed do's and don't's. You may remember the signs in municipal swimming pools – 'No Bombing! No Smoking! No Running! No Petting! No Ducking!' – well, this is the gig-related equivalent, minus amusing illustrations.

1.   **DON'T BE LATE FOR SOUNDCHECK** - the success of your gig is at least 47.6% related to the quality of the sound in the room. Yes, I understand that traffic can be bad around Birmingham on a Friday evening and that the drummer has an incredibly small bladder and needs to pee at every service station you pass, still – account for these things and do your best to get to venues in good time, so that you give yourself every chance of getting a great sound.

2. **DO BE CIVIL TO SOUND ENGINEERS** - I've worked with sound engineers for many years. They can't believe the amount of artists they encounter who are brusque with them, treating them like a 3rd class citizen. Neither can I. Remember who's controlling how good – and more particularly, how bad – you can sound. Even if the engineer is grumpy with you, it's best to earth them with a beaming smile and irrepressible positivity.

3. **DO REHEARSE A SET / DON'T JUST BUSK IT** - there are exceptions to this rule, quasi-shambolic geniuses like Jonathan Richman and Daniel Johnston. Giving your set a shape – a beginning, a middle and an end – will make your sets more effective. See the **Chapter 19:** *'Band Practise'* for more details.

4. **DO BE PREPARED TO SHARE BACKLINE** – if there are other artists on the bill, contact them and the venue in advance to sort out who brings the drumkit and whether other elements from the backline can be shared. This can help a night run much more smoothly. Sound engineers will already be on your side if you've arranged a shared drumkit in advance of a gig. (You still bring your own snare / cymbals / bass drum pedal / guirro… every drummer has a guirro, right?)

5. **DO, WHEREVER POSSIBLE, HAVE A SPARE INSTRUMENT, WHERE APPLICABLE** – OK, a trumpet is unlikely to break… but it's wise for guitarists to travel with a spare guitar. Nothing interrupts the flow of a gig quite like having to stop for a few minutes to change / stretch and tune a string.

6. **DO, ALSO, CARRY AN EMERGENCY BOX OF SPARE EVERYTHINGS** – 9V batteries (for FX units, if applicable); strings; drum skins; snare; WD40

(handy for bass drum pedals); switch cleaner (handy for cleaning dirty pots on guitars / amps etc.); Gaffer Tape; a MagLite (or equivalent – venues are dark and instruments are made of little dark things that love to fall onto black floors); a spare guitar strap (unless you're up for playing the guitar on a stool or looking like a hunchback crab); plectrums; leads (power and jack-to-jack); power adaptors (for FX boards / laptops etc.); fuses; painkillers; drumsticks; wire snips & screwdrivers; amp valves… just draw up a list of whatever you have that's breakable and try and include a spare for it and whatever tool is required to fix it.

7. **DO USE TUNERS** – see rant in **Chapter 22:** *'Recording'*. Being out of tune will ruin the vast majority of gigs. It's unnecessary. If my 11yr old daughter can keep her guitar in tune, while being distracted by Minecraft, increasingly uninnocent thoughts of Harry Styles and aspirational American T.V. crack, so can you.

8. **DON'T GET SHITFACED / SMOKE YOUR LUNGS TO TATTERS BEFORE YOU GO ON STAGE** – I don't want to sound like your mother, G.P. or social worker, but – fun and liberating as playing after half a bottle of rum is, it doesn't sound a quarter as good to the audience as it does to you. Smoking – and I've never managed to entirely shake the habit – totally screws your voice up, if you're not particularly careful… and careful probably isn't your watchword if you're a smoker.

9. **DON''T FORGET YOUR MERCH OR YOUR MAILING LIST** – I know bands who do this. It's a little akin to a market trader leaving their daily take behind when they go home.

10. **DON'T TALK BOLLOCKS ON STAGE** – avoid stretching the audience's patience. Few bands

manage to be humorous between songs without making the crowd want to garrotte them slowly.

11. **DON'T BORE US, GET TO THE CHORUS** – not so much a comment on your song structures, more a metaphor for not titting about aimlessly while you're on stage. People's attention is there to maintain, not to fritter away while you fiddle with your knob(s).

12. **DO PLAY AS IF YOUR LIFE DEPENDED ON IT, REGARDLESS OF AUDIENCE SIZE** – converting one person to your cause is, potentially, as valuable as preaching to a hundred of those who are already converted. Give that handful of people a great show and they will tell their friends. Every band in the history of everything gig-shaped has played to 10 or fewer people. That's why pubs are filled with bores who saw U2 / The Smiths / Radiohead / The Stone Roses / Razorlight play to just them and a deaf sheepdog. Obviously in the latter band's case, that was at the end of their career, not the start.

13. **DO REMEMBER THE 'ONE WANKER RULE'** – every crowd has at least one wanker in it. Someone who'll think it's amusing to heckle between songs; who'll try to get up on stage; who'll maybe throw something at you, while hiding in the shadows. These brave founts of bastard shouldn't sour your experience of the gig, or be allowed to ruin proceedings for everyone. Get them removed. Do it without drama and without bestowing upon them the attention they crave. If you can't get rid of them, ignore them as if they're double glazing salespeople on your doorstep on a bank holiday morning.

14. **DON'T LEAVE YOUR EQUIPMENT UNATTENDED** – this applies to when you're in the venue as well as when the equipment is stowed in your transport. Nothing derails a band as surely as getting all of

their equipment nicked because they thought it'd
be OK while they all went for a quick loo break.
Van doors are easier to jimmy open than dandelion
seed deadlocks (with a hair dryer). When a band
get their equipment nicked, it's not so much the
loss of equipment that splits them up as the
acrimony and recriminations as to whose fault the
theft was.

15. **DON'T OVER PLAY** – leave an audience wanting
more. Any band playing for more than 45 minutes
had better have very good reason, and at least 3 hit
singles, to justify doing so.

16. **DO LISTEN TO THE SOUND ENGINEERS** – if they
have asked you to keep an amplifier turned down
on stage, do so. They're not trying to sabotage your
sound. Sound engineering is all about limited
control over a chaotic environment. Don't make it
more chaotic than it needs to be. Chaos isn't good,
not even in rock 'n' roll. The controlled, sonic
illusion of chaos is, however, very good, thrilling
and entirely in the hands and ears of your engineer.
Trust them. They can hear it all better than you can.

17. **DO USE IN HOUSE ENGINEERS WHERE YOU
CAN** – I've worked in a venue every weekend for
the best part of 20 years. I can't tell you how
frequently an uppity band have brought their own
engineer in, simply because they think that makes
them look like a proper band, only for the engineer
to completely screw their sound up. In house
engineers are, generally, very good and a much
better option. They know the rooms they work in;
which frequencies are problematic and likely to
feedback; the volume limits for the venue. Bringing
your own apprentice engineer along, just because
they know when a guitar solo kicks in and they can
lift it in the mix, is a false benefit and a potential
disadvantage. However if you have a great,

experienced pro engineer with you, all well and good. They'll know to liaise with the in house engineer, anyway. But until you can afford someone better than the engineers provided, use the engineers provided!!

18. **DO HAVE FUN** – enjoy what you do up on that stage and that joy will be transmitted to the audience. You can have fun playing the dourest and darkest music imaginable. You don't have to behave like a wacky Eurovision entry. Take your music seriously, by all means, but have serious fun with it. Finding an audience while you're stuck up your own arse is much more difficult than finding an audience outside your own arse. And you can quote me on that.

34: <u>Clwb Ifor Bach On Getting A Gig</u>

Clwb Ifor Bach is a historic music venue in Cardiff, Wales. It has been a cornerstone of Welsh music and culture since 1983. As well as having provided a vitally important platform for (now) internationally-recognised indigenous artists like Super Furry Animals, Catatonia, Gorky's Zygotic Mynci, Funeral For A Friend, Future of the Left, High Contrast et al, Clwb (as it is generally known) is a vital touring venue for international artists: the likes of Autechre, Pavement, Coldplay and many hundreds of others, played key, early shows at the venue... bringing inspirational live music to a city that had, previously, been too easy to overlook for touring artists.

Clwb (pronounced Club) is a proactive supporter of the Welsh language: its staff, its website and its promotional materials are all bilingual, and valuably so, when it comes to nurturing the Welsh language. Its PA – and its facilities, generally – are widely-regarded in the industry as being amongst the best for its size (up to a capacity of 380) for gigging artists in the UK.

It continues to support a very wide range of music (bands, solo artists and DJ's, covering most imaginable musical denominations) across its three floors, more-or-less every night of the week.

Richard 'Chill' Hawkins manages the venue, books artists and oversees a team of excellent, independent promoters.

What is Clwb Ifor Bach's music policy?

We're open to anything, although the phrase "we can do a covers set" doesn't sit well. I'm not against covers or

358

tribute bands but would always prioritise original material bands.

What proportion of the bands who play are booked through agents?

It varies, although we do have a lot of bands through agents, I'd say it's a fairly even mix.

Do bands ever get gigs at your venue via submitting unsolicited demos?

Yes, they do. It tends to be links, like a soundcloud that I listen to. We have fewer and fewer CDs or tapes through nowadays.

What is it that can make an artist submitting a demo / link successful?

Usually just my own personal taste, but we (the team of promoters at the venue) do all give submissions a listen. Sometimes, it's if we think they'd work with a touring band. Quite often, it's timing, when you happen to listen to it and maybe they fit something you need to fill. For example, a support slot may need filling and I'm hoping to put on someone new.

Does an artist need to have a following before they approach you or one of your promoters?

If I have a touring band, that I think will sell well, I'm more willing to try new bands, despite their perceived following. Otherwise, I think the combined bill of bands is more important than the following of an individual band. There has been occasions, during quiet periods, where I have looked at well-supported local bands, to do a prominent weekend night gig.

New bands get frustrated. They understand that to get a good gig, they need a following, but they can't get a

following without doing good gigs. It's a chicken and egg conundrum. What is the solution to that conundrum, from your point of view?

For myself, I don't think that a following, is an issue, although it does help.

Honestly, some of the issues I have are local artists playing too many local shows in a short period of time. Bands complain that promoters aren't doing their job, but it needs to be supported on both sides. I've put on a 3 band bill, which I think is exciting and will work well for the bands and us, only to discover some of those bands then go on to book a show down the road or, even, a free show at a funded local arts centre, the day before.

Is an OK band who work hard to galvanise their following, and who work hard to promote a gig, a more attractive proposition to you than a genius band who are lazy buggers and do little / nothing to co-promote?

Yes. I could tell you about a few bands who do nothing and then complain about ticket sales.

What can a new band do to improve their chances of getting a gig?

Hard to know. A good band will always garner attention, but it will always be a venue's personal choice. There're bands now that we don't book, as they appear to have found a home elsewhere, as that venue, bar, restaurant, hipster joint, suit what they play.

How much can being an active and supportive member of the local scene – being a recognised face in the audience at gigs in Clwb – improve a band's chances of getting a gig?

It helps, because as much as discovering new music is a joy, having it handed to you on a plate makes life easier.

How do you recommend a band approaches the subject of payment?

Ask outright. I'll ask for availability for a booking, the band agrees, then they need to ask about money. Sometimes I honestly forget to discuss money, as it's a Facebook conversation, but will try to agree a fee then and there. When I talk money, sometimes we'll negotiate, but I will always suggest that if they're not happy with what I can offer, then I would rather they said "no".

What is it that you, as a venue, notice about a band that makes them viable for you and your business? (Is the amount of 'likes' they have on Facebook, for example, ever persuasive?)

The amount of likes would help, but I think it often paints a false picture. There's nothing in particular, as it varies from band to band. Sometimes you just hear a demo you like. It could be word of mouth or seeing a band playing elsewhere.

I put Foals on after seeing them support Battles in Oxford in 2006, they had no agent but I spoke to them at the gig. They then played Clwb 4 or 5 times, supporting, headlining and acquiring an agent on the way.

Can a business like yours afford to take a leap of faith on an unknown band? I imagine you have to be pragmatic?

Taking a leap of faith on an unknown band would mean it has to sit alongside something that is viable. Possibly any of the following options; playing a support slot, playing a downsized show, whilst we have another event upstairs, or suggesting the band hire the venue themselves.

Throughout the book, I've stressed the importance of not relying just on social networks to promote music or gigs. Would you echo that?

Yes. As we come from a different generation, it's very

evident, that bands can be very savvy with social networking, but a lot of old methods, like flyers posters, word of mouth, bullying friends to come, is no longer the case.

Find out more about this excellent venue at their website: http://www.clwb.net
You can find them on Twitter, too: @clwbiforbach

35: <u>Catfish & the Bottlemen On Getting A Gig</u>

Unusually, but appropriately for this section of the book, Catfish and the Bottlemen were one of the few Welsh bands who I grew to love as a live entity before I ever heard their recordings.

They started playing the venue where I'm a resident D.J.1, in 2009 or 2010. When they first graced our stage, they were still a good few years off having legal ID in their back pockets, but they were already very good. Even then, when they were leather jacket-clad Bambis finding their guitar-toting hooves, it was clear that they knew exactly what they wanted to do.

They had determination in their eyes and were very complimentary about the music I played before they went on stage. Butter me up once and I'm a friend for life.

They've gone on to become one of the hardest working live bands in the UK. Now, hard work doesn't, in itself, make rock 'n' roll transcendent. Applying a work ethic isn't a guarantee that you'll turn into a great band.

However Catfish and the Bottlemen also know how to write a great song. And they look good.

All of the important elements were there, and they managed to align the heavens in their favour by driving up and down the country, for the last few years, playing anywhere that would have them.

Soon, the venues had to get bigger to accommodate

their burgeoning audience. Management and an agent came calling. This momentum, and the excellence of their singles, earned them praise and significant support on national radio.

It was, almost, an old school, rock 'n' roll tale. One you mightn't have thought possible in the cynical tweens of the new-ish millennium.

Catfish and the Bottlemen conquered the U.K. by gigging it to death out the back of a transit.

Apt, then, that Van is their singer's christian name. He very kindly took time out during a frantic, sold out tour and the recording of their debut album, to answer a few questions about their ascent, and about gigging.

How did you get your first gigs? Was it all a disadvantage coming from a sleepy north Wales town?

I used to get all our first gigs. I used to manage us, really. We started off playing in pubs around the North West to raise enough money to tour. We eventually got our own van and just spent about two years of our lives in it.

We never really got given anything and that's still the case. We've always had to work from nowhere, if you know what I mean? We consider it a blessing as well as a curse, to be honest.

Living so far away from everything disciplined us massively at such a young age. We got so used to the long drives up and down the motorways at all hours of the morning, it made us so strong as a band and mentally. I was heading off to a gig midweek in somewhere like Sheffield and then getting home at about 6am, going to bed for two hours and then getting straight back up for school in the mornings. It was hard, man, but really worth it.

What was it that made you 'attractive' to promoters, in those early days?

To be honest I think it was our persistence. I never gave up pestering promoters for gigs. 'Cause I was like fourteen and the lads were sixteen, I don't think we got taken too seriously. But I knew if people gave us the opportunity then we could do them proud. After playing for a lot of promoters, I made sure they knew how appreciative I was of them. I used to go up and knock on their doors after the shows and thank them and all their staff. We've stayed close to a lot of promoters we played for at the start as they've been so good and loyal to us growing up as a band.

You've always had a reputation for being thoroughly excellent people – obviously the music is the major reason you're doing well, do you think that having manners and being good to people (audience / promoters etc.) has served you well, too?

Haha, That's lovely to hear that mate. I think that having manners and being good to people serves you well in life, not just in music. Why would you not be? My Mum and Dad brought me up to look after everything you love. So I do. I'm so in love with my life, the people in it and the people I write songs for, man.

Does the experience of touring match up to the expectation?

Yeah, It's beyond expectation! We were happy playing to ten people in Dorset, in a pub we'd never been to before. We've always loved this. It's what our band's been about from the ground. We never wanted to make music to sell it, we just wanted to tour it, and get to know cities and the people in them.

So, to come here (to Guildford) tonight... and the whole

tour's been sold out… is amazing. It's a lovely town. Good people. Last time we played here was to about three people and tonight it's sold out!

We make sure we stay behind for hours after the gig and meet everybody, have a drink with everyone. We couldn't be more pleased. It's the nicest thing possible, we're just enjoying ourselves. It's crazy that people are really into it. We're overwhelmed by it all.

Hanging out with your audience, was that something you picked up from the bands you went to see when you were younger, or is that just a natural part of your personalities?

When I used to go and see bands, like everybody else I thought they were gods! I'd loved to have met them but I never got a chance to meet anyone, really. We were always jumping on the last train back to Llandudno.

There's a lot of bands who are a lot more stylish than us, and a lot cooler than us[2] – we know that… we're just about making music. All we wanted to do was to play for people.

I've always been about bands like Oasis, when they first came out, and The Stone Roses – not necessarily from a musical point of view, but the side of it where they could have been your neighbour all their lives. They became massive bands but it was still like they lived next door to you.

Tonight we've turned up in Guildford and there's two girls here who've been waiting since one 'o' clock this afternoon, and I said, "You're mad, waiting round for six hours, what are you doing?" I went in to get them drinks and t-shirts to say 'thank you'.

It's just in my personality to do that. I just love meeting people.

Some of it's a little strange. I met this girl the other week and she asked me to sign something, I did and she started crying her eyes out, as if I was some kind of immortal, which is mad. I said, "don't get upset, we're just normal people... obviously!" I just wanted to make it really clear to everybody who's into the band that we're the same as them. Shouldn't need saying.

I don't know many other bands who are like that, so maybe inside of me probably thought it was good to be different to everybody else.

I think it is. My experience of touring with bands is pretty limited. But I have spent time in the States with The Joy Formidable, and they're like that with their audience. To me it seems like the most natural thing in the world to do, but some artists feel they need to closet themselves away. Do you think that that's to try and maintain mystery? Or is it because they have quite shy personalities?

A bit of both, probably. I think a lot of bands like to stay mystical and that kind of thing, and a lot of them... well, the hours are exhausting... you go to bed at five in the morning and you're up at seven. You go soundcheck; you barely have time to eat anything and, when you're done, you are buggered! Maybe it's down to that as well. Because at the end of the night, when you've finished a gig and you're all sweaty and horrible, the last thing you want to do is meet people.

It's just the thought that hanging out for an hour or two could make people's night. That's the difference between not doing it and doing it.

I don't blame anyone for not doing it because I guess a lot of it is down to personality and, you know, I've been told that talking after a gig is the worst thing for singers, and this girl I spoke to told me that Tom Jones, singers like that, don't go out and see their fans after gigs because if they went out, and there was loud music on that they'd have to talk over to be heard, it'd wear out their voice.

So there could be lots of different reasons. I don't know. I just think it's really nice for people to think that it's their band, you know? Not just us four making the music, they're part of it, too.

On the last tour, I was saying to the crowd, let us know which songs you like and which you don't, and we'll put the ones you do like on the album. And the ones you don't like, we'll rewrite, or take off. I wanted people to pick the album for us, to be involved in what we're doing.

How do you think gigging has improved the band. If you look at those early gigs you did for us in Telford's (Warehouse, Chester - see below), you were tight – which isn't really a compliment for a band, I don't think – but you were also good. Now, 3 or 4 years later, you have great songs and a real, natural musicality… is that the result of so much touring?

Well, you know what you say about bands being called 'tight'. There's a good story about Roy Keane… I think it was Alex Ferguson who said: "the thing I love about Keane is that he'll cover every blade of grass, right up until the last minute" and Roy Keane was a bit offended by that because he was thinking, "shouldn't everybody do that? Shouldn't everyone run until the last minute for their team?"

He was offended at the thought that that was his quality. So, when you say about the 'tight' thing, if you weren't being described as tight then you haven't earned your crust, you're not good enough.

Unless that's your thing, like The Libertines or someone, which is based around the looseness or spontaneity of being together. But there's still a togetherness, whether it's loose or not.

So with the tightness thing, I just think it's quintessential for a band to have that.

In terms of gigging, yes it was massively important in making us better. We couldn't have been one of those bands that got picked up after a month of gigging. I know a load of bands who are together now, who are blowing up now. Bands like Royal Blood who have only been together for under a year. You know, they're awesome. I think that it's because they're naturally gifted people. We weren't born good. We were crap. We had to graft. I think anybody can do anything. I think, if you wanted to, you could walk on the moon, if you wanted it that much.

So we were one of those bands that weren't gifted from birth. We literally worked and worked and worked at it.

Sometimes when bands work that hard, they can sound pedestrian, like they've put the spark out, but there's a real spark to your music… is that something that you found through working hard?

I think that if there's a spark to something, it's to do with the way we write. I don't record anything or note it down. If I don't remember an idea I have for a song the following morning, then 60,000 people in a stadium aren't going to remember it.

I never write anything down. If I write a chorus and I think it's brilliant but I wake up in the morning and I can't sing it, I know it wasn't good enough.

A lot of the songwriting I do is done at night. So it'll maybe take me two hours to write a tune and then next morning, the bits that I remember I just glue up with other memorable bits, and then that's done. I try not to overthink it.

I read something interesting about John Lennon. He would write something down and then do his best to never go back and correct it, because what he was singing there and then was the most natural and right thing for the song.

I've portrayed you in the introduction as if you had a

370

conscious philosophy from the start to 'conquer the country' by playing live. Some people thought that that wasn't possible any more, but clearly it is. Was it a considered strategy for you or were you following your instincts, just doing what you wanted to do?

It definitely wasn't considered. If someone had come and offered us a record deal and said "you're going to be massive in a month", would we have taken it or would we have done it our way? It's an interesting question. Because we have literally slept in the back of a van for years and we've still got nothing. We do it for the love of it.

The main reason we did it was, we started in Llandudno and there was nowhere we could gig, really... nowhere really close. Chester was probably the closest place to home, or Bangor, where we could get a gig.

You know, a lot of people wait for their door to be knocked on by a label but we had to go and do it ourselves.

I've been to record companies, pretended I had a meeting with the head, and I've gone to them: "you need to check this band out..."

I met Geoff Travis once (head of Rough Trade) and I was just a bright-eyed little kid and I said: "Got the new Strokes on this CD, here..." and I gave it to him, and I was expecting a phone call... as if I was going to get one! I was just a little kid and the CD was probably rubbish.

We've always been about banging on doors. I've had it drilled into me from a young age. I was told, if you want to make something of yourself, don't wait for it to happen, go and do it.

That's a lot of the mentality and another reason was because this is what we like doing. Me, personally, I don't like being in a studio... I hate recording... I really struggle with photos and videos. For us it was just about imagining that we could sell out arenas. It was never about imagining we could get a number 1, it was just about imagining we could sell an arena out.

Back to that point about banging on doors. Some bands, in removed areas, do struggle getting those out of town gigs, how did you do it? How did you approach promoters? It was more than just knocking on doors, wasn't it?

If you speak to any promoter from our early days, they'd probably say that I was the most annoying person that you could ever meet, because I wouldn't give up. Now I'm friends with them all. In Telford's, people like Stew (Etcell, who used to book the bands at the venue… a great, hairy Aussie) would book us just to get me off his back. Because I'd tell him lies and exaggerate a bit, tell him we were on tour with such-and-such-a big band… and eventually he just said: "All right, you little shit! Come and do a gig for us…" And he stuck with us and we stuck with him.

I used to play football with the older lads in school and they used to kick the shit out of me, but I kept getting back up and towards the end they admired me. Me and my other mate got in their team. It's one of those things where you keep on getting up and asking people to give you a chance, and don't stop until you get that chance.

A lot of it was to do with that.

Another thing we used to do was, we'd put guerrilla gigs on. Once we turned up to a Kasabian gig and I told the promoter we were on the bill, trying to sneak on, and he said "No way. You're not getting on." So we thought, while we're here… so we revved up a generator in the car-park and, you know when thousands of people come out of the venue after a gig? We were there in ninja masks and we had a mate giving CD's out for us, and we basically played to the crowd that Kasabian had just played to. And we've got fans who come to our gigs now because of that, you know.

372

We played in Warrington the other day, an acoustic set, in a full shop, and I mentioned that story and a dozen or so of the people there came up afterwards and said: "we were at that gig!"

It's about empowering yourself, isn't it? It's just about being positive.

Yeah, exactly, that's what it was all about.

Ever since I've been a kid it's been about that. When I was with my mum and dad, raised in the back of the car, just with love, every challenge, we'd find a solution.

I used to live in a B&B when I was a kid. Sometimes my mum and dad would have to let the extra room out, our bedroom, because they needed the money to keep going, you know? And they would let our actual bedroom out, with my little bed in it. They'd trick me and say that we were playing a game of hide and seek, and we'd sleep in the living room. Just to get by.

I've been raised to feel that wherever you are, see the positive in it.

No matter what happens, we're bursting with positivity.

How important is it for your set to have a beginning, a middle and an end? Isn't it important for a gig to have a shape to make it more memorable?

I think it's massively important to have a good end. Our last song in the set, and the last song on the album, isn't really a song... I don't really see the point in writing a song, at this stage of the band, that is too deep. I just think it's about writing songs that people can party to and really feel good about.

Until you've built up a really big audience, save your deep songs for then.

I think the last song should be about making the audience feel "Fuuuuck… they're really tearing the place apart!" So, our last song… I wouldn't even really rate it as a song, but to watch it live it's just about that moment… this is big!

I think it's good to start with a bang. It depends, really. I think I know what the set's going to be if we start playing bigger venues, you know – two thousand capacity and above, I think I know what we would start with. I like the idea of starting with a slow song.

Live it's important that you put your singles, or your hits, in the right places so that people have a sense of anticipation and of that expectation getting rewarded throughout the set. Because a lot of bands put their new single last. I always put our new single first! I think it's quite a bold move to do that because you're basically playing your best song, or the one that most people are likely to have been hearing.

I like starting with a bang, ending with a bang, and in the middle just maintaining enough energy and power for the audience to think that we've really got it.

We've always thought that every one of our songs are as good as each other, so exactly where we put them in the set doesn't worry us.

Thank you Van McCann, the least worried man in rock 'n' roll. Which goes some way to explaining why Catfish and the Bottlemen are one of the most life-affirming bands you could hope to see.

Keep an eye on http://catfishandthebottlemen.com for details of upcoming dates (in the U.S. and Europe too). Their excellent debut album 'The Balcony' is out now on Island / Communion Records. Follow @thebottlemen on Twitter.

If we enjoy the ride even a quarter as much as they are, we're in for a very good time indeed.

[1]*Resident D.J.* - *Telford's Warehouse, Chester. Every 2nd & 4th Friday.* http://telfordswarehousechester.com *- my spiritual home. A great venue that has been supportive of my musical adventures for over 20 years now.*

[2]***There's a lot of bands who are a lot more stylish than us, and a lot cooler than us*** *- I'd dispute that strongly. Catfish do things their own way, regardless of fads, what's 'cooler' than that?*

PLAYLIST:
Catfish & the Bottlemen - The Balcony (2014)

36: <u>Critical Reaction</u>

It's very good when you have a new song to play it to somebody. Play it to a few different types of people and see what the reaction is. And part of being a singer-songwriter is to learn / have the ability to make a judgement on what other people think about it without them stating it explicitly. It's almost like a sensory thing. You can pick up what people really think about things just by body language and the way they respond. Look at the people you're singing at. It's very important to look at the people you're singing at because you can more accurately gauge their reaction.

Ray Davies, The Kinks / solo

Ray Davies has written some of the greatest, most acute, sensitive and grittily romantic songs in pop music's canon. Even he – the man who penned such undisputed classics as Tired Of Waiting, Waterloo Sunset, Days, Shangri-La, Deadend Street and Lola – cares what other people think about his songs.

He's also careful to not care too obviously.

There is even a word for giving the impression that you don't care, overtly, about your art. The Oxford English Dictionary defines *sprezzatura* as: *"Ease of manner, studied carelessness; the appearance of acting or being done without effort; spec. of literary style or performance."*

It's a word that dates back to 1528. Seems that insouciance in art predates rock 'n' roll by a good few hundred years.

Rock 'n' roll, you see, is supposed to be the antithesis of caring and conformity. Whereas conformity and being a functional member of society is predicated on caring what other people think and behaving accordingly (making sure that you stick to the rules or pay the consequences); rock 'n' roll is about giving the impression that you really don't give a fuck what other people think, breaking the rules, unconformity, brandishing a middle finger to the establishment and their 'consequences'.

At least, that was the unwritten manifesto when rock 'n' roll blew up and out of the rubble of post-war austerity and conservatism.

That was almost sixty years ago. Rock 'n' roll hasn't been seen as subversive for a long time. When prime-minsters invite bands to 10 Downing St., and they actually go, it's a symbol that the art-form has become as quaintly gentrified as Volkswagen camper vans.

A lot of the time music is to do with people saying "I don't want to be like everybody else, I'm a rebel" and I think that kind-of rock 'n' roll rebellion thing is wearing a bit thin somehow because it's been done to death for so long.

I was always more frustrated that I was considered marginal and that we as a group were considered to be on the margins of society. Whereas I always thought that we were a pop band and mainstream.

People always thought we were very strange just writing about normal people doing normal things. Whereas I find it more strange that other people write about riding a motorbike going down Route 66 when they've never been to America in their life.

Jarvis Cocker, Pulp

The impression that music has become an agent of conformity, not rebellion, is further highlighted by X-Factor.

The most popular music show on T.V. (*still*) is one where anodyne wannabes sing karaoke for the judgement of a panel made up of the similarly anodyne.

Yes, it can be a fun viewing, if you enjoy watching the deluded being humiliated by the overblown. Yes, its questionable merits certainly shine brighter in the face of those dour-faced killjoys who advocate campaigns for 'real music'. (I prefer X-Factor to that prescriptivism, truly.)

This televisual juggernaut's most depressing legacy, though, is the impression it gives its legions of impressionable, young viewers that success is about conforming, publicly, to the views of the judges and the wishes of an audience.

Designing pop stars to conform to an audience's desires is nothing new. It's just the shamelessness of how it's done now that gives the impression that rock 'n' roll / pop music is all cadaver, no spirit, ready to be wheeled off to the morgue in a neon fanfare, preceded by copious, crocodile tears cried to camera 3.

It's up to *you* to defibrillate pop's body. And one philosophy that will help is for you to have a healthy disregard for other people's opinions.

The majority of the artists I support on my show would claim that they make their music for themselves, first and foremost. The hoariest cliche in music adds, "but if anyone else likes it, it's a bonus."

I don't doubt that a high percentage of the creative beasts I have parasitically milked for the last two decades are oblivious to other people's opinions while they're hammering away at the forge. But the moment a song is finished and they reveal it to their audience, they start to care a great deal.

There's nothing wrong in that. The notion of pleasing an audience, or acknowledging that you set out to please an audience, is somehow seen as lacking integrity and of less artistic value.

Motown was pretty much built on a strategy of selling a large amount of hit records. The likes of Carole King, Phil Spector and Burt Bacharach would clock into the Brill Building with the express intention of writing hit singles. So some of the greatest examples of pop music were written expressly and unashamedly to please an audience. It's no bad thing.

My advice would be, don't listen to anyone. Just do what you believe is right. If you think your music is good, stick by it and work it really hard. Don't change your style, your image your artwork or anything for anyone otherwise it's kind of pointless and you could just go on X Factor.

Those things might not mean that much to you – like artwork – but they did to me and I'm very glad that I stuck by everything that I've done, pretty much. If it happens to work and takes off for you then you can be truly proud that this was your thing and just be confident in what you've done and don't be made into something that you don't want to be.

Manda Rin, Bis

Other people's opinions only matter if you let them matter. And, naturally, their influence over your music will differ according to who they are and their role in your life.

There are five groups of people who will offer an opinion on your music:

1) **You**. If you're satisfied with the music you make and you've already been your own worst critic (as has been implored in earlier chapters of this book), then other people's opinions shouldn't tarnish any pride and

satisfaction you have in your work.

Your opinion on your music is unlikely to influence anyone else's because, of course, you're biased. But your enthusiasm for what you do can draw people to your work.

If your own assessment is an accurate one, it will be much easier for you to find the right level for your releases and people who are willing to work with you.

If you haven't been your own worst critic, and you've over-valued your music, finding people (an audience / the industry) to support you will be much more difficult. No one in the music industry will be impressed by bravado alone.

The important thing is to keep monitoring how you're doing, how the songs are going down. Don't take comments off your friends and your family as gospel. It's strangers that you need to be watching. And if you're winning over strangers then you're on the right track. If your songs aren't really winning over strangers then you have to stay a little bit humble and not just dig the same hole deeper. Be prepared to abandon a well-worn path and go back and start again from first principles.

Tom Robinson, songwriter / 6Music new music guru

2) **Your friends and family**. Friends and family are likely to be especially supportive of your musical efforts. They provide invaluable support through hard times, buoy your ego when it has been pierced by a scathing rejection e-mail, but take any opinion they have of your music with a gritter-full of salt.

Think of all those embarrassingly exploitative occasions in the early rounds of X Factor when family members stand in the wings, completely oblivious to their progeny's awfulness as it's beamed into the nation's living rooms in the name of entertainment. When did you ever hear a mum say: "I don't know what my daughter's doing here, it's obvious to anyone with an eardrum that she's got a voice like a knotted fox."

An excellent independent record label I know was besieged by an irate builder, convinced of his son's musical excellence, despite that music's obvious and awful shortcomings. Threats were made, the police had to be called, it was a frightening example of how delusions of excellence can be propagated by your nearest and dearest.

My dad would drag his mates upstairs into my room and ask me to play for them:

"He's better than any of that lot on Top of the Pops[1]," he would say to his drinking buddies. But I wasn't. Parents don't so much see things through rose-tinted spectacles as hear you through DNA-tainted headphones. Ones with built-in AutoTune and a device that can turn pedestrian songwriting into something olympic.

So, do value any support you get from your family but don't let it delude you as to your music's absolute qualities. Music is subjective but the decisions that the music industry makes are based on subjective authority, not DNA. Labels, radio stations, blogs, agents and promoters support who they like, in the main, but they do it having listened to everything else that is pushed their way for appraisal. Your friends and family have no real benchmark to judge you against, and because they love you, it's difficult for them to be honest and objective with you.

3) **Your audience**. Your audience's opinion on your music is as important as you want it to be. As mentioned earlier, a high proportion of the artists who submit music to my show say they make their music, resolutely, for themselves. The audience aren't in their mind while they're creating. It's only after the fact, when a hotly-forged new

song is ready to be unveiled (either live or recorded) that the audience are considered.

The size of your audience, and its preparedness to buy tickets to see you or your releases, is the determining factor on whether you will be a success, or not.

Being wise to their opinions, without consciously shaping yourself for them, is the recommended course of action.

One of my absolute favourite bands keep themselves very accessible to their worldwide following, and have a regular dialogue with them, but they would never base an artistic decision on their audience's opinion. The audience doesn't write the songs, after all. One of the reasons this band has endured and been successful is that they don't patronise those who follow them. They're respectful of their audience but don't let them determine the direction of the art. The art is off limits.

4) **Critics**. The critic is anyone who, like me, is detailed with finding the best music that they can and then directing it towards an audience.

Critics run record labels, radio shows, write for blogs and music magazines. They promote shows. They have 'subjective authority' in that their opinion counts more than that of the everyman on the street, because they make the decisions as to which bands get signed, played, booked and written about. This 'authority' is vested in them by whoever it is that buys their label's records, reads their writing, listens to their shows or podcasts or goes to the gigs they promote.

When critics have significant authority – say the authority that Zane Lowe has on his BBC Radio 1 show because of the size of his audience – their opinion on your music can be decisive in whether or not you find a bigger audience.

The more powerful the critic, the more music they will be bombarded with, the less likely it is that they will listen to every piece of music (or close) that is sent their way.

Powerful critics rely on other filters: word of mouth, labels, radio shows, publications, promoters whose booking policy they trust.

There is an unwritten hierarchy of critics and there can be a stifling etiquette amongst them, and those who sue for their attentions. This is why influential radio shows have exclusive first-plays of singles, access to sessions etc. It's why agents book bands into a hierarchy of venues, mostly according to size, but not always.

Aiming above your place in the hierarchy, when you're not ready, isn't advised. Yes, it looks like a class structure for a cultural form that was partly, at least, supposed to be a poke in the eye of class-ridden institutions. Sadly music has its own old boys network. Be aware of it. Let's hope you can do something to help dismantle it.

5) **Anonymous strangers**. Beware the *anonymous* stranger. Anonymity can be a powerful and necessary weapon for the disenfranchised, fighting against a corrupt regime. In the context of hurling insults and negativity about on the internet, though, it's the first and last bastion of the shameless coward.

Opinions are like arseholes, everybody has one, and the most gutless also have an anonymous Twitter account to air theirs, whenever they like.

I am fully immune to criticism. I don't mean that I arrogantly don't listen to it, I'm just immune. They said on TV that I was violent, my sons have seen that! I don't care what anyone writes about me, I was falsely accused and it puts all of that in perspective.

Ian Brown, The Stone Roses

I suspect that contemporary music-makers get used to negative criticism early on. Whereas artists from a previous age might have heard the occasional Chinese whisper of inter-band banter, and perhaps had to tolerate a negative review from a fanzine or the music press (if they reached the sanctified level where they were being written about by the national music papers), these days the potential anonymity of social networks has meant that poisonous and negative views about your music are more easily-aired than ever before.

My view is that if someone isn't willing to put their name to a criticism, it isn't worth *anything*. An opinion only has validity when you know who it came from and what motivated them to say it.

The best rebuttal is a silent one; one that underlines, without you having to go to the trouble of saying so, that you're confident in what you are and the music you make.

Music is an emotive subject and humanity is bogglingly complex. Not everyone will, or should, like what you do. Engendering a bland conformity with your music would indicate that your music is blandly conformative.

Be prepared for pettiness and back-stabbing. Rise above them. They're a sure sign that you're moving in the right, envy-inducing direction.

So that's the five, broad groups of people who will hear you. Your audience won't be made up of just one group. A wide variety of people will come to your music for different reasons: some will listen to you because they want to, others will have to be persuaded; some will approach your music with enthusiasm, others with weary cynicism.

You can't please everyone. That is why the most important person to please is there at Number 1. It's you.

Please you, make music that satisfies you, and other people are more likely to be satisfied, too.

As soon as you feel like someone has walked up and plonked a name tag sticker on you you're just going to rip it off as soon as possible.

Elliott Smith

The criticism you receive will either be positive (i.e. praise), negative, a combination of the two, or you'll get no response at all.

A positive response is, seemingly, the most desirable. It could, after all, lead to a record deal or radio exposure (if it comes from one of the critics). Positive responses, from people with little authority (friends / family) are a nice fillip, but little more. A positive response from your audience, similarly, is the kind of thing that makes practising in hypothermic rehearsal rooms bearable. Or a drive to Exeter, from Leeds, when the fee is a pasty and half a crate of flat Panda Pops.

A positive response, with some provisos and constructive criticism is, if anything, more desirable. I think I'd be suspicious of a label who had no ideas of their own on how to improve my music, or the delivery of that music. Similarly an agent who, having witnessed my live set, couldn't offer some feedback as to how it could be improved, or how I could better present it, is a suspiciously un-agent-like agent.

A negative response is the hardest to deal with. Because of dwindling staff in almost every environ of the industry, negative feedback most frequently manifests itself as: no response at all.

Which causes understandable confusion. If you don't

get a response , does that mean that your e-mail / upload or package hasn't been received?

It's important to check but I'd leave it a week, at least. As I've mentioned elsewhere in the book, every industry type you send your music to will have a teetering pile of unsolicited demos they know they need to get through (unlistened to demos manage to teeter, even in inboxes).

They have guilt-ridden nightmares about that pile. They know that it's as much a pile of individual dreams as much as it is a pile of music. It's not all about altruism, though. They understand that somewhere in that pile could be the future of music. It's like being given a pile of free lottery tickets but assuming that a winning one isn't in there because a winning one never has been, before…

And that "before…" will nag at them, ulcerate their stomach, until they respond to its call and listen through the pile, with growing despondency, because great music is rarer than white crows.

Their despondency won't be improved by receiving an email from you, the day after your submission, enquiring why you haven't had a response, yet?

"Because I'm still listening through this endless, teetering pile… trying to get to you like a free climber reaching for Everest's distant peak in a 200mph storm…"

We industry types like to over egg our position. It helps us feel important. As we can't make good music ourselves, being obstinate and demanding as to how we listen to other people's is the surest way we've found to bolster our egos.

Don't provoke our outer child.

Industry folk are looking for people whose music they like, first and foremost, but also for people who they can envisage working with. If you come across as impatient, rude or ignorant, it'll reduce your chances of a positive response significantly.

I try to offer constructive criticism where I can but even a provincial carthorse like me can't find anywhere near the time required to respond to every demo submission. Which is why I wrote this book. And why, particularly, I wrote the next chapter.

Contained therein you will find a glittering, narcissistic trove of the reasons why I reject demos. I suspect it will reveal much more about me than it will about you.

Still, read on, dear friend. You've made it this far and we're almost at the end.

[1] *Top of the Pops* - *prime time TV show 'enjoyed' by all the family, that featured performances and videos from a broad selection of that week's Top 40 artists.*

37: <u>Reasons For Rejection</u>

I imagine that you've learnt – inadvertently, unless you're my mum – more about me while reading this book than you anticipated or desired. I have tried to keep myself in the background, honestly I have. However gobshite radio presenters don't do 'background'. We're the animated .gif's of background.

I've sought numerous other voices and opinions in the writing of this book, so that it had more gravitas and authority than 'just me'. 'Just me', however, is what this chapter is all about.

Over the next few pages I will detail what I regard to be the most common mistakes that people make when they're submitting music for airplay on *my* radio show. These are *my* **Reasons For Rejection**, the errors of judgement that render music unsuitable for broadcast, purely from *my own point of view*.

What I say here is written entirely from my own perspective. I'm not representing BBC-wide Introducing policy. These thoughts are my own and not the corporation's, Zane Lowe's or George Orwell's. I've always felt uncomfortable with department-wide music policies (not just at the BBC... anywhere). If music isn't subjective, and driven by the individual passions of those who present it, or release it, or promote it, it may as well come via a North Korean dictate.

Music is about freedom. Your freedom to make it; my freedom to say exactly what I think about it.

Honesty is the greatest respect I can pay you for your time and creative efforts.

I don't think that original music-makers are best served

by the stock responses automatically fired out by the music industry…

Thank you for taking the trouble to submit your demo to us. Unfortunately it's not quite what we're looking for at the moment. Please do send us any recordings you make in the future, though, so that we can consider them for airplay. Good luck x x

But what was it you didn't like? WHAT **ARE** YOU LOOKING FOR?

My responses are usually more along the following lines:

I stopped listening to your first track when it was clear you hadn't bothered tuning the guitar. In fact, I was so horrified by how out of tune the guitar was, I dropped my favourite mug and smashed it. Could you reply with an address that I can forward a bill to, please?

I don't know whether it's arrogant or rude (it is a real example). I think it's honest. It leaves the artist in no doubt why I'm not playing their recording and what, if I were them, I'd aim to improve next time I'm in the studio.

Every Saturday morning, as I plough through new submissions to the BBC Introducing Uploader, my Tweets can read as if they're mean-spirited, castigating artists (anonymously… I never mention names) for obvious shortcomings in their music or their biogs. Especially their biogs.

I don't derive any joy, whatsoever, from criticising people by proxy. I do, though. derive some satisfaction from airing my frustrations publicly, in a manner that I hope will let music-makers know what I expect from them.

Oh, how high and mighty that sounds! There is a lot of false modesty in this book. The honest truth is that, when it comes to assessing the relative merits of pieces of music for my show, I do think that I get things right the majority of the time.

My starting point is this, always this: I want to be able to enthuse about every piece of music that you send me.

I don't think I'm God, or more important than you, but the responsibility to compile a 3 hour new music show every week has been bestowed on me by the BBC. I take that responsibility very seriously – 400 pages-worth of seriously. I can only choose things based on my own (very wide) taste. That is the only criteria that can ever apply to a half-decent music show.

Try and do things by committee and you end up with androids serving gruel.

Over the years, artists I have rejected have made the argument that, because I'm funded by the license fee… a license fee that they pay… I should provide a platform for their music regardless of what I think about it. It's a flawed argument because the service I provide is for an audience, not for the artists. My responsibility is to make the best radio show I can for the listeners, not to showcase every piece of music that is sent to me without exercising any quality control.

That thought horrifies me! The nation's airwaves would be awash with cruise ship cabaret, Duplo trance, horribly generic pop punk, over-earnest folkish tapioca, creatively-throttled Arctic Monkeys wannabes, hilariously un-Welsh gangster rap, and terribly serious (and terribly terrible) overweight metal.

There has to be a filter, somewhere.

Reasons For Rejection

I'm that filter, and this is what I filter out.

1) BAD MUSIC (*See chapters on Your Sound, Songwriting, Lyrics, Arrangement, Recording and The Perfect Demo.*)

Let me reiterate something about the people you send your music to. The majority of them do not make a living out of what they do. They write their blogs, run their labels and promote their nights *for the love of music*.

They do not, in my long and wide-ranging experience, sit smugly in their palaces of bitterness, high on the schadenfreude of inviting people into the throne room, only to delight in slamming the door in their faces, while cackling wildly.

Highlight this bit, it's important.

WE WANT YOU TO BE GOOD.

WE WANT TO HELP THOSE OF YOU THAT ARE.

WE ARE VERY SAD – SOUL-SAPPINGLY SO – WHEN YOU ARE SHIT.

Sadly – very, very sadly – most of your recordings won't pass muster. This is a fact of musical life. An absolutely level playing field, where I played *everything* that was submitted to my radio show, would be HORRIFIC. No one would listen, not even the artists themselves.

The music business isn't a communist collective or a cosy, back-patting democracy, it is more cut-throat than Sweeny Todd's daydreams, more dog-eat-dog than a letterbox-shaped room filled with pitbulls on hallucinogens.

Don't expect charity.

Do expect undignified enthusiasm if your music has

any magic about it whatsoever.

Remember: no one owes you their ears. If you're going to ask for people's attention, be deserving of it.

2) BAD RESEARCH *(See chapters on Writing A Biography, What Next? And The Perfect Demo.)*

The bane of my otherwise comfortable and pampered musical existence is the profusion of books, guides and websites out there that list my contact details as someone who helps and supports new music-makers. These guides don't qualify that information – at all. They don't explain that I'm seeking leftfield, underground music from artists of Welsh origin. So I get thousands of submissions from all around the world, at least 99% of which I could never play.

I am *astonished* how many of those artists haven't done any research into who they're sending their music to, not even the smallest iota.

The artists have taken these mailing lists, all those hundreds of e-mail addresses, and mailed everyone regardless of their role or musical preference.

There's a word for unsolicited communication: it is SPAM. No one in the history of music in the digital age has been signed because of a random, hit-and-hope email.

How do those who spew out these missives believe they are received, and what kind of impression do they think they give of their music?

Most of the time they aren't received at all, ending up siphoned by your mail provider's heavy-handed spam filters into Junk folders from Timperley to Timbuktu. Once an email address is blacklisted by spam filters, it becomes difficult, if not impossible, to guarantee future e-mails sent from that address will reach their intended recipients.

If that is your primary band e-mail address, that could cause you significant frustration.

So, do the scantest research. Send your music to the labels, blogs, radio stations, agents et al that you *know* share an aesthetic, a sound, a similar philosophy to you.

You have a much better chance of getting listened to if you demonstrate real knowledge of the tastes and roles of the people you send your music to.

3) BAD VOCALS *(See chapter on Recording.)*

If there are vocals in your music, make them as good as is humanly possible. A poor vocal – either performed badly or not recorded well – will curdle the whole recording.

Listen to the vocal takes as if your artistic life depends on it. Because it does.

A bum note on the guitar is sometimes forgivable. Recording a song with a bum vocal note in it advertises the fact that you have pretensions to make music but can't hear the most elementary of mistakes.

I'm not demanding that you sing like Leona Lewis. Don't sacrifice the character in your voice to the note. But do still hit the note. Bob Dylan and Tom Waits are two of my favourite singers. Their voices are rich and challenging, provoking extreme reactions, but they never hit bum notes. Tone is different to 'in tune'. Make it in tune.

4) BANDWAGONS WILL CRUSH YOU*(See chapter on Your Sound.)*

Bring something new to music and someone, somewhere will love you for it.

Hitch a ride on a bandwagon and your Best Before End

date will be the day before you jumped aboard.

5) BAD TUNING *(See chapter on Recording.)*

Out of tune means out of luck, and in the bin.

6) BAD NAME *(See chapter on Choosing A Name.)*

Unimaginative, derivative, common band name = unimaginative, derivative, common band music.

7) DON'T BORE US... *(See chapters on Arrangement and Recording.)*

Try to ensure that every moment is necessary to the overall effect of the piece.

Music-makers can be very precious about their parts in an arrangement. Try, as best you can, to consider the music ego-lessly. Is that 14th guitar track really adding something to the whole? If it isn't, or you're not sure, ditch it.

Less is more.

Always.

The two minute intro that you think brings scope and drama to the song probably doesn't. Half of the The Ramones finest songs have entered the finishing straight by the two minute mark. Not everyone, sadly, should sound like The Ramones but even masters of the longer recording – Pink Floyd, Sigur Ros, Soft Machine – ensure that every moment is there for a reason. Not just to repeat the guitarist's perfunctory new riff again. And again. And again.

And again.

And, yes, again.

394

See?

8) **LACK OF ORIGINALITY** *(See chapters on Your Sound, Songwriting and Lyrics.)*

I don't want to hear a new Arctic Monkeys, thanks. I hear hundreds of new Arctic Monkeys every year. I am heartily *sick* of new Arctic Monkeys.

Banjos, as re-appropriated by men-in-tweed-in-strummy-folk-bands are fucking annoying, too.

If you want to dress as if it's 1955 and you're your own granddad, that is your prerogative. Good luck with it. *Anything* you do to fit with a fashion that has reached the supermarkets, whether that's musically or in the way you present yourselves, makes you less interesting.

When Tesco started stocking tweed and Brylcreem, it marked the death of gentleman folk. Thank Christ for that.

9) **CLICHED LYRICS** *(See chapter on Lyrics.)*

Similarly, 'fire' 'desire' 'higher' lyrics – or something equally sub-pedestrian – are likely to give my hate gland a good squeeze. I'd rather you spewed nonsense and idiocy in my ears than magnolia.

38: <u>A Manager?</u>

I'm afraid you're going to need a manager. They're a necessary evil. Ideally you'll find a trustworthy one — but trustworthy managers are a little thin on the ground. You need a manager to negotiate record deals, organise tours, arrange transport, book hotels, hire crew, cater for your every whim, alert the media to your every move, get you on the Jools Holland show and fend off the amorous attentions of Kate Moss who's seen your picture in the tabloids and wants to know if you might be interested in a brief but turbulent love affair.

Do you want to do all that yourself?

No, of course you don't. You need to be free to create musical extravaganzas that will one day change the face of popular music.

Finding a suitable manager is a matter of trial and error. Every musician of my acquaintance has had at least 5 different managers during their career. Managers are an occupational hazard and severing managerial connections can be a messy business often ending up in savage litigation.

So before you sign anything be absolutely certain you've got the right person. And if he or she turns out to be a shyster, swallow it, move on and chalk it up to experience. It's called paying your dues.

Deke Leonard, Man

My first brush with management came in 1987 when I was 16. A man called Tony, who said he was – if my backfiring memory hasn't entirely failed me – bass player with Sweet Sensation (No.1 hit with 'Sad Sweet Dreamer' in 1974), offered to lead my band and I to the promised land. I have no idea how he'd heard of us. I remember we did an audition for him in one of Chester's less salubrious nightclubs, murdering Rain by The Cult and U2's 11 'O' Clock Tick Tock. We were nothing if not supercool crowd-pleasers.

"You're okay. Need a bit of work. And you could do with rethinking your material…"

He had good ears, then.

Tony took us to his palatial bungalow on the outskirts of the city. He opened his garage with a flourish.

"If you sign with me, I'll let you have this…"

There was a Rickenbacker bass hanging on the wall. Paul, our bass playing singer's eyes widened. He may even have said "wow!". Poker faces weren't our strong suit.

Sadly my mum and dad weren't as impressed by the promise of the bass guitar on the garage wall. Nor were they all that impressed by Tony's credentials.

"Sad sweet what now? Take your 'A' levels and you can do what you want," they lied.

I often wonder what might have been had we signed with Tony.

It was only while writing this opening salvo for the 'Management' chapter that I thought to look Sweet Sensation up on Wikipedia. It transpires that their bass player isn't listed as a 'Tony'. Maybe Tony worked under a nom de plume? Lots of 70's artists did, after all. Maybe the Tony we met replaced (the listed) Barry Johnson late on, and wasn't part of the original, hit-making line-up?

Or maybe time, and Guinness, have sozzled my brain to such an extent that the guy's name wasn't even Tony and the band he'd been in weren't Sweet Sensation.

Absolute truths, especially those sought from the

shifting eddies of rock 'n' roll's past, are rare.

Welcome to the mysterious and morally fluid world of music management.

I can't think of a worse job in music than a band manager, no-one's friend with every fucker on your case, second only to being a label manager. No thanks!

Scott Causer, founder of Northern Star Records

Old school managers remind me of sideshow hawkers in travelling circuses, trying to tempt the innocent and unwary with the most persuasive ballyhoo:

"Roll up! Roll up! The wonders hidden within aren't for the dull or weak-minded. You sir, in your brown suit, are too normal to enter. Your accountancy brain would blow a gasket if exposed to my phantasmagoria. And madam, I'm afraid that that age and fragility of heart disbars you. Walk on! Find salvation in our travelling show's lesser attractions.

Now, those of you who remain... I can see from your lustrous hair and glittering eyes that you have what is required to meet the challenge, to go within and take The Ride Of All Lifetimes!

But please, please put your money away! Do not sully our glorious inner sanctum with the grime of finance. Just simply sign my assistant's document as you walk in. It's nothing to worry about. Just a list of names... the tiniest of agreements to protect both of our interests... a mere trifle."

There was something undoubtedly roguish about rock 'n' roll management in the late 50's and early 60's. Back then, rock 'n' roll was regarded as pervasive a threat as communism, an immoral force threatening post-war stability and conservatism. Managers like Andrew Loog Oldham (The Rolling Stones' manager in the mid-60's / founder of Immediate Records) stoked the flames, provoking the semi-detached, suburban mothers and fathers by asking them: 'Would You Let Your Daughter Marry A Rolling Stone?'

There can't have been a more horrifying notion for the respectable parents of suburbia. Apart from the threat of nuclear apocalypse. The Stones still managed to get more column inches than an imminent Armageddon.

Their ascent was powered mostly by great music, but also by teenage hormones and parental outrage, stirred and aroused by Oldham's canny brain. He perfected the art of headline-grabbing. After all, contriving a headline was much cheaper than paying for a full page ad in those same newspapers.

Oldham was a kitten compared to some of his contemporaries. Don Arden (manager of The Small Faces) is alleged to have conducted some business negotiations by dangling competitors over balconies by their ankles.

Peter Grant (The Yardbirds then Led Zeppelin) would use his 6 foot 5 inch frame to ensure that business dealings with promoters went in his favour.

Despite the notoriety, the likes of Grant, Albert Grossman (Bob Dylan) and Allan Klein (The Rolling Stones '65 - '70, then The Beatles)[1] did much to fight for the rights of their charges with promoters and record companies.

Klein may have been instrumental in the break-up of The Beatles but his negotiations with EMI (on behalf of three of The Beatles) helped to create fairer contractual conditions for songwriting artists. However Klein was also the man who tied The Stones up in a contract that signed away the rights to all of their early hits, to him.

There's a real moral duality to many of these historic figures. They shaped the industry more in an artists' favour, but were very happy to exploit their artists' ignorance about the business affairs they were handing over.

Now that the power of the major record labels has subsided, you're more likely to find yourself having to operate on an autonomous, DIY level. Having some knowledge of business-related matters is important, regardless of whether you find yourself a manager or not.

There's a commonly-held belief that creative brains can't be organisational brains, too. For some people that is undoubtedly true. For others, that's just an excuse to ignore the (much) more mundane part of your artistic existence. I delayed and prevaricated over writing these last two chapters for the same reason. However the cold reality is that forcing yourself to pay attention to the business side of music-making can enable and prolong your very ability to make that music.

Some of the logistical tasks associated with being a music-maker are:

- planning release / tour / promotions schedules.

- handling cash-flow.

- knowing how to get a gig and negotiate a fee for it.

- putting money aside for recording sessions or equipment.

- finding and paying for rehearsal space.

- booking or maintaining transport.

- generating interest from the media.

- running your social media and mailing list.

- planning / paying for releases.

- approaching record labels / publishers / agents.

- registering with collections agencies and other necessary authorities (PRS, PPL, MCPS).

- keeping accounts (for tax purposes).

- applying for any grants / subsidies to which you're entitled.

- ensuring you have a valid passport / travel documents, if you're gigging out of the country.

- Insurance.

- keeping you / the other band members motivated.

These are also, pretty much, the tasks handled by a manager. As my friend, and infamous Welsh music chronicler, Neil Crud[2], more succinctly defines the role: "babysitter, counsellor, Samaritan, bank, taxi, cook, doctor, dogsbody, punchbag."

When you start out, your only responsibility is to write and make great music. As momentum builds, if you find your ability to make great music is being compromised by having to fulfil the responsibilities listed above, you'll need to find a manager.

I think that the internet has demystified what a manager does and what can be done by a band, with the right skills. That is not to say a good manager cannot be helpful, or in some cases essential, but I sense bands are now in a place where it's about doing everything for yourselves. I think the number one thing a band should get is a good booking agent. That is the difference for me: the ability to gig regularly and get on bigger / better shows.

Marcus Warner, musician / former music P.R. in

South Wales punk / D.I.Y. scene

Music-makers who have organisational skills, too, *can* successfully manage themselves, even at a high level: Frank Black (as a solo artist), Cat Power, The Smiths, Jello Biafra, Aphex Twin.

Clearly handling all of the details of your own affairs is time-consuming. The clear advantage is that all of your dealings will be transparent to you; you'll have complete autonomy over the decisions you make, and you're very unlikely to do a runner from yourself with proceeds you illegally siphoned from your own accounts (as Leonard Cohen's manager did.)

The disadvantages of self-management are that you can only benefit from the contacts you have made yourself; you may be at a disadvantage when negotiating deals and fees (frequently negotiation is better-handled and more effective through a third party); time management challenges (keeping the books, but ensuring that you have the time to write music that keeps entries going into those books); that you may be too emotionally involved with the music to make objective decisions about it; and that there will be less time for you to be dissolute, to enjoy your music and the lifestyle it brings.

So, managers, where do they grow?

It's good to have people you trust around you, obviously, and that's a knack in itself, finding people you can trust. I think we managed it a couple of times with Touch 'N' Go and Bloodshot Records — they were basically people we would hang about with. And that's always a good sign, if you can trust people.

Jon Langford, The Mekons / The Three Johns etc.

A Manager?

Before we talk about the professionals, let's look at some alternatives closer to home, or – maybe – in it. A number of prominent artists have kept it in the family when it came to management. Paul Weller, Beyonce Knowles, The Jackson 5, Enter Shikari and Miley Cyrus were all managed by their parents…

It's relatively rare, in the lawless and subversive world of rock 'n' roll, for an artist to be represented by their mum or dad. It's worth remembering, though, that rock 'n' roll is old enough to be your grandparent. And what your grandparents were doing, round the back of the Metro Dancehall in 1962 would probably make our refined, 21st century eyes water. Parents, then, aren't as uncool as they used to be; although, as I am one, I may be rather clutching at drainpipe-tight straws here.

Rightly or wrongly, many people within the music industry think that being managed by a parent is likely to cause unnecessary complications, but these complications are as much of a risk with a manager who's not a relative: over-protectiveness, lack of objectivity, unrealistic expectations when negotiating.

The real risk when employing a parent is the same risk as employing anyone else to manage you, that they won't know what they're doing. Of course, that's to be expected for anyone starting out, at anything.

Whoever you get to manage you, whether it's your mum, your girlfriend / boyfriend, or the cute spaniel next door, ensure that they learn the ropes before they start trying to throw their weight around. There's a temptation for amateur managers to be overtly demanding in order to demonstrate to their charges that they have 'power'. Management, in this era, is mostly about quiet authority and being efficient and business-like, not shouting your mouth off and making ridiculous demands.

It is eminently possible for an enthusiastic friend to

grow into the role as you progress. That's how a lot of managers start out, as a trusted friend who has some ideas and an ability to organise things.

'Trust' shouldn't be undervalued.

It's also very important for a manager to be able to get on with people. One of my band's early representatives had a reputation for being a bit of a headcase. We thought that might work in our favour, following in the lineage of Andrew Loog Oldham and Don Arden. But doors were quietly, and permanently, shut in our faces. No one wants to work with someone intimidating.

If you're keen to self manage, or to use a family member or a friend, it may be worth them considering one of the (many) music management courses or degrees that are offered by universities and colleges across the country. These courses, covering the gamut of music management scenarios (from artist and venue management through to managing the affairs of orchestras and opera groups) are the antithesis of the cheap cigar impresarios and entrepreneurial wide-boys that dominated music management in the early days.

However doing a degree is an expensive and time-consuming business. The value of these relatively new qualifications, especially with the industry in such a state of flux, isn't proven. Anyone thinking of undertaking such a course should check that it matches their needs and that the tutors have authority in the required fields.

In the majority of cases, music management isn't book knowledge, or a qualification, it's learnt as you go along: a combination of common sense, accruing experience and persistence, according to the needs of the artist.

That last point is key. The more leftfield artists I play on my show need an entirely different managerial strategy to someone whose music is aimed at daytime playlists and arenas. That's two polarised examples, but every artist is unique, has unique requirements and a unique place in the grand scheme of things. The right plan for an artist has to come from knowing them and their music intimately. And believing, absolutely, in both.

Most of the managers I know either started off in bands and learnt about the industry the hard way (making mistakes or having managers of their own plot the wrong path for them), or they happened to be friends with incredibly talented people, with a managerial position developing out of that friendship. However there is a lot to learn. *Just* being a friend doesn't qualify you to be a manager.

I like to use this analogy: "just because you brush your teeth every morning, it doesn't make you a dentist", likewise 'being into music' doesn't make you a manager. A true manager will have an understanding of making music, contract law, the workings of every department in a record label, publishing, touring, international markets, distribution, digital, merchandise, accounting, business management, finance, grant applications, collection societies, how to run their own business & have a contact list as big as the music week directory (and that's omitting general parenting skills).

Jo Riou, studio manager (& former artist manager)

So, a good manager needs to be personable, trustworthy, organised, a good motivator, ruthless when required, to have good contacts and strategic ideas for the artists they represent, and to understand how the music business works now, in 2014, not how it worked in 2004 or 1994 or… well, you get the point.

Whereas the music industries of 1994 and 1984… 1974, even… were mostly comparable, the music industry of 2014 is a very different place to 1994... 2004, even.

A manager in the modern age has to have a grasp of all of the new, digital ways to sell, distribute and promote music. That is essential.

If you have have a friend or family member working on your behalf and they're personable, trustworthy, organised and they can motivate you, they can learn the other skills as they go along – experience is earned, contacts can be made and collected. It does take effort and a certain amount of courage, though. Your manager needs to have the gumption to knock on doors and enough belief in you to continue knocking on doors, even when no immediate answer is forthcoming.

And a good manager knows which doors are worth knocking on. Some doors should be avoided as if they have a red cross daubed on them and a handcart filled with putrefying musical dreams parked outside. They're the ones that lead to insultingly exploitative contracts, questionable battle of the bands competitions, pay-to-play gigs, or vanity release 'record labels'.

Mistakes are part of the learning curve. As Deke sagely points out in the quote that opens this chapter: "move on and chalk it up to experience. It's called paying your dues."

Still, it's best not to be blithe about charlatans and errors of judgement, regarding them as an inevitable part of your education. Music-makers have limited time to make a reputation and earn an audience. Poor management, pursuing dead-ends and making too many bad choices, will waste valuable time and limited opportunities.

The music industry is a tough game to play. You're lucky if you have one life to lose. As the artist, it's important for you to be vigilant as to how you're being represented and the decisions being made on your behalf. Don't let a bad manager screw things up for you.

Experienced and knowledgeable managers are fewer and further between than they once were, despite all of the college courses.

A good professional manager will understand the vital importance of a good booking agent, and will have the contacts and influence to secure you one.

A good professional manager will also understand the wealth of opportunities enabled by a deal with an esteemed publisher.

A good professional manager will unburden you of the logistical burden of being (in essence) a self-employed transient, so that you can focus on creating music.

But good managers who have the contacts to achieve the first two, and the wherewithal to enable the latter, are as rare as great bands.

Generally, as with an agent, a professional manager is likely to approach you once the momentum behind you and your music warrants it. Yes, it can look like yet another unsolvable chicken and egg riddle to the music-maker who can't progress and who isn't generating momentum...

"Without a manager or an agent, how am I supposed to get the good gigs I need to generate the buzz that'll get me a manager and an agent?" <slams head against wall!>

It's a very valid question and an understandable frustration.

Don't forget that it's all about great music. Make great music, work hard to make get that great music heard at an entry level (local gigs and local media support), and the other elements will start to fall into place.

I'll leave the final words on management – a thoroughly informative and neat summation of its role in the 21st century music industry – to Paul Gray from the British Musicians Union.

From my work at the Musicians Union, the majority of bands are now able to manage themselves perfectly well if they have great songs, using good advice (from the Musicians Union) and the plethora of aids now available on the internet. Often, though, bands want to delegate this to a manager. When asked why, the usual answer is "to get us more gigs". But managers generally don't get gigs – agents do.

Artists now need to prove that they have been able to generate a viable market for their wares before they can attract "wider industry" interest, including both managers and agents. The simple reason is that as royalty rates contract, there are fewer deals on offer and less dosh for a manager to earn commission on.

A great manager IS critical when an artist has done as much as they can, under their own steam, and needs someone to take them to that mythical next level by building a solid business plan and utilising their experience, knowledge, enthusiasm and contacts. Yes, generally, they find you via recommendation, although you can find details of managers via the Music Managers Forum or Music Week. Or simply google your fave band and find out who manages them - but not until you're more than ready. Because in the 38 years I've been doing this , "they're not ready yet" is often the reason wheeled out to not work with someone.

And don't sign anything until you have sought expert legal advice - there are still too many jokers out there, and I've seen many contracts cut and pasted from the net, where one clause renders another meaningless, meaning that the person who's given it to you doesn't understand it either, which doesn't bode well for either party.

You get unlimited free advice and contracts vetted for free as a Musicians Union member, a blatant plug but absolutely crucial if you're serious about your career. This is all very simplified of course, every artist

A Manager?

is at a different point and so needs different guidance.

Paul Gray, former Regional Officer for the Musicians Union / musician (bass player - The Sensible Gray Cells, Eddie & the Hot Rods, The Damned)

Paul's words underline how much really good advice is out there, from authoritative and august organisations, if you're prepared to ask for it and you're prepared to do a little research into who the best people are to be asking.

Start with the Musicians Union. Also find out if there is an agency in your geographical area whose remit is to encourage music industry development.

As a final point for this chapter, remember that no amount of managing will make your music great. Management can help create the time for you to make music and then spread the word about it once it has been written. However great music is till the fundament, and – fundamentally – that is your responsibility and no one else's.

You don't need a manager, an agent, a psychologist or a neatly-trimmed chihuahua in a bowlful of blue Smarties to make great music, you just need you and your musical ideas. Everything else subsists off those sounds.

If you're suffocating yourself with the frustration of not being able to find a manager, an agent, or a label, go back to the music. That is your reson d'etre. and your route upwards and outwards. Liberate yourself from the frustrations you can't control by investing yourself in the one thing that is, resolutely, in your control: the music.

[1]*the likes of Grant, Albert Grossman (Bob Dylan) and Allan Klein (The Rolling Stones '65 - '70, then The Beatles)*

- It's a very testosterone-driven list. Music management is still male-dominated, but with a growing number of excellent managers, who happen to be female: Mairead Nash (Florence & the Machine / Violet); Estelle Wilkinson (former manager of Coldplay); Rhiannon Morgan-Bell (Charlotte Church); Niamh Byrne and Regine Moylett (Blur / Gorillaz / Damon Albarn et al).

[2]*Neil Crud* - runs, writes for and collates a vast repository on Welsh music past and present (as well as music from Liverpool) at: http://link2wales.co.uk – well worth a visit.

PLAYLIST:
Man - Bananas
Sweet Sensation - Sad Sweet Dreamer
The Cult - Rain
U2 - 11 'O' Clock Tick Tock
Andrew Oldham Orchestra - The Last Time
The Small Faces - E Too D
The Yardbirds - Over Under Sideways Down
Led Zeppelin - Communication Breakdown
Charlotte Church - Little Movements

39: <u>Turnstile On Management</u>

Turnstile are a management team and record label based in Cardiff, Wales. They look after the affairs of such internationally-renowned artists as Gruff Rhys, Perfume Genius, Cate Le Bon, Los Campesinos, Christopher Owens, R. Seiliog and Sea Lion.

Alun Llwyd, who co-runs Turnstile, was one of the founders of Wales' most revered and influential record label, Recordiau Ankst. That label's back catalogue is a history of much of the finest underground rock and pop music that has come out of Wales since 1988. For a quick, and eminently-rewarding sightseeing trip through many of the peaks, I highly recommend Ankst's two Radio Crymi compilations.

Alun's (and Turnstile's) managerial relationship with Gruff Rhys grew from releasing his first, proper band Ffa Coffi Pawb on Ankst, through releasing Super Furry Animals' first two singles (also on Ankst), to managing them over the course of all of their remarkable albums, and now managing Gruff's equally superlative solo releases.

Their enduring relationship with Gruff is testament to the commitment they have to their artists. The quality of the rest of their roster is testament to their excellent taste.

Turnstile also functions as a thoroughly contemporary record label. They've embraced new methods of distribution and communication. Their physical releases – the vinyl pressings, in particular – are remarkably desirable works of art in their own right, even before the needle drops and reveals the musical marvels contained in the grooves.

Alun kindly agreed to answer some questions about management.

What is the role of a manager?

Everything, is probably the closest description. Thinking of the now, the short-term, the long-term and everything in between. Predicting problems, fire-fighting and being a good friend, all at the same time.

How has that role changed over the last decade?

It hasn't really. The realities – both economically and creatively – have changed but the ultimate responsibility remains the same. The main added responsibility is to ensure artists are aware of the relative contexts of the world they live and work in.

You also run a record label, did that grow out of your management responsibilities? Or was it always an intention?

It grew as a logical extension of wanting to plan long term for artists we work with. And these days, no one wants to think long-term record-wise so it made sense that we do it hand-in-hand.

What do you look for in the artists that you manage?

Music that we will still listen to once we retire. and artists that are happy to get involved and work hard in building their own career in partnership with us.

How have you found the artists that you manage / have

managed, who weren't already known to you?

A combination of recommendation and word of mouth. We are proud that our roster is our best and only calling card.

The artists you look after have remarkable (and, may I say 'unparalleled') artistic value, but none of them are commercial certainties. How much of that is a risk?

Always a risk but you can only go on belief and faith in the long-term.

At what point in an artist's trajectory do you think they should start thinking about management?

As late as possible. An artist ideally would have the sense to grow things to a level where a manager would then come in and able to help in taking things to the next level.

In the early days of Ankst, you worked with people that you knew (obviously I'm aware it was a label but managerial responsibilities quickly grew out of those relationships, didn't they?)... do you think there is still scope for an artist to be managed by a mate? Or has the industry changed so much that professional authority and experience are now vital to the role, from the off?

I had no idea what I was doing when we started. I was blessed in being surrounded by people who did know something and wanted to see us succeed. A mate manager can work in the right environment.

I make the point that managers and agents aren't found by sending out unsolicited demos, but I've made that point

based on an assumption rather than any real knowledge. Have you ever signed anyone (label or management) based on a demo? Have you ever heard of that happening?

Never done it ourselves.

Managers cover the business side of projects, that's the general stereotype – but how important to you is that you like the music that your artists make? How important are you to them in terms of an objective voice on their work?

It varies. We would never work with someone we didn't enjoy listening to at home. As to our voice on their work, then we do feel it's nice to voice an opinion but ultimately it's always the artist's call.

You work with some of my favourite artists of all time. You know this is true and not just me trying to butter you up! Do they make revenue in different ways, or is there a pattern across them all (and across other similar artists in the industry)? i.e. is live music the main source of income, or music sales, or merch? Obviously I'm not trying to probe specifics! Just generally, without having to refer to any names.

We work on a partnership basis so therefore benefit from all income streams. And most bands make their money in different ways. The key is to realise that all the incomes streams e.g. merch, live, synch, record sales, publishing are all as important as each other now. An artist needs to find their key income stream and focus on it.

You're a principled bunch, too. It's a staple part of SFA's story that they turned down an ad deal with a major soft drinks company. Is it increasingly difficult to have values and principles when more traditional revenue streams have changed / dried up? Or is having those principles, and not selling to the highest bidder, part of the philosophy of Turnstile that makes it a great home for artists and a kitemark of quality for punters?

We have our principles. But ultimately it's the artists' principles that decide what does (or doesn't) happen. And as long as artists are aware of how crucial, in this day and age, it is that all income streams are maximised then decisions can be taken on basis of principle and strategy within a context.

You use the internet and social networking well. How important is it to have an understanding of these new platforms?
Absolutely crucial.

You know how hard you work for your artists (and I've heard how bloody hard you work for your artists) – given that, do you think it's possible for a new artist to self manage and build themselves up to an international level, or is management something that they will have to engage with at some point?
It varies. I think management can be viewed as a part of the general partners any artists need to make to achieve global success. But as in any aspect of those partners, an artist can do with or without any element. It all boils down to the nature of the artist involved.

Diolch Alun.

Keep an ear on what's happening at Turnstile, and shop for their excellent releases, here:

http://turnstilemusic.net

You can read more about Recordiau Ankst, and buy the

releases, here: http://ankst.co.uk

PLAYLIST:
Gruff Rhys - Patterns of Power
Gorky's Zygotic Mynci - Merched Yn Neud Gwallt Eu Gilydd
Topper - Something To Tell Her
Tystion - Byw Ar Y Briwsion
MC Mabon - People Are So Stupid
Cate Le Bon & Perfume Genius - I Think I Knew
Ffa Coffi Pawb - Valium
Super Furry Animals - Hello Sunshine

40: <u>Paper Work(s)</u> – <u>Making Money From Your Music</u>

It's not like anybody's going to make any money out of the music industry.

Kim Gordon, Sonic Youth

Remember, the EU has 500 million people, the US only has 300 million people, don't come to the USA. If you want to go anywhere after your record starts to sell, go to the EU. Don't emigrate. Don't move to London. Live local, think global.

Kim Fowley, record producer and impresario

It's a portentous, intimidating and sexless chapter heading for a book with music, self-expression, fearlessness and instinct as its intended cornerstones. I'm about to drag you into a Kafka-esque nightmare of bewildering forms, unmarked doors and endless corridors... or am I? That's what it felt like when I ran a label some years ago, and was faced with reams of intimidating paperwork.

I spent a week neck-deep in acronyms: "but I just want to put a few singles out. I'm not arsed about making any money..."

Which was fortunate, really, as I lost a lot.

If I'd paid more attention to the paperwork, that might

not have been the case.

There is an idea, perpetuated by a lot of music-makers – many of whom, it has to be said, haven't investigated the subject any further than just echoing the myth themselves – that the paperwork associated with music-making is inordinately difficult, something so anti the rock 'n' roll spirit that by signing any of the related forms, you'd destroy your mojo forever: the opposite of the deal that Robert Johnson signed with Satan at the crossroads.

Musicians don't make money by writing or recording songs, but by filling in the paperwork which says they wrote the song or recorded the song. There's a reason it's called the Music Industry, not just 'Music'. There's work that has to be done to ensure you're 'in business'.

John Rostron, former Chief Executive Welsh Music Foundation / co-founder Sŵn Festival & Welsh Music Prize

I had thought of the bureaucracy, paperwork, the dull grind as being an arduous and unnecessary evil, but having done some poking around in the subject, rather than just trusting my own jaundiced preconceptions, I've changed my opinion. The organisations who you ally yourself with via all of this onerous paperwork can be a positive force for creating, and exploiting, opportunities for your music.

Music-makers, both composers and performers, register with different agencies so that they can collect the royalty payments that their music generates. Those royalties can be earned by having composed or performed on a piece of music that earns airplay on the radio / television / film; from monies due to a live performance; from sales of downloads / CD's / vinyl; via royalties generated by plays on streaming services (Spotify / YouTube etc); and from publishing royalties (say someone covers your song or synchronises (synchs) it for use in an ad / video game, or quotes one of your lyrics).

There is no "one size fits all" for the admin. side of the music industry. The same questions and problems arise time after time.

If you are an artist or a songwriter or a band member it is your responsibility to understand how PRS, MCPS and PPL will provide you with an income. You will need to learn how your situation and circumstances should be dealt with.

Owen Powell, Catatonia / songwriter

Owen's advice is key and borne from experience. Make the effort to learn about these agencies and sign up with the services that you think will be most useful to you, as soon as you can, because it's no one's else's responsibility to look after your interests, only your own.

A day's worth of head-scratching with a pile of forms will benefit you, perhaps greatly. Don't be intimidated. If you are confused, PRS / MCPS / PPL/VPL / Eos et al will be only too happy to help you. You're a potential customer and source of revenue for them, not an inconvenience. And – as the extensive FAQ sections on their websites demonstrate – they're used to answering a broad range of questions, from the apparently simple to the very complex.

Depending on where you are in the world, there are other organisations who can help lead you through the business side of things more objectively. In Wales, we had, up until June 2014, the Welsh Music Foundation (now defunct, with no clear indication as to what has replaced it – a great loss), in England and Northern Ireland there is Generator, and in Scotland, the Scottish Music Industry

Association (see the links section at the end of this chapter.)

Do make use of these services. It's not like phoning up a bank or a tax office. They're run by music-minded people. They'll understand where you're coming from and won't boggle you with jargon or ask you why you haven't got a 'proper job'.

To reiterate: if you don't have a manager or a knowledgeable label behind you, it is in your interests to attain a basic understanding, at least, of these income streams and how to claim them.

If you don't know anything about the business you're working in why the hell are you doing it? Learn about it. You're going to get ripped off if you don't. Try and understand how it works and try and understand how it works now and not how it worked 10 years ago.

Colin Newman, Wire / Githead

If you're a DIY music-maker, you'll need to grasp the fundamentals of the music industry in parallel with encouraging your creativity. Don't believe people who state as fact that a creative brain can't be an organised brain, too. There is no authoritative scientific evidence to back that up. Finding and maintaining the inclination to get organised is the main challenge.

Don't sign your songs away because they are your pension fund.

When you're old and grey – and one day you will be – the publishing royalties will still be rolling in and their size will be dependent on how well you've managed your songwriting portfolio.

Deke Leonard, Man

Publishing rights are the crown jewels. If you ever make any serious money in the long-term it will be from having composed the songs. The composer of the songs needs to protect that absolutely.

Be really careful if somebody comes along and offers you a publishing deal because somebody offered me a publishing deal and said they'd give me £400, back in the 70's, and I thought: "well, that sounds brilliant"... so I signed it and within 2 years I had to pay £20,000 to get out of it again and give them 13 of my best songs.

If you do sign a publishing deal make sure you get re-version of copyright. The copyright in the song isn't given to the publisher forever. You just lease it to them for 10 years, 12 years, 15 years at the most — and then it comes back to you so that ultimately you own your songs. That's your pension.

You may want to share that with the other members of the band, like U2 - they split it four ways. Or you may want to keep it all for yourself but pay the musicians generously out of the rest of the income that comes in. That's a decision for you and a whole other debate that you need to have. But don't forget that publishing is where the real money is.

Tom Robinson, songwriter / 6Music presenter

For those who secure the services of a good one, the most productive relationship a music-maker is likely to have is with their publisher. Good publishers seek opportunities for your music. They have contacts who trust their judgement and their catalogue, and can get music placed (i.e supported and played) in a welter of different, potentially lucrative environments: in adverts, films, TV shows, covered by other artists, on compilations, game soundtracks, apps, with agencies that provide music for gyms / restaurants / clothes shops etc.

Established music publishers are also experts at

tracking down potential revenue from more remote geographical locations.

In essence, a publisher grants permission for third parties (radio / TV / games companies etc.) to make fair use of your compositions, for which those third parties pay an agreed rate, a rate that is then split with you according to the deal you have signed with the publisher.

Music publishers administer the rights to the melody and lyrics of your compositions, not the actual recording. So a publisher would collect royalties for your song regardless of who was performing it. This is the 'publishing right'. The 'master right' covers the actual recording of a song, and songwriting / performance royalties generated by the use of that recording are administered by agencies like PRS, MCPS and PPL, who we'll come to in due course.

Effective music publishers have close relationships with related, creative industries. Someone at a film company may be looking for a piece of music to soundtrack a particular scene in a movie. They'll send a rough cut of that scene to the publisher who will then consider which of the pieces of music they have in their catalogue is best-suited to the scene and the film.

Similar scenarios are played out with TV companies, advertising agencies and game / app designers.

This sort of opportunity is almost impossible to eke out for yourself, without contacts or a proven track record. If you have no problem with your music being used commercially like this, there is potential for it to be heard by huge audiences across the world, with the raised profile and renumeration that that can generate.

Forget about quaint ideas of 'selling out'... you want to sell in to where the action is: the market place, the listeners.

Jeremy Gluck, The Barracudas

Of course, not all artists are comfortable with the idea of allowing their music to be exploited for commercial reasons, by the highest bidder. Integrity is an important quality that can be worth protecting. Think carefully about any offers that come your way and whether they fit with your music's philosophy.

If the phrase "your music's philosophy" makes you guffaw, you're probably good to go with whoever offers you the shiniest shilling.

Whatever you do, try to make it right for you and for your music.

If you can't secure the services of a good publisher, it is feasible to start your own publishing company. I know some good independent labels here in Wales who have set up in house publishing. They won't, initially, have the contacts to drum up big synch deals, and the like. They do, though, recoup a little more in the way of royalties for their songs and they also have absolute ownership of those songs, which could prove to be an invaluable resource as the label and its artists progress.

Aside from publishing, the next port of call in your paperwork quest to collect any monies earned by your music is **PRS for Music**.

PRS for Music is the brand name used by the Performing Right Society and its operating company PRS for Music Limited (formerly the MCPS-PRS Alliance Limited). PRS for Music also provides services to the Mechanical Copyright Protection Society (MCPS) under a service level agreement.

PRS pays royalties to its members (songwriters, composers and publishers) when their songs / compositions are used in a broadcast, live event, played in a public place or online.

In essence, every time a piece of copyrighted music is played publicly, the law stipulates that the copyright holder's permission needs to be obtained. PRS have the authority to provide that permission on behalf of the songwriters, composers and publishers they represent, usually via blanket agreements.

Eos represents some composer and publisher members in Wales for UK broadcasts only.

All premises where copyrighted music is played in public – even if it's in the background in a workplace – are legally obliged to buy a licence from PRS for the permission to do so, whether they're large retailers like Tesco or much smaller businesses, like hairdressers, cafes or garages. Broadcasting organisations like the BBC pay PRS for the permission to broadcast their members' music.

PRS distribute the funds generated by licences for airplay amongst their membership according to who was played, where and when. National stations like Radio 1 generally pay a higher rate than local stations, due to their larger audiences and reach.

PRS also distributes public performance royalties collected from businesses such as pubs, shops, hairdressers, cafes etc. 'Public performance' doesn't mean that you, the artist, has to have played live in these places, it simply means a public airing of your music... for example, via a radio or hi fi.

To calculate who is being played where, and how frequently, PRS often use details of songs that have also been played on the radio.

If you're not a member of PRS and are not published,

you will miss out on royalties. If you're not a member of PRS and your music is played abroad you are likely to miss out on royalties even if you are published.

You pay a one-off, lifetime fee (£50 for a composer, £400 for a publisher) to become a member of PRS. The administration for logging your compositions is done through their website.

Please ensure that the details of the songwriter(s) registered with PRS for a piece of music are mirrored exactly in the songwriting credits you list on your packaging (including promos). For example, if you list on the sleeve of your CD single that a song played on the radio was 'written by The Silent Atoms' but the PRS registration is under the songwriters' real names (as opposed to the band name), there is a chance that you will not get paid the royalty you're due as a PRS member, as they cannot always guarantee to be able to resolve band names to their individual registered members.

When you join PRS, royalties can be backdated to the 1st of January or the 1st of July of that calendar year. As an example, if you join in September, PRS can backdate to the 1st of July. None of the plays before this date, however, would count or earn you money.

Songwriters can generate a significant amount of money from airplay, even on smaller stations. It's worth becoming a member for that fact alone.

Every question you could ever want to ask, and a number more, are answered on the PRS for Music website: http://www.prsformusic.com – where you will also find a full and comprehensive definition of.......

MCPS. The Mechanical-Copyright Protection Society licenses your mechanical (reproduction) rights and pays your mechanical royalties. Sources of mechanical royalties include record companies, TV production companies, downloads, films, adverts, videos, computer games etc.

If you are unpublished, (or have songs / compositions which are unpublished) and are generating mechanical royalties outside of a physical self-release, you should consider joining MCPS. Like PRS you pay a one-off, lifetime fee of £50 to become a composer member. If you are a publisher who publishes works which generate mechanical income you should consider joining MCPS. Like PRS you pay a one-off, lifetime fee of £400.

As an example, if you join MCPS, and register your songs and compositions with them, your record label are obliged to pay you a mechanical royalty for every reproduction of your music they make (whether that's a download, a CD, a vinyl pressing etc).

Sometimes this can be prohibitive, for self releases or low quantity runs on small independent labels. In those instances, MCPS can grant waivers.

Read the FAQ's on their website, or contact them directly, if you have any queries.

The next agency you should consider registering with is **PPL**. Phonograph Performance Limited pays royalties to its members (record companies and performers) when their recordings are used in a radio or TV broadcast, live event, played in a public place or online.

PRS pays its members a royalty if a song they have composed is played on the radio; PPL pays its members a royalty if they played an instrument on that recording.

Anyone who has made an audible contribution to a recording can earn royalties from PPL (if they are members and the recording has been registered).

If you are recording with a producer, it is their job to file Session Sheets, indicating who played what on a track. These Session Sheets should be passed on to your record label who will use them to register recordings

427

with PPL.

If you are a band or artist producing yourself, then you should provide your label with the information and check that they complete the PPL registration correctly.

Getting PPL information changed once a registration has been made, is really difficult. So get it right first time.

Owen Powell, Catatonia / songwriter

Like PRS, PPL grants permission for fair use of its members' musical performances via licenses and blanket agreements.

Membership of PPL, as a performer, is free.

If you also run the record label that your music is released on, it's important to note that you need to join PPL as a rights holder, too. You then register your recordings, and the performers who contributed (including you), via the PPL website.

This will generate a unique ISRC code for the recording that can be used by broadcasting organisations, say, to ensure accurate payment of PPL, to all of the performers (and the record label) involved.

If you self submit your music to radio / TV / for streaming etc, it is very useful to include ISRC information (and your PRS ID number).

Another option is to have the ISRC encoded into your recording during the mastering process. This makes it easier for agencies to track where your music is being played (on the radio, for example) and improving the efficiency with which you get paid any royalties that are due to you.

Do bear in mind that administrative errors can be made

with any of these agencies. PRS / MCPS and PPL handle catalogues containing millions of songs and compositions. They digest playlist information from broadcasters and the like, that must amount to many hundreds of millions of plays. It's inevitable that mistakes will be made:

Don't rely on your manager, label or publisher to keep an eye on things for you. In fact adding these layers of admin. means that you should be checking song splits and registrations more often. Mistakes do happen. Catatonia's publishers Sony/ATV registered the song Mulder and Scully as "Mulder and Skully." A tiny typo right? Yes, but on the sleeve of the record, the song is called Mulder and Scully. So when a radio station play the song they log the fact that they have played a song that doesn't match with the registration held by PRS. Luckily only one song called Mulder and Scully is registered with the PRS so most radio plays are picked up but it goes to show why you should check.

Every time you receive a PRS statement check the following:

1. Are the song titles correct?

2. Are they spelt correctly?

3. Are song splits correct? If you wrote 50% of a song make sure that you are being paid 50% of the royalty.

4. Are all your songs appearing on your statement? If a song that has been paying royalties suddenly vanishes from your statement, get in touch with PRS.

Owen Powell, Catatonia / songwriter

If you're making money as a self-employed music-maker, you need to register with the **HMRC** / **Inland Revenue**.

You don't pay tax until you've earned over a certain

threshold of income (taking into account your expenses, as well.) There's not much point in my mentioning specific figures because the personal allowance for self-employed people changes every year (and those changes can be significant).

Firstly, find out whether you should be declaring a taxable income (via an annual tax return). You can read about self-employment and check the earnings threshold on the H.M.R.C website (http://www.hmrc.gov.uk), or call your local tax office to explain your situation and check your employment status.

Ignorance (of the necessity to pay tax) isn't regarded as a valid excuse for not doing so. Tax avoidance is a criminal offence.

Keep records of what you earn (via gigs, sales, the royalties from the agencies listed below) and a record of / receipts for your allowable expenses (which would include fuel, office costs, maintenance for your instruments etc. etc. Discuss what is / isn't allowable with an accountant or tax officer.)

Yes, it is dull and about as far-removed from music-making as you can get, but the risks of not paying tax outweigh the inconvenience.

It's worth getting into the habit early on.

Remember that a good accountant will handle your tax return for you and that their fee, as your agent, is an allowable expense, which means that – in essence – you're not paying for their services.

Let's talk a little about **distributors**. Distributors get your music into the shops / onto online download stores. There are, broadly, two different types of distributor, although – frequently now – there are companies who can offer both services.

Physical distributors get your physical product

(records / CD's / cassettes) into record / music shops and collect any income generated from sales (for a percentage). Although this side of the business has changed markedly since the implementation of download stores and streaming services, there are still distributors out there, working with (mostly) specialist music retailers.

They can be very helpful in getting new releases stocked in shops on their recommendation alone. It mightn't seem like the biggest logistical challenge for you to do it yourself, but it's prohibitively difficult to get any shop to take a release from a barely-known band, with the margins of survival in retail being as tight as they are.

Even sale or return deals (where, in essence, you send your music for free and, if the shop doesn't sell it, they send the product back... theoretically, no risk for the vendor) are difficult to forge because many music shops have limited shelf space. They can't take everything and are much more likely to make an order on the basis of a trusted distributor.

Digital distributors charge you (either an annual fee / per release / a percentage of the sale price, or a combination of all the above) to upload your songs to music download stores (iTunes / Google Play / Amazon / eMusic et al) and music streaming services (Spotify, LastFM et al). Whilst it's theoretically possible to do this yourself, it would be time consuming, in the extreme. Also, many of these digital distribution services (Tunecore, Distrokid, CD Baby etc) have a much better success rate for getting music into the music stores and have experience in correcting any errors (if there's a typo in your song title, for example) and collecting royalties on your behalf.

Royalty collection rates differ across the different digital distributors, and their deals can change on a regular basis.

The final organisation I would advise you to consider joining is the **Musicians Union**. The MU offer a boggling array of information for the self-employed musician. Please visit their website for a full appraisal of their services.

Remember that should you find any aspects of the business side of music-making difficult to grasp (and it's taken me two decades to make the effort to understand these technicalities), all of the agencies detailed above have in depth FAQ's on their websites and will be happy to answer your questions.

Not only that, but as mentioned earlier, here in the UK, music-makers in England, Northern Ireland and Scotland can take advantage of the free advice on offer from their national music industry development agencies: Generator (England), Generator (Northern Ireland) and the Scottish Music Industry Association (see links below).

I hope this chapter has helped, too.

I'm off for a lie-down until I stop hallucinating acronyms.

SOME USEFUL LINKS:

http://mpaonline.org - *Music Publishers Association*

http://www.prsformusic.com - *PRS For Music (including MCPS)*

http://ygynghrair.rhysllwyd.com - *Eos*

http://www.ppluk.com - *PPL*

http://distrokid.com - *Distrokid*

http://awal.com - *Awal*

http://www.tunecore.com - *Tunecore*

http://www.cdbaby.com - *CDBaby*

http://www.hmrc.gov.uk - HMRC / Inland Revenue

http://www.musiciansunion.org.uk - The Musicians Union

http://www.generator.org.uk - Generator (England)

http://generatorni.com - Generator (Northern Ireland)

http://welshmusicfoundation.com - Welsh Music Foundation

https://www.smia.org.uk - Scottish Music Industry Association

PLAYLIST:
Sonic Youth - Kool Thing
Catatonia - Strange Glue
Robert Johnson - Cross Road Blues
Catatonia - Mulder and Scully

41: <u>DIY Releases</u>

If I'm not careful, this next chapter could turn into a full-on Marxist rally, a rant about collective empowerment and having access to your own means of production that'd have the Daily Mail's slavering coyotes baying at the BBC door. But the call to musical arms over the following paragraphs has nothing to do with politics. This is about creating your own opportunities in a digital landscape that encourages them, and forging your own path, either because no other is open to you, or because you desire autonomy and creative freedom.

Some original music-makers find that an incredibly liberating notion.

Many of the aspects of being a DIY music-maker (that is: self-managing, self-releasing, self-promoting) have been touched upon elsewhere in On Making Music.

We haven't, yet, talked about self-releasing and setting up your own record label.

DIY labels have been a tremendously important part of indie, punk, hardcore and dance music culture for decades, a mark of integrity and unwillingness to 'sell out' in order to sign to the highest bidding record label.

The seismic upheavals in the music industry of the last couple of decades have made DIY labels and self-releasing a necessity for more artists. With less money sloshing about, the record companies that remain are taking fewer risks.

Traditionally those companies have been the banks of the music industry; banks that charged a high rate of interest and who were likely to ask you to tour incessantly, on an income somewhere south of the minimum wage, to pay your advance back.

Setting up your own label looks like a wise choice when the situation is couched like that, doesn't it?

However, understand that if you want to self-release, the logistical burden becomes yours. It takes a rare kind of organised mind to be able to run a label, promote its wares, manage the artist (you) *and* write enough great music for the whole machine to fuel and oil itself on a cyclical basis. There is no simple test or BuzzFeed quiz to determine whether you have the necessary skills. You'll just know whether or not you're fit for the challenge, or you'll very quickly learn.

Be reassured that it is possible. In the next chapter, we'll hear from Julia Ruzicka from Future of the Left, an incredible band who set up their own record label to release their 2014 album, How To Stop Your Brain In An Accident.

The huge advantage of DIY is that it gives you complete artistic control. As long as some form of quality control runs parallel to that, this can make for a great record label.

Mute Records, Dischord, Creation, Stones Throw Records, Frenchkiss, Night Slugs all started out with a DIY, self-release ethos... it's true that none of these seminal labels are most renowned for releases that involved their founders (other than Dischord), but there are enough examples here to show that DIY can work, and, indeed, prosper.

Finding the money to record, press, release and promote a physical release 'properly' is the big challenge with a DIY label.

It would be prudent to start with digital releases only. The wisdom of this will become more apparent when we talk about the costs involved in a physical release later in the chapter. A digital release is much cheaper than its physical counterpart.

You can raise funds through gigging; through having a 'normal' job and funnelling that money into your music (which is an increasingly common scenario); from a patron or benefactor; or via one of the increasing number of crowd-sourcing initiatives: KickStarter, Pledgemusic, IndieGoGo, PeopleFundIt etc.

Whichever approach you decide on, it's wise to have an idea of your costs and your potential sales in advance. These can be difficult to predict even for seasoned artists, let alone newbies. Throughout the rest of this chapter we'll look at the costs involved in the different ways there are to release your music, so you're better prepared to make a decision that won't ruin you financially.

Self-releasing your music can start the minute you have made a decent (preferably mastered) recording. iTunes, as one example, allows individuals to register their music to sell on the iTunes music store. However it can be a drawn out and frustrating process. One of the requirements to become an iTunes music provider is for you to first obtain a US tax ID by registering with the IRS, which involves an international phone call (at your cost).

If that sounds too intimidating (and I'd hope that it shouldn't – it is only a phone call, after all), you can – instead – register with a digital aggregator (like TuneCore... see **Chapter 40:** *'Paper Work(s) – Making Money From Your Music'* for more information) who will place your music on a number of digital marketplaces, simultaneously, without you having to register with anyone, other than them.

TuneCore charge a fee per release (more for an album than a single, understandably).

CDBaby also charge per release.

Distrokid offer a membership model of payment. You can upload as many recordings to their service as you like, for an annual fee of $19.99.

The services listed above allow you to keep 100% of the royalties earned by your musical sales on the digital stores. It's important to note that that is 100% of the royalties *after* the digital store has taken its percentage for hosting and selling your music.

Another option worth considering is bandcamp. Bandcamp is a free service, but once you start selling your music via their site, they will take 15% of the revenue from digital sales and 10% of the revenue from merchandise sales.

Bandcamp liaise with whoever distributes / stocks your physical product so that they fulfil (package and post) orders (this could well be you if you want to keep things determinedly DIY). Bandcamp doesn't offer its own fulfilment service.

So, there is a boggling range of alternatives when it comes to services that will sell and propagate your music digitally. Choose carefully according to the cost implications for your planned releases. Also take into consideration the other services, above and beyond digital aggregation / distribution, that are offered by these companies: publishing, sales of physical items etc.

Weigh up which is best suited to you, if doing the whole thing yourself (registering with iTunes, Amazon, beatport etc.) looks like a series of unnecessary, logistical complications, pay to use a digital aggregator.

Once you have made your music available digitally, the next logical step is to consider pressing up some physical product: CD's, vinyl, memory cards, cassettes, or whatever the future may throw back at us from the past, in an ironic and slightly kitsch style (MiniDisc revival, anyone?)

The key thing when planning physical copies of your music is to be very, very realistic about the amount you can sell. This is difficult to determine accurately, especially if it is your first proper release. Regardless of format, you don't want to be stuck with boxes and boxes of unsold music under your bed.

In our enlightened times, vinyl appears to be the format of choice for many of this new breed of DIY labels. No doubt a reaction against the impersonal, vapid nature of downloads.

Most eschew CD's, certainly with regard commercially duplicated CD's (they may burn a few CDR's themselves and package them in DIY artwork).

Cassette-only releases have been a hipster affectation of recent years. I have a great deal of affection for the format but it's a movement that struck me as self-limiting and somewhat style over substance. But pop music is supposed to be style over substance, and if your style is best represented on a cassette tape, don't let my cynicism put you off.

One of the UK's quickest growing independent labels is Cardiff's Shape Records. They've released excellent records by Islet, Sweet Baboo, H. Hawkline and Truckers of Husk (all Welsh artists) and started putting out releases from international artists in 2014 (Wakes and Flamingods).

We specialise in limited edition vinyl so I would do a run of 250 or 300 for that scenario. It never sounds like many, but when it comes to actually selling them, it is!

I suspect we are a bit of an unusual case. We don't really have a 'normal' set up – I treat each release a bit differently. We always do CD's if we have a plugger working the release as they require them.

Ideally, for environmental and financial reasons, I'd prefer it CD's were phased out as a promotional tool. The faster internet we get and easier it becomes to share music I'm hopeful that will happen. I don't like doing CD promos as it's another thing to get done: artwork, deadlines etc!

Mark Daman Thomas, Shape Records

Physical promo copies of a release are a necessary evil. Some radio stations still prefer to receive their music physically (a CD in the hand can be deemed more reliable than a download link, for example.)

Having your promotional strategy in mind when you draw up a business plan for your label is wise.

"Business plan for my label?"

Oh, yes! It's vital you have some kind of business plan in mind otherwise your release is likely to be late, over-priced and either hideously over, or under, subscribed. But don't worry, I don't think it's as complicated as it sounds.

The first question you need to ask yourself is, realistically, what can I sell? This applies to the format and the number of copies to be pressed.

We'll consider the prices of both a 7" vinyl and CD single release. The example prices are taken from one of the UK's leading pressing / duplication services. I'm not presenting these prices as the cheapest available (they're not). For the sake of this discussion, these figures give you a ballpark idea of how a vinyl release compares to a CD release.

I will quote figures for 500 copies of each, that isn't to suggest that this is the right amount of stock for you to produce.

In the UK, an independent band who earn significant local radio airplay and some national support too, and who have started working with a live agent (i.e. tour small-mid sized venues nationally) sell in the region of 200-250 copies of a vinyl single, in the first few weeks of release.

This is very much a benchmark figure, derived from conversations with people in bands and people who run labels. Some artists sell significantly more (generally those who tour more widely and garner more airplay and blog support). Some sell significantly less.

It's important that you don't overshoot your mark, or bankrupt yourselves, with your debut release.

It's *really* important that you only press physical product if you know you can sell it. This is more than a vanity exercise. Having a nicely pressed vinyl single, in a beautiful full colour sleeve, might elevate you, in your mind, to the level of a 'proper' touring artist, but it's a very expensive form of delusion.

Only press what you believe you can sell. If you're going to promo your release with physical copies, take that into account, too (generally 10-20% of the copies you press).

A sold out, low quantity pressing of a single is far preferable (and much more collectible, in the long-run) than one that you've over-ordered.

I sold 10 copies of the first single I pressed for my label, back at the end of the last millennium. TEN COPIES. That's despite it having been played a couple of times by Steve Lamacq on BBC Radio 1. The band split up a couple of weeks after release. I was left with 490 copies in boxes in my shed. They're still there. Even the mice don't want them.

That was an almost crippling blow for the label. Fortunately the next two releases sold out, otherwise I'd be writing this from a debtor's prison.

Let's look at those figures:

500 *copies of a 7" single with a white label, in a white* *paper bag: £624 inc VAT. Price per unit: £1.25*

500 copies of a CD single in a clear wallet: £402 inc VAT. Price per unit: £0.80

They're the prices for the most basic and unadorned products on offer. Often bands take up these options and make their own artwork for the releases. Or source it more cheaply elsewhere.

With comparative artwork and packaging taken into account, the prices are these:

500 copies of a 7" single with a full colour label and sleeve: £888 inc VAT. Price per unit: £1.78

500 copies of a CD single in a full colour printed card wallet: £540 inc VAT. Price per unit: £1.08

As you can see, printing artwork adds a significant premium to the final unit price. However if it's good artwork, it also adds significantly to the aesthetic value of your product.

People go to the trouble of buying tangible copies of your music, as opposed to downloads, because they want something that has an aesthetic value beyond 1's and 0's, that compliments the music. Don't scrimp on your artwork. Nothing makes a release look less appealing, or undersells the music more, than ill-considered, cheap-looking artwork. Remember to factor the cost of designing the artwork into your business plan, too.

As a guideline, the artwork for the cover of this book, designed by an excellent illustrator and graphic designer from Cardiff called Caroline Duffy (http://www.carolineduffy.co.uk), cost in the region of £500.

Caroline is a brilliant illustrator who works through the whole process with you: from initial discussions about any ideas you may have, through conceptual drawings that offer choices around your brief, to a final draft and any subsequent modifications you may require.

Professional designers know how to deliver the artwork in the correct format to the printers too, which is vitally important. It's very dispiriting to receive a box of singles you've been anticipating eagerly, only to discover that the sleeves have been printed in the wrong colour (which happened for my label's final release... the subsequent ulcer being a determining factor in why it became my final release.)

Mastering your recordings before they are pressed / duplicated is important too, if you want your release to be heard at its optimum quality. Please refer back to **Chapter 24:** *'Mastering Your Recordings'* to remind yourself of the difference mastering can make.

At the time of writing, mastering a track professionally can cost anywhere from £50-£150, depending on the engineer you want to work with and the extent of their facilities. Many mastering studios offer discounts for unsigned / DIY artists.

As with any of the services I've detailed in this book, use your favourite-sounding recordings as a guide to who you would most like to work with. There is no better word of mouth than a great sounding record – the people responsible for recording, producing, engineering and mastering that record are usually listed in the credits. Their fees mightn't be as out of your league as you imagine.

Most pressing plants will send you a certain number of test pressings so that you can check that the master they cut your records from sounds as you want it to. Again, Chapter 24 underlines why obtaining and listening to test pressings is vitally important.

Don't be reticent in voicing any concerns you have about the sound of the test pressings. A record lasts for longer than you or I will. And our children. And their children, too. You are the customer and you are king!

It's important that your release plans take into account the fact that there *will* be challenges and issues with a vinyl pressing (and, occasionally, CD duplication too) that will delay the final delivery of your stock. If the pressing plant say that their turnaround is 4-6 weeks from the date of your order, double it, otherwise you will overshoot your release date and that swanky single release party you've organised, which you'll be committed to playing, minus your guest of honour: the single itself.

Avoid making orders with any degree of urgency in the weeks before Christmas and Record Store Day. There are only a few decent pressing plants in the whole of Europe, they're overwhelmed with orders at these times of the year.

The moment when your stock is eventually delivered is a magical one, once you've got over the shock of what 500 boxed 7" singles look like in the flesh, and worked out where you're going to keep them.

When ordering your 7"s, consider paying a premium to have download codes included with each item. Larger pressing plants will handle the hosting of your audio files and the generation of the download codes. You do, of course, pay for this service. The cost is approximately 10% of the fee for the vinyl pressing plus a setting up charge.

A third party – like Bandcamp – can offer this service at a drastically reduced rate.

Some smaller labels prefer to operate a vinyl-only policy for their releases (but they still promo the release digitally). Obviously, vinyl-only releases are limited in reach to the number pressed. This increases desirability. If the release goes on to sell shedloads, you can always re-press (at a cheaper cost because you already have the master cut.) You can also make the release available digitally at a later date, if you wish.

Let's go back to the costs we've listed and see how many copies of our releases we need to sell to break even.

Please note: these are, very much, guide figures.

R E C O R D I N G & **MIXING 2 songs:**	£600
MASTERING 2 songs:	£200
ARTWORK	£300
PRESSING: 500 x 7" **vinyl copies (with label &** **printed sleeve)**	£900
5 0 0 x p r i n t e d **download codes (pressing** **plant)**	£190
100 x CD promos	£90
TOTAL:	£2280
Cost per 7" single	£4.80

When was the last time you paid £4.80+ for a 7" single? It's an eye-watering total, isn't it? Please note that these figures are a worst case scenario, of sorts. Your recording costs, for example, would also be recouped by any digital sales that you made via iTunes / bandcamp etc. Some studios offer a cheaper daily rate for new, unsigned artists. If you have the skills and the necessary equipment, you could always record (and master) the single yourself, trimming 25% of the single's cost in one fell swoop.

Mastering the single could come in at half that price – again, if you're prepared to haggle and search around for a better price (but still with confidence that the job will be done well).

The price for the artwork is based on a day of a graphic designer's time. If you employ (and pay for) professionals, your final product is much more likely to look professional and appealing to the customer. DIY sleeves are part of the fun, though. I have hundreds of singles with photocopied sleeves! People buy records, first and foremost, for the music captured in the grooves.

I know of some labels who have devised ingenious workarounds for the costs of artwork and presentation. Popty Ping Records (popty ping is a Welsh colloquialism for 'microwave') use the cheapest pressing options (with regards to the 'extras' – the vinyl itself isn't scrimped on, at all) and get their artwork, which is designed to look like the packaging for a microwave ready meal, printed elsewhere, slashing the artwork costs, whilst still making their records look distinctive.

Other DIY labels I'm familiar with have used ink stamps on the standard, lowest cost white labels, giving their releases a handcrafted, guerrilla look.

With a single oodle of creative thought, you can turn a limitation in budget into a great DIY aesthetic for your label.

Let's look at those costings again, but with haggled and cheaper alternatives to the expensive prices I quoted earlier.

R E C O R D I N G & MIXING 2 songs:	£300
MASTERING 2 songs:	£100
ARTWORK	£100
PRESSING: 500 x 7" vinyl copies (with white label)	£624
5 0 0 x p r i n t e d d o w n l o a d c o d e s (Bandcamp)	£15
100 x CD promos	£90
TOTAL:	£1229
Cost per 7" single	£2.49

That's a much more affordable proposition than the original costing. Especially (again) when you consider that the full cost of the recording session can be spread across both the digital and the physical releases.

The costing above doesn't take into account any of the peripheral expenses involved: office costs (phone / internet); the (significant) costs of a radio plugger, should you choose to employ one; pre-production costs (rehearsing) etc.

At a unit price of £2.50, you can realistically sell your 7"s for £4 (£5, even) at your gigs or via social media (with postage and packaging to be added on top, of course). Even at that price (£4), you'd need to sell 308 copies of your single to cover the costs quoted above.

Are you still sure that a self-released vinyl single is a good idea?

You need to haggle, cut some corners and be unstinting in your promoting of that single (gigs, radio, music blogs, music papers and magazines etc. etc.) in order to make it financially viable. Either that, or you resign yourself to regarding your physical releases as promotional items in their own right, to draw people to your shows and, eventually, an album release that has the potential to recoup more money for you.

DIY releases are fraught with financial challenges but also replete with the wonder of complete artistic control.

If you can get the balance right, there is no more rewarding way to get your music to an audience.

You need good people around you. I think it's very hard for musicians to do all of the jobs that have to be done. I've tried running a record label a number of times and that's a really hard thing to do... especially when you're a musician and you're going out on the road and trying to play gigs, trying to do all of the things you need to do... write songs, get the artwork together, it's a big, big leap to think you can actually then successfully market your music yourselves. Even on the smallest level.

Jon Langford, The Mekons / The Three Johns etc.

A big leap, but not one that's impossible. Over to you, and – almost – over and out...

PLAYLIST:
The Normal - TVOD
Minor Threat - Straight Edge
Biff Bang Pow! - 50 Years of Fun
Islet - Triangulation Station
Truckers of Husk - Awesome Tapes From Africa

Sweet Baboo - Bounce
H. Hawkline - Clown Catches Fly
Big Leaves - Sly Alibi
Mowbird - HAHO

42: Julia Ruzicka On Running Your Own Label

Future of the Left are one of the UK's most uncompromising and brilliant bands. They've been mentioned on a number of occasions throughout this book because their originality, intelligence and courage to do what is right by their music and their audience, makes them inspirational: a high-water mark of noise and integrity in a landscape that's rare in both.

There is no commercial imperative behind their music. They make phenomenal pop music that doesn't doff its cap to radio or tug its forelock to mass popularity. It's pop music that isn't all that popular, in other words. It would be much more popular if the UK media had the guts to play harder music, instead of always shaping itself for focus group approval, but as things stand, the piss-weakest X Factor finalists sell more music than Future of the Left do. What a soul-strangling thought.

In the Utopian parallel universe that I've oft mentioned in this book, where music of all hues is embraced by a mixed race, multi-gender, ageless and expansively-minded audience, Future of the Left's Manchasm was No.1 for as long as Whitney Houston's version of I Will Always Love You.

Kevin Costner had a much better time in that dimension's film, I can tell you.

Future of the Left's relative lack of commercial clout makes them a difficult proposition for a record label that isn't similarly courageous. Those labels are difficult, if not impossible, to find.

So rather than making another great record that a label would fail to do justice to, Future of the Left set up their own label, Prescriptions, to release their phenomenal 2014 album 'How To Stop Your Brain In An Accident'.

'Phenomenal' wasn't typed lightly.

The money for the release was raised via a Pledgemusic campaign (in 5 hours!).

Julia Ruzicka is Future of the Left's bass player and much of the brains behind the logistics of Prescriptions.

What made self-releasing and setting up your own label the right option for Future of the Left?

Being completely honest, it was half-choice, half-necessity. We knew we wanted to create and put this album out, it was an important one for us, and it needed the right home.

The recording industry, as we all know, is operating in a very different (online & financial) climate now. It's more cautious and a little more desperate due to dramatic financial drops thanks to internet-influenced market trends and changes to lifestyle which, in turn, has altered numbers and changed how people obtain their music. And in terms of newer fans, how much longevity is there, how much do they invest in music these days?

We used a crowd-funding platform to raise the finance to launch the label and make the record. That was suggested to us for the previous record but we we were't keen on the idea as we thought it might look desperate and didn't fit the band's ethos.

However after once again putting a record out through a label where it was quite hard work for very little return, we came to the conclusion that for the next record we should give crowd-funding a go. This decision didn't come lightly. It was a year's worth of deliberation, investigating and realisation. It was a slow dawn.

After talking to other bands we knew who'd tried it, and that it had worked for, it seemed silly to not give it a go with our existing fan base. There was also the realisation that we could make it suit us, and that we didn't have to succumb to the cliches attached to it (playing people's living rooms, writing a birthday song for someone's cousin, doing the dishes in a gorilla suit, any of these silly promises bands made for a bit of dough) and could pitch it how we want.

Also, between Andrew and myself, we had years of experience behind us releasing records so we knew we could put out the record ourselves in a professional manner.

How much of a bureaucratic and logistical challenge is it to do properly?

There is more bureaucracy and logistical challenges than an artist would care to deal with, sure; but without wanting to sound like a cliche, they are necessary evils, I'm afraid.

I don't think there are many people left who think that some magical talent fairy comes along and brings this wonderful new music to the front door of all those who will love, cherish and donate towards it. The word has to be out there and, depending on what kind of band or artist you are, it's a delicate balance between appealing to your existing fan base and reaching new ones as well. If it grows, it means you can too, hopefully with more flexibility.

We have plateaued a little, but I am pleased to say that our two last albums certainly did contribute to a small growth in audience numbers but it's quite normal for that to happen, and if that levelling off is small it makes it harder to expand as time rolls on and new trends emerge, but it's not impossible! You just have to be clever, imaginative and work that bit harder.

Enter logistical challenges! Namely, timing your promo activity so that it falls in line with your release, and choosing the right time to put your record out.

I won't go into too much detail and turn this into a music business tutorial, but you need to think about things like: release schedules of other labels, i.e., who you are in competition with as this can impact on review space and editorial in press. Broadsheets especially have very limited print space so if you put your record out the same week as, say, Radiohead, Bjork, QOTSA, Nick Cave and One Direction, then you will clearly struggle to get that space and attention, as no matter how mind-blowingly-amazing-blow-your-pants-off your release is, you still won't be able to compete fairly.

Of course, you never get artists that big releasing new records in the same week anyway as the labels know what they are doing and find out who is releasing what, when... but you get my drift. This can be infuriating or disheartening, but is still very much the way of things within the realms of the press. You don't NEED to get that kind of press, sure, but if you can it does make a significant difference in terms of how many people you can reach.

Logistically there was a lot to think about in terms of coordinating press and radio promo activity, as well as touring the record, and online promo, and working the Pledgemusic campaign as well, to make it all run efficiently.

Due to having worked for different labels and being in bands over the last 13 years I felt very well versed on the whole business of a well executed record release and confident, so I knew what was coming. What I hadn't done before, though, was release a record totally DIY, so I wasn't as well prepared for the bureaucratic shit storm that lay ahead, especially when something goes wrong!

To prepare anyone who wants to do this, put aside a huge

amount of time for data entry, and make your song titles short!

To set up the manufacturing and consumable part of the record release you will be met with a common scenario: just when you think you have completed everything needed, there is another code to generate for something else, or another error in artwork to fix, another delay to deal with for some silly reason like vinyl manufacturers running out of the actual black gunk they use to make your records with, packaging not meeting requirements, slits in the vinyl bag on the wrong side, sending a million couriers all over the country for more infuriating reasons beyond your control. It feels like it will just go on and on and on.

However, it does end! And once you have completed your first release, learnt through that, the second should be easier. Like having kids, right? Is that how they work too?

In short, the key word here in your question is 'properly'. Anyone can put a record out. It is pretty darn easy, if you don't care too much about how it's done, perceived or sells. If you want to be proud, and see some results from your efforts and feel your music is worth it, then you want to do it properly, and properly means forethought, hard work and focus I'm afraid. Bummer right?

What were the surprises? The aspects / challenges of releasing something through your own label that you hadn't anticipated in advance?

I have to admit, I'm sitting here struggling to come up with any surprises. I can't recall any right this minute. I'm guessing this is down to the fact that I had worked for labels previously and knew exactly what to expect in terms of the normal process. ie when nothing goes wrong. But this is the music industry! It's going to go a little wrong along the way somewhere.

Julia Ruzicka On Running Your Own Label

Even though we put our own record out through our own label we still had other people involved who we chose to work with, like press, radio, merch printers, artists for artwork, manufacturers, distributors, agents, publishers, etc. so when you work with a team of people you need some contingency in place for errors that may occur. That contingency should be extra time and extra budget, to catch those little disasters that are bound to happen.

Even while we were prepared for little bumps, what we didn't expect was a major colossal, big, fuck off mountain of a bump! Which was receiving faulty stock and dealing with a broker who wasn't willing to rectify their mistake quickly.

I will try to not go into too much detail, but, essentially, they delivered 3500 scratched CDs and argued that because they were playable they were deemed commercially viable. As one of our dear friends down at Music Box rehearsal studios said (where the CDs were delivered to), and I quote, "I could draw a cock on it and it'll still play, but you won't want to buy it". That's pretty much it.

If you go in to your local record store, or order your album online, when you do get that item, tear the shrink wrap off, and excitedly open it to take out and play, if you discovered scratches on the surface of this brand new cd you wouldn't be happy. I personally wouldn't!

There is no way on this earth we were going to let faulty stock hit the shelves, or be sold like that to our fans, who had showed an incredible amount of faith in us. It was no secret the label Prescriptions was our own, so it's not just the label's reputation at stake but also the band's.

To this day I still shudder at the thought of what would have happened if we had let them bully us into releasing stock like that. It would have cost us dearly. All the replacing of stock coming back from stores around the country, from gigs, from our own online store, from everywhere. The loss would have been tremendous and could have destroyed everything.

We were very lucky to find an excellent lawyer who was a fan of the band and he graciously helped us in our fight against this broker. Before we even knew the outcome of our case (we just wanted our money back for the faulty stock, we didn't pay for scratched CDs funnily enough) we decided to quickly go through a different company who worked ridiculously fast to turn around another 3500 CDs so we could make our week late release date. Due to this palaver, we knew we had lost our release date, but we also knew we could get away with delaying the release by a week (too many factors to list here which were considered in these decisions) so we made the decision to make a new batch.

Cash flow was depressing for a few months due to this, but I'm glad to report that we succeeded in our case and the broker settled out of court and we didn't have to pay for the faulty stock. Pretty challenging and outrageous really. Didn't really anticipate it at all as they were a very reputable broker who we had used previously.

Do business concerns run counter to an artistic philosophy / mindset, do you think? Or can the two work parallel to each other?

The two can run parallel to each other certainly, however, it's what many labels miss and struggle with, and understandably.

Most of the time label owners are music fans, yes, but they are also putting a lot at risk financially, so their business heads have to kick in to enable them to survive. Being a fan of music and getting your business head on does mean you are coming from a different angle to the artist and clashes are on the cards, no doubt.

When you are the label and the artist though, it's pretty darn easy avoiding those clashes! As no one else knows what you do better than you. Hopefully you're switched on enough to recognise it, at least.

You need to be open with your band mates, you must be on the same page every step of the way.

While you must respect and keep your artistic integrity intact you must also understand how to work with each other on the business side and work in a cooperative manner, that's the best you can ask for and is key to the record's success.

If you decide to release another band's record, then again, it's about understanding their vision and remaining faithful to it while in the process of promoting it. It has to be clear and thoughtful communication from both parties. It's the label's responsibility to adhere to the artistic vision amidst the release, and it's the artist's responsibility to be able to communicate their vision clearly.

Future of the Left funded their (brilliant) How To Stop Your Brain In An Accident L.P. via a Pledgemusic campaign (which was remarkably successful)… is the biggest challenge raising the funds?

We were lucky. As was widely-reported, we reached our target very quickly, so raising funds through Pledgemusic came surprisingly easy for us, and it really was the nicest, and biggest surprise amongst this whole process.

A month was the pencilled target. We thought if we reach our target in a month that would be amazing, so raising it in five hours was spectacular and humbling, all at the same time.

Saying that, though, as we set our target realistically (no glass bottom boats in the budget and the like) in hindsight, we are thanking our lucky stars we hit 200% as our initial target would no way have been enough. No chance! That showed a little naivety on our part with budgeting. Of course, there is also the fact that the more pledges we received we had to order more stock, hence budgets growing. Demand and supply.

You offered a variety of different packages, including a beautifully pressed vinyl edition of the L.P. – how important is it to cater for all different budgets and to also offer a desirable physical item, too?

We were able to demonstrate full autonomy with this release and therefore, could finally put together exactly the kind of packaging we wanted, which was important to us. I think a lot of bands can relate to this. Most of my experiences with bands and musicians are that how their music is packaged up and presented is crucial to them, and it makes total sense! So when a label restricts what you can do with that it can be disappointing, but understandable due to financial reasons.

When you do it yourself, however, you can see exactly how much it's all costing and make those decisions. Do you spend an extra 50p per unit to get that gatefold? Or stick to a single sleeve and make that money back instead? You can weigh it all up and it's a great freedom to have.

As this was our first album release through our own label we wanted it all to look amazing, without it costing the earth, either, as we didn't have an infinite amount of money to play with but we were able to make those aesthetics versus profit decisions.

Can you gauge, yet, whether having the freedom to cater directly to what your audience wants has had a positive effect in negating the piracy of your music?

Theoretically, you'd like to think that, since your fans know this is your own investment and enterprise, they are less likely to download your music for free from some torrent site (I actually have no idea how illegal downloading works, not taking a moral high ground here, just never been bothered enough to find out, and yes, I like paying for music! Moral high ground back in there), but it would be impossible for us to say conclusively that our recent approach has effected illegal downloading positively.

I couldn't say. I hope it has! Sales were certainly healthy and something to be very proud of considering the low key nature of it in comparison to a major label release.

How much does crowdsourcing a budget in advance help you to not overstretch yourselves? It's a good gauge of market interest, I'd imagine.

Yes, it was a great gauge of market interest, but as not everyone knows about Pledgemusic, or likes using it, we also offered a special pre-order via our own site which was a great move as it gave people a choice and helped us gauge our position even further.

So yes, it helped us determine initial stock levels. Budgeting was still tricky though, it was a careful and stressful balancing act, due to cash flow problems, as when you do a Pledgemusic campaign you don't get your cash straight away! But you need your stock for release date and to fulfil orders, so you need money for the stock, but you don't have your money for the stock, you need to get your orders out to get the money, but you don't have your money??

It was difficult managing it, keeping invoices at bay, but not pissing people off, either, with late payments. A financial juggling act!

We made it work, though, through people being patient and showing faith in us.

Did you have to compromise any of the time you wanted to spend writing / rehearsing doing office tasks?

No, not really. While we were in the creative throes of the record there were some small set up, admin tasks to do, but the real bulk of the heavy office / admin work kicked in three months prior to release and continued on afterwards, so we made sure all the writing, rehearsing, and recording was completed by then,which it was, and that is definitely the way to go!

It worked well. Shame to get the fun stuff out of the way first, though.

How onerous and demanding is the paperwork side of running a business? Tax returns / PRS & MCPS registration, and the like.

I won't lie or hold back, it's incredibly tedious and it grates. I don't think anyone enjoys it, really. It's just something you have to deal with and do.

We are very lucky to have one of the best music accountants in the industry and he helps a lot in terms of accounts, and VAT, and HMRC and all the stuff that makes me want to run away and bury my head in custard as my brain melts.

When it comes to PRS, and MCPS and anything like royalty collection, again, it's time consuming and insanely frustrating as they themselves have archaic, bogged down systems which make things extremely annoying if there is a problem.

Who could you turn to for advice, if required?

Luckily, due to my background, being in bands previously and also working within the industry, I had a lot of good people I could call on for advice, which I did on a few occasions.

I realise, completely, that it would have been a lot harder without those connections, but again, we are very lucky to be living in a world now where a lot of the answers you need can be found online, with a bit of research.

I mainly went back to a manager who looked after my previous band, Million Dead, as he was always excellent with the financial and business side. He was a great help.

Our accountant, too, David Hitchcock and his wife who's a music industry lawyer, were also an enormous help with company queries, publishing and tax.

In advance, did you draw up a business plan? And how (roughly - I'm not HMRC!) did you break down the costs, percentage-wise, for pressing / recording / promo / tour support etc.?

We definitely had to draw up a rough business plan so we knew what money was needed, when, and how much. We didn't break down the budget into percentages, though. It was just getting quotes in advance and tallying them up so we could see what we could and couldn't do.

A little bartering helped too, of course!

Again, due to the band's established reputation, a lot of the people I approached wanted to work with us so were willing to shave off some costs here and there, especially when they knew we were self-releasing.

All of the Pledge money went to the record, all of it! Recording it, manufacturing it, and promoting it, we didn't use that money for tour support or anything of that ilk.

Were there any aspects of the traditional record industry

that you missed or wished that you'd had access to?

Interesting question! As we approached the release in practically the same way as a label would, it wasn't anything like know-how that was needed and, if anything, it was much better for us to be able to choose exactly who we wanted working the record for us. But I did miss the support of say, extra people, those extra pair of hands, a proper in-house team, just to alleviate the workload really.

I also think people in radio (not you Adam!) on commercial stations, or presenters or producers who work on the commercially notable programmes pay more attention to releases on established (major) labels.

Sometimes I think we are taken less seriously by the industry as we are self-managing and releasing. We are a bit of an outsider and underdog, in that respect.

Since writing this, I also read an interesting article on radio playlist meetings[1]! So let's add, not enough hits on YouTube or twitter followers as well.

Similarly (I suppose) what are the limitations of setting up your own label? Was there anything that you couldn't do, that you wanted to? (other than the gold-plated splitter van).

The only limitation was financial, but to be honest, with the way most labels operate now anyway, we would have had the same financial limitations on a label, even more so due to their overheads, which we didn't have. Unless signed to a major of course! Even then it's a little more restricted there, too, these days. And at the end, in majority of cases, you end up owing them money, they own your music, and you're paying them back for years. Not all cases, but that tends to be the most common scenario, especially in the instance of a major.

Overall, though, to actually answer your question, we were happy with what we did in terms of the release and did everything we wanted to, nearly.

Yes, we could have used a tour support budget and more money so we could make some decent videos, that would have been extremely useful, but as mentioned above, even if we were on a label, I doubt there would have been the funds there to provide those things anyway. Unless we were very lucky, of course, and found someone who was willing to front up those costs!

We were able to actually make a little money off the record to pay ourselves something... not much, but something... and we wouldn't have seen a penny yet on the record if we went through a label, just because their costs would have been higher and royalty rates lower.

What did you learn from doing the first release that you'll implement next time?

We were pretty happy with everything we did straight off the bat really. Sounds smug right? Haha! But we honestly were. I wouldn't change a great deal at all.

The only thing we might do is give it more time before manufacture to perhaps shop around a bit more, and compare manufacturing costs against each other. That's such a boring answer isn't it? More midgets and cocaine in the office?? More cake?

How did you handle distribution to your significant fanbase in the U.S. and Australia? Was it literally a case of packaging albums up & distributing them through the post?

Interestingly enough, and you can't get more rock and roll than this, but yes, we sorted a franking machine, stocked up on mailers and labels and got posting.

With Australia, the label Remote Control picked up the record which was great, and they distributed throughout Australia.

Even though we had distribution there, we still took a lot of orders from that part of the world via our site, and packaged up those ourselves. We did this for the US as well, where we sent a lot out, and many other far and away places, which was nice to see.

Our distributor in the UK, Republic of Music, sold the record and EP into stores, and to online sellers… they did a top job incidentally… as well as exporting into Germany, France, Spain, wherever there was demand or orders coming in from.

Even with their distro, we still sold a lot of copies of our record within those territories via our site, as with Pledgemusic, there is something very appealing and rewarding to fans, I think, buying direct from the artist. They feel closer to it, as well as understanding we benefit more from direct sales.

In retrospect, has setting up Prescriptions been a more positive experience for the band than your previous experiences releasing through record labels?

For where we were at last year, yes, it absolutely was the right thing to do and was a positive experience overall.

While I touched on some stresses and bumps in previous answers, it still – in some ways – wasn't as draining as it can sometimes be with a label.

With a label you are dealing with a group of people, and unless they are ALL totally behind your record, it can be an arduous task making others think creatively, work efficiently, or just be excited by it and give it their all.

It's a highly competitive music market out there, with many

in advantageous positions, so to be able to stand out from amongst all that, and have even a remotely small chance at grabbing that all important music fan attention, you have to be persistent, focused and well, love what you do! So by running every aspect of the show we were able to put that across and, dare I say, enjoyed the process too.

Thank you so much, Julia, for these valuable insights into the challenges and rewards of self-releasing.

Discover more about Prescriptions here: http:// prescriptionsmusic.com

I can't recommend their releases highly enough, without drowning you in hyperbole.

[1]*radio playlist meetings* - http://www.theguardian.com/ media/2014/may/25/radio-1-playlist-secrets-uncovered-battle-of-brands

PLAYLIST:

Future of the Left - How To Stop Your Brain In An Accident (LP)

43: <u>Alan Holmes On Making Music</u>

I have done my very best to keep On Making Music as un-prescriptive and un-sanctimonious as possible. I'm aware that there is no 'right way' to make music; no set of dictates that need to be adhered to. I hope this book has encouraged you to make the noise you want to make, however you want to make it.

Music's choked with do-gooders trying to gentrify the fuck out of it. People who think that money and talent shows and battle of the bands and schemes and focus groups and workshops are the way to encourage interesting music when, patently, they aren't.

The most interesting music *always* has something subversive about it. Or, at the very least, has stolen something from music that was subversive. Which in itself, in its brazenness, is subversive, I suppose.

I thought it would be timely, here at the end, after dense thickets of well-intentioned, beige advice, to remind you – as if you needed reminding – that you can do what you please. There are no rules.

A music-maker chasing success for success' sake is a dog chasing its tail. A music-maker who digs up original sounds for the pure and simple enjoyment of those original sounds gets to be a content dog, sleep-chasing massive, slow moving bunnies into burrow entrances that are far too narrow.

Alan Holmes, or as I sometimes call him out of earshot when he comes on my radio show – The Godfather of the Welsh Underground – makes, and releases, some of the most beautiful, unsettling, uncommercial and accessible music that I've ever heard.

His music is riddled with such contradictions. One moment, it's napalm thunder; the next, it's peachy tufts of cloud ghosting over a blood orange sunset.

It's music made with with the joy of making music at its heart, and little or no concern for commerce, accessibility or an audience.

Alan's most renowned for being a member of Fflaps and Ectogram, and for producing Gorky's Zygotic Mynci's phantasmagoric early albums. The recordings he has made with Parking Non-Stop are also brilliant and occasionally unfathomable. His record label, Turquoise Coal, released my favourite album of recent years, the similarly unconcerned, original and remarkable 'HaHa' by Irma Vep.

I know that Alan feels a little uncomfortable that his words on the subject of making music should be arranged on any kind of plinth of suggested import, but that's precisely why I wanted to talk to him here at the glorious end. To remind us that making music needn't be about anything more than, you know, making music.

Why do you make music?

I often ask myself the same question and am not sure whether I've ever come up with a satisfactory answer. All I really know is that the urge to do it hasn't diminished at all over the 40 years or more that I've been doing it. It might be a bit trite to compare it to breathing or eating – maybe more like a drug or alcohol addiction – certainly something that I have no conscious control over.

Although my first ever record was "Bits and Pieces" by The Dave Clark Five, which I got when I was 4 in 1964, it was another couple of years before I got fully hooked on pop music by The Monkees – when I heard their first record in 1966, I knew straight away that it was what I wanted to do with my life.

This might sound a bit pretentious and pompous but one reason is a quest for immortality. Having no children, the only way I might outlive my body is through any art I create while I'm here. I don't feel an immediate need to be appreciated by other people, but in the back of my consciousness I suspect there is a romantic notion that 20 years after I die, some hip young group will chance upon a copy of something that I did and hold it up as an influence. Clearly that's not going to happen, but knowing that doesn't dampen the urge.

One crucial reason I'm still driven to make music is that I haven't got it right yet – I don't think anything I've done is very good, and I'm determined that before I die, I will do something that will make someone, if only one person, feel the way I felt when I heard the first Modern Lovers, Television or Pere Ubu LPs. If I achieve that, and I almost certainly won't, it would make my existence worthwhile.

I think we should refer back to your chapter on self-criticism here – if you already think you are great, then where is the motivation to go further? I know I'm not good enough, but one day maybe I will be... at which point I'll retire.

You have a love for pop music, don't you, but not for music that's made with an audience in mind – isn't that a contradiction?

Well, that depends on how specific your idea of an audience is. It's certainly nice to believe that there's an abstract group of people out there who share your own aesthetics and so would connect with what you do if they got to hear it, but as soon as you start targeting a specific demographic and making creative decisions with appealing to them in mind, it inevitably compromises your artistic intention.

When you treat 'the audience' as anything other than a bunch of people who are the same as you, and would therefore be open to what you do, then you're being offensively patronising. A good example is the power battle within The Beach Boys, where Mike Love wanted to formularise the music with the group's audience in mind, while Brian Wilson insisted on following his instincts and making "Pet Sounds" – complete commercial suicide at the time, but 48 years on, few people would side with Mike Love.

Can an album be a truly great album if only 5 people hear it?

Oh I think so... I guess the more pertinent question would be whether it would still be great if none of those 5 people actually liked it. Personally I only judge things by my own criteria, but having made neither a great record that nobody has heard or an unsatisfactory but popular one, it's difficult to answer that one honestly!

If cornered and plied with a couple of pints, what advice would you offer to someone who makes music?

Make music that feels like it's yours, preferably with other people. The chemistry between people throws up completely unexpected and exciting results . The thing music has over literature or painting (for example) is that it lends itself to collaboration, the whole being so much more than the sum of the parts.

Don't advertise for band members as 'bassist wanted – must be into The Doors, Chas & Dave, Marmalade, Phil Collins, Metallica, Nick Drake etc' – just get together with any other people (bassoonists, theraminists?) who also *want to make music and see what the clash of your influences produces. The chances are that it won't sound like those other people and will actually sound like YOU. I've spent the past few months writing and recording with a young woman half my age and we've never once spoken about anybody else's music – no idea what each other listens to – we just play together, but the results are pretty great. Don't try to be someone else.*

I'd also suggest playing several different types of music with different people – it can be so easy to get stuck in a rut – when I play a lot of horrid noise, I long for subtle melodies and vice versa... so do all of it simultaneously. If you only like one type of music, you don't really like music, and might well be more fulfilled in accountancy or waste management.

Are there any rules in music worth paying attention to? If you start being choosy about which rules you adhere to, and which you don't, aren't you in danger of being something of a hypocrite? (Not 'you', you... people who espouse a philosophy of chaos / anarchy, but who still manage to make albums and tour and function in modern society.)

My instinctive answer to that is no, of course there are no rules... but then I considered the question a bit more deeply and decided that no, of course there are no rules (that sentence is not quite as flippant is it sounds.)

I tend to have a few 'rules of thumb', but they are all made to be broken. Look around and see what everyone is doing, and then do the opposite. If people like what you are doing, then stop doing it. If you've done something once, don't do it again ...that kind of thing. My only real 'rule', and it's more a philosophy than a 'rule' is to keep open to whatever might come along. I genuinely love people, but I also love testing their limits by pissing them off. I don't think I ever really play 'extreme' music, but I have every respect for those people who do - Merzbow, Whitehouse and the like, but I equally love gentle, pastoral music. One of the reasons that possibly my all time favourite group is The Velvet Underground is that they could follow 'I'll be Your Mirror' with 'Sister Ray' – that's life, it's multi-dimensional, and your music should reflect that. At this point I should refer you to the wonderful Half Man Half Biscuit's splendid 'Irk the Purists'.

Which are the artists who've managed to sell records, earn some kind of renown, and influence people without compromising their music, do you think?

Well... do you mean sell records at the time or retrospectively? The Velvet Underground and The Stooges have both sold plenty of records and influenced people, but after a pretty long time delay. Leonard Cohen and Bob Dylan come to mind... The Kinks and Sex Pistols too, and I guess that Throbbing Gristle and The Fall have also influenced a lot of people and earned renown, although I'm not sure how many records either of them have sold. Nirvana of course, were tragically uncompromising despite selling millions of records. The problem with them was that although they they were both great and influential, everyone they influenced was shit... hence Kurt's premature exit.

Probably the most uncompromising yet successful artist I've ever encountered is Steve Albini – his own music isn't massively successful, although it is both popular, well-renowned and wonderful, but he also applies his principles to the groups he produces – Pixies, Breeders, Nirvana etc. I had a beer with him once in Chester at a Rapeman gig, and he was thoroughly charming despite his contrary reputation. I most recently saw him playing with Shellac a couple of years ago and was pleasantly surprised to see that he set up all his own gear and didn't use roadies – something the group had in common with Television... a trivial detail, but sometimes these small things matter.

How did the many years working behind the counter of a record shop (the much-missed Cob Records in Bangor) affect your opinion of music, particularly music commerce?

It came very close to killing my love of music. I miss Cob enormously as a customer, but as for working there, its demise saved my life. In one way it was great to be just listening to music all day every day, but after a while it just numbs you to the wonder of it all and it becomes something that's always just there in the background... I have totally rediscovered the wonder of music since it closed. I do not recommend working in a record shop if you're a music fan, it's like an alcoholic working behind a bar – not healthy.

Do you favour instinct over technical ability? You once told me you hated the word 'talent'... why?

Yes, I'd say I do favour instinct really, although that's not to say that you shouldn't rationally formulate your ideas – it would be pretty horrendous if all music was just people banging on bongos and 'expressing themselves' – we'd all be begging for the return of X-Factor. I think there's a pretty wide area between pure instinct and technical ability where most of the interesting things happen. If you want to express yourself, then please do it in private.

I do indeed hate the word 'talent' because it implies elitism – the idea that there's some tangible quality that some people intrinsically have and other people don't. I believe that everybody has the ability to create something worthwhile if they can envision what they want to do and figure out how they might be most able to do it.

Yet there are some very technically-gifted musicians out there who make great music, too? Zappa, for one. How do you think some manage to not be a slave to their ability, instead using it to reach higher and more interesting places?

I've never been a huge fan of technique, at least not for the sake of it. I have however in recent years got to know several of the ex-members of Henry Cow, who are arguably the most technically proficient musicians to have ever been involved in the UK rock scene. What really struck me about them was their continuing desire to reach out further, just do things they'd never done before and to connect with as many different people as possible. Despite their iconic status in 'serious music' they all seemed as open to connect with the likes of me as with cutting edge contemporary composers like Iancu Dumitrescu.

I think it's all about attitude and openness rather than merely showing off. I think that the value of technique is to enable you to do things you haven't done before – which of course applies at every level of technical ability. If you are just out to impress people with your technique, then you belong in the world of sport, not art. Despite that, I do sometimes find myself impressed by technically accomplished drummers, possibly because it's one instrument I have no ability on myself; I have sat open mouthed in astonishment through live performances by Can's Jaki Liebezeit and This Heat's Charles Hayward, for example, but then again both of them use their considerable talents to make great music rather than to merely impress.

You started your first bands round about the time punk was just beginning (depending on what you regard as punk's year zero). How inspiring was punk? If it was inspiring, what was inspiring about it?

Oh, punk was infinitely inspiring. I don't think that people who didn't live through it could possibly understand the extent that it liberated us all.

I find it offensive when groups like Green Day and Blink 182 are classed as punk – there are no groups on Earth further from punk than them – Yes and ELP... even the Moody Blues are far more punk.

Punk taught us to be be participants rather than spectators, and has informed every aspect of my life ever since. Mind you, I think it's a cop-out to claim that punk was all about attitude and that the music wasn't important – listen to 'Crossing the Red Sea with The Adverts' or Alternative TV's 'The Image Has Cracked' and play me a contemporary record that even comes close.

The attitude was life-changing; the music was incandescent. The first punk group I saw live was The Slits – my life was instantly, irreversibly transformed. Punk also acknowledged women as people rather than the accessories the previous rock culture had classed them as.

What keeps you excited about making music?

I never know what's coming next. I've been making music since around 1976 (I did have a short lived 'group' in 1967, but I don't think that really counts) and the most enjoyable and satisfying year yet has been 2014. I just find that collaborating with new people opens up whole new worlds. Some of the music I'm currently making is delicate, intimate, melodic, yet still a bit odd – it takes me into areas I've never been before – it really stretches my limits and I'm constantly excited that I can actually do this stuff. The one thing that would kill off my enthusiasm was if I restricted myself to one area of music, like so many people seem so willing to do.

What keeps you excited about listening to music?

474

There's just so much of it out there – most is pretty rubbish, but even that 0.001% that isn't will fill up the rest of your life to listen to. Every year I go to the Schiphorst Festival in Germany and the bill is usually filled with people I've never heard of, and yet they are all pretty much guaranteed to be great. There's so much fantastic music being made, and much of it isn't from the UK/USA and is unlikely to be heard on any form of mainstream media. The fact that you (Adam) can fill three hours a week with good new Welsh music just demonstrates how much is actually out there that gets passed by by the mainstream media.

Would you still make music if no one, other than yourself, was going to hear it? *Really?* Is that philosophy rare, in your experience?

Well, the short answer is YES. I was, for example, once in a group (early 90s) that played garage rock type stuff with Punjabi and Welsh lyrics – we wrote and rehearsed a whole set worth of original material over a few months and we were pretty good – and like nobody else. Unfortunately people moved away and not a single person outside the group ever heard our music – we never played in public and no recording was ever made. I still remember the group most fondly though... the lack of documentation or public acknowledgement takes absolutely nothing away from the music we created.

As to whether that's rare, who knows? The very nature of the question implies that we couldn't possibly know!

The only negative to writing this book has been that it ate up all the time I had to make music. Alan's words have underlined where the itch is. I can't wait to scratch it.

He didn't do the interview so that I would point you towards his music. I'm going to do that, anyway:

http://turquoisecoal.com

http://ectogram.co.uk

PLAYLIST:

Fflaps - Greddf Pioden Gwern
Ectogram - Glove Soup
Gorky's Zygotic Mynci - Merched yn Neud Gwallt Eu Gilydd
Irma Vep - Be a Mother
Dave Clark Five - Bits and Pieces (*first record I ever 'bought'*)
The Monkees - Sometime in the Morning (*the group that hooked me on music & also a tribute to the late Gerry Goffin*)
The Modern Lovers - Hospital (*from my favourite LP of all time*)
Television - Venus
Pere Ubu - Final Solution
Beach Boys - Surf's Up (*original Smile version*)
Merzbow - No More Exploitation of Animals
Whitehouse - Mindphaser
Velvet Underground - I Heard Her Call My Name (*the first song I ever heard by the VU - life changing*)
Half Man Half Biscuit - Descent of the Stiperstones
The Stooges - Loose
Leonard Cohen - The Future
Bob Dylan - Visions of Johanna
Kinks - Waterloo Sunset
Sex Pistols - Did You No Wrong
Throbbing Gristle - Very Friendly
The Fall - Rebellious Jukebox
Nirvana - All Apologies
Rapeman - Steak and Black Onions
Henry Cow - Beautiful as the Moon, Terrible as an Army with Banners
Iancu Dumitrescu - Pierres Sacrees
Can - Halleluwah
This Heat - Rimp Romp Ramp
Charles Hayward - My Madness
The Adverts - The Great British Mistake
Alternative TV - Nasty Little Lonely (*the only song ever recorded good enough to survive the presence of Jools Holland on it*)
The Slits - Love & Romance (Peel session version)
Spectralate - Water Table

44: <u>Last Notes</u>

Anything else you should know? Never give in and never give up.

Kim Fowley, record producer / impresario

Thank you for reading this book. It was fashioned mostly from the world of making music as I see it and have experienced it. I haven't pretended to be anyone other than who I am. I have only lied to you 3 times in, more or less, 500 pages. Sorry if you've been offended by my antipathy to Muse.

You know better now, though, right?

Please share the link to: http://onmakingmusic.co.uk wherever and with whomever you feel it would be useful / appreciated.

If you think you've learnt something and benefited from On Making Music, please also consider making a donation via the site. It took me a year to write this book. I trust you to do whatever is right, according to the value you've found in these pages.

If you have any questions, observations, additions or corrections, please contact me via @adamwalton on Twitter. On those occasions when I'm not ferreting for interesting new demos or making my daughter tea, I will be very happy to help, where I can.

45: <u>Thank You</u>

Ava, Mum and Dad for the patience and support.

Ritzy Bryan, Rhydian Dafydd, Andrew Falkous and Martin Carr for their encouragement (and contributions).

Anyone who ever sent me a demo, for fuelling the fire.

Alan Daulby, Alan Holmes, Andy Black, Angharad Trwbador, Badly Drawn Boy, Ben Hayes, Carwyn Ellis, Charlie Francis, Charlotte Church, Clive Langer, Colin Newman, David Gedge, David Wrench, Deke Leonard, Donal Whelan, E, Elin Angharad, Elliott Smith, Frank Black / Black Francis, Georgia Ruth, Grey 'n' Pink Records, Gruff Rhys, Huw Stephens, Huw Williams, Ian Brown, James McLaren, Jarvis Cocker, Jeremy Gluck, Jeremy Grange, Jesse Von Doom, Jim Bob, Jimi Goodwin, Jo Riou, Joe Goodden, John Hywel Morris, John Rostron, Jon Langford, Julia Ruzicka - Prescriptions, Kim Fowley, Kristin Hersh, Liam Gallagher, Manda Rin, Marcus Warner, Mark Daman Thomas - Shape Records, Mark Foley, Matt Robin, Matthew Evans, Mike Peters, Neil Innes, Owain Trwbador, Owen Powell, Paul Draper, Paul Gray, Polly Thomas, Ray Davies, Richard Hawkins, Richard Parfitt, She Makes War, Stephen Moshi Moshi, Telford's Warehouse, The Anonymous Promoter, Tjinder Singh, Tom Robinson, Turnstile Music, Van McCann and William Tyler, for the music, the generous wisdom and the music, again, because fundamentally that is all that matters.

Scrivener, for being a boss piece of software.

Sainsbury's raspberry jam doughnuts

CPSIA information can be obtained at www.ICGtesting.com
Printed in the USA
LVOW10s1652270115

424564LV00017B/800/P

9 781502 724663